THE LONG RANGE
DESERT
GROUP
IN WORLD WAR II

OSPREY
PUBLISHING

THE LONG RANGE DESERT GROUP
IN WORLD WAR II

GAVIN MORTIMER

First published in Great Britain in 2017 by Osprey Publishing,

PO Box 883, Oxford, OX1 9PL, UK

1385 Broadway, 5th Floor, New York, NY 10018, USA

E-mail: info@ospreypublishing.com

Osprey Publishing, part of Bloomsbury Publishing Plc

Every attempt has been made by the Publisher to secure the appropriate permissions for material reproduced in this book. If there has been any oversight we will be happy to rectify the situation and written submission should be made to the Publisher.

A CIP catalogue record for this book is available from the British Library.

Gavin Mortimer has asserted his right under the Copyright, Designs and Patents Act, 1988, to be identified as the Author of this Work.

ISBN: 978 1 4728 1933 8
PDF ISBN: 978 1 4728 1934 5
ePub ISBN: 9781472819352

Index by Alan Rutter
Page layout by Myriam Bell
Typeset in Bembo
Originated by PDQ Digital Media Solutions, UK

Printed in China through World Print Ltd.

17 18 19 20 21 10 9 8 7 6 5 4 3 2 1

Front cover: Left: Two men of a Long Range Desert Group patrol, dressed in greatcoats, make use of available cover while on a road watch. (Imperial War Museum E 12434). Right: A Chevrolet truck about to set off on patrol from Siwa in 1940. (Imperial War Museum E 12373)

Page 2: Stuck in the mud: an LRDG patrol uses sand channels to extract a vehicle from a desert quagmire. (Courtesy of the SAS Regimental Archive)

Imprint page: Two LRDG men aboard a Chevrolet truck, the preferred mode of transport in the desert. (Courtesy of the SAS Regimental Archive)

Osprey Publishing supports the Woodland Trust, the UK's leading woodland conservation charity. Between 2014 and 2018 our donations will be spent on their Centenary Woods project in the UK.

www.ospreypublishing.com

CONTENTS

DEDICATION

To the men of New Zealand, Britain and Rhodesia whose courage created the
LRDG legend.

ACKNOWLEDGEMENTS

First and foremost I would like to thank Lofty Carr, Mike Sadler and James Patch, three of the handful of LRDG veterans who, 75 years later, still talk with pride and affection of their time in the unit. This book is dedicated to you, and your former comrades, who served with such gallantry and guile in the Long Range Desert Group.

I am also grateful to Grenville Bint for his assistance in my research, particularly in the supply of some many of the wonderful photographs in the book, and my thanks, too, to the SAS Regimental Archive, who allowed me access to their treasure trove of LRDG records.

Similarly, I am indebted to Jonathan Pittaway, author of the excellent history of the Rhodesian members of the LRDG, and John Valenti, who does such a fine job running the LRDG Preservation Society, and who generously granted me permission to reproduce some of his photos in this book.

Thank you to the staff at the Imperial War Museum, the National Archives in Kew and the Churchill Archives in Cambridge.

Several relatives of LRDG personnel exhibited great kindness during my research in unearthing documents and diaries, notably Barbara Atherton, daughter of Harry Horton, one of the unit's most efficient signallers, and Ian Chard.

Thank you to my agent, Felicity Blunt, and her assistant, Jessica Whitlum-Cooper, at Curtis Brown for their diligence on my behalf.

Finally, I'd like to thank the team at Osprey on must be congratulated for their enthusiasm, efficiency and editing. Thanks for an excellent job.

INTRODUCTION

The desert campaign of World War I is a largely forgotten theatre in the minds of the British and their allies. One hundred years after the 'war to end all wars', the perception is of a conflict of carnage fought in the trenches of France and Belgium. Mud, blood and barbed wire. Of course, Australians and New Zealanders still recall with pride the bravery and fortitude of their troops in the Dardanelles campaign of 1915, but few are aware of the consequences of that failed campaign to knock Turkey out of the war.

It resulted in Britain diverting 80,000 of its soldiers from the Western Front to Egypt and then a march up through Palestine into Syria to engage the Turks. Turkey's reaction was to call on Muslim states to wage a jihad against Britain and her allies. The appeal met with a mixed response. In the Arabian Peninsula, thanks in part to Colonel T. E. Lawrence – Lawrence of Arabia – Prince Feisal and his warriors fought with the British against Turkey. But in the Egyptian Desert, the vast arid tract of land west of Cairo, the Senussi tribesmen embraced the call to jihad against the European 'Crusaders'.

Armed by Turkey and Germany, thousands of Senussi, led by Sayed Ahmed esh Sherif, began attacking British outposts. The raids caused little in the way of material damage to the British but they were nonetheless a concern, and forced their commander, General Sir Archibald Murray, to transfer troops from Palestine to reinforce the British position in Egypt. An innovative general by World War I standards, Murray organized his troops into the Western Frontier Force, combining infantrymen with units of cavalry and artillery, further strengthened by a squadron of light bombers from the Royal Flying Corps (RFC).

The innovation didn't stop there. A Camel Corps was formed, but, bold as they were, the men were no match for the Senussi who had grown up on the awkward animals. If they were inferior to their enemy in tradition, Murray reasoned, why not gain the advantage by using their superior technology. And so in early 1916 the Light Car Patrol (LCP) was formed.

OPPOSITE
Ralph Bagnold, seen here in Egypt during the 1920s, founded the LRDG in 1940 and his vast experience of the Libyan desert proved invaluable in the North African campaign. (Getty)

9

Comprising a fleet of 20 horsepower, four-cylinder Model T Fords, the Allies – the volunteers were all British and Australians – now had the mobility but more importantly the firepower to take the fight to the Senussi. Operating in conjunction with the RFC, the patrols were provided with the location of a Senussi camp by the reconnaissance aircraft and they would then drive into the desert and launch a hit-and-run attack. 'They,' said Lawrence of the Light Car Patrols, 'were worth hundreds of men to us in these deserts'.[1]

T. E. Lawrence, also known as Lawrence of Arabia, recognized the worth of vehicles in the desert during World War I. (Getty)

The small but significant contribution of the LCP in the Desert War was quickly forgotten following the Armistice. But in 1925 a young British captain was posted to Egypt, an officer who had survived the horrors of the Somme and who in North Africa found a land of enchantment and unlimited adventure. Ralph Bagnold's keen and enquiring mind devoured a mountain of literature about his new posting, including an account of the Light Car Patrol's activities nearly a decade earlier. Then, when he saw the desert for the first time, he was captivated. It reminded Bagnold of Dartmoor, where he had spent many happy times as a boy. 'Both had the strange aura induced by the physical presence of the remote past, and also by the great bare trackless expanses where the careless might well get lost,' he later wrote.[2]

Bagnold set off to explore the interior of the Western Desert, and as he disappeared into the towering dunes he was unwittingly blazing a trail for a special forces unit whose name, in time, would come to be a byword for intrepidness.

An LRDG patrol rests by a small desert oasis during a 1942 operation.

CHAPTER 1

FROM SCIENTIST
TO SOLDIER

On 15 August 1939, a 43-year-old scientist was recalled to the colours. In the four years since leaving the British Army, Ralph Bagnold had made something of a name for himself within the scientific fraternity as a writer of crisp prose. His area of expertise was the North African desert, a region he knew intimately from the years he had spent exploring it in the late 1920s and early '30s. Two of Bagnold's papers appeared in the Royal Society's journal, and in 1939 his first book was published, *The Physics of Blown Sand and Desert Dunes*. In the summer of that year Bagnold was commissioned to write a long article for the *Scientific American*, entitled 'A Lost World Refound'. The piece, a blending of science with exploration, recounted one of Bagnold's adventures in Egypt's Western Desert. The desert, he explained, made one feel very small and insignificant, not just because of nature's vast splendour but also the realization that they were retracing the footsteps of men throughout thousands of years. 'The most lasting memory of the expedition doubtless will be a trivial incident which happened in a cave in which we had taken shelter for the night from the cold wind,' wrote Bagnold. 'The beam of a torch fell on an artificial rock ledge. On the ledge lay a solitary stone knife, left behind by the last occupant untold centuries ago, just as we ourselves would empty our pockets before going to bed.'[1]

OPPOSITE
The key to successfully surmounting a sand dune was for the vehicle to accelerate towards the crest, slow, and then with wheels aligned, gently topple over the tip and surf down the gentle slope on the other side.
(Author's Collection)

Shortly after Bagnold posted his article to the editor of the *Scientific American* in New York, he received through his letter-box his call-up papers. Ordered to report for two and a half months' training with the Third Signals Division at Bulford, Bagnold arrived on Salisbury Plain feeling a little apprehensive. His last war had been a quarter of a century ago when, as a young officer in the Royal Engineers, he had survived three years on the Western Front. What skills could he bring to the British Army, an out-of-shape middle-aged man, against the enemy that Britain would surely soon be fighting – Nazi Germany?

None, seemed to be the view of the British high command, who on 26 August appointed him commanding officer of the East Africa Signals. It was a backwater appointment if ever there was one, and Bagnold believed his contribution to any conflict would be negligible. 'War declared' was his curt diary entry for 3 September. Germany's invasion of Poland had little relevance for the East Africa Signals.

On 28 September, Bagnold was one of several hundred military personnel who sailed from Britain bound for Kenya on board RMS *Franconia*, a requisitioned

The Italians were responsible for the 400-mile barbed wire fence that ran south from the coast along down the Libyan frontier with Egypt. (Courtesy of the SAS Regimental Archive)

Cunard liner. There were no German troops in East Africa, but there were plenty of Italian soldiers stationed in Abyssinia (present-day Ethiopia), Eritrea and Somaliland, the three countries conquered on the orders of the fascist Italian dictator Benito Mussolini earlier in the decade and formed into the Africa Orientale Italiana.

Seven days into their passage to East Africa, the RMS *Franconia* collided with the merchant cruiser *Alcantara* as the two vessels manoeuvred their way through the Mediterranean. Bagnold saw the incident from the deck and believed that the *Alcantara* 'must have mistaken starboard for port for she ran straight into us'. Neither ship sank, but the damage required the vessels to limp into the nearest port for repairs. The *Franconia* arrived at Malta on 6 October and the following day Bagnold transferred to the *Empress*. The ship was not the only change to Bagnold's schedule: instead of sailing directly to East Africa, he was first heading to North Africa, to Port Said, where he disembarked on 9 October while they waited for the next available troopship to take him onwards to Kenya.

Bagnold wasted no time in exploiting to his advantage the unexpected change to his itinerary. Catching the first train to Cairo, he arrived in the Egyptian capital and began looking up old friends from his time stationed in the city a decade earlier. One of his first calls was on Colonel Micky Miller, chief signals officer at the headquarters of British troops in Egypt. The pair went for a drink in the Long Bar of the Shepheard's Hotel, the favourite haunt of the officer class, and Bagnold asked Miller to have a word with the War Office. Surely even they must see the nonsense of packing off arguably Britain's foremost expert on the Western Desert to East Africa when Libya was of far greater strategic importance, particularly as the Italian commander, Marshal Rodolfo Graziani, had an estimated quarter of a million men in 15 divisions at his disposal.

Miller promised to submit his friend's request to the War Office, but unbeknown to Bagnold he had a more powerful ally by his side. He and Miller had been spotted in the Shepheard's by a reporter from the English-language newspaper, the *Egyptian Gazette*, and the next day an article appeared in the 'Day In, Day Out' gossip column praising the War Office for wasting little time in bringing to Egypt an expert like Bagnold. The War Office, of course, had done no such thing. If it had its way, Bagnold would be swatting away flies in Kenya not Cairo, but the information reached the ears of Archibald Wavell, General Officer Commander-in-Chief of Middle East Command. Instructions were issued and Bagnold was soon sitting in front of Wavell in his cramped office at the top of the 'Grey Pillars' HQ.

Wavell knew all about Bagnold, how he and a group of like-minded adventurers had put their spare time as army officers in Egypt to good use, driving Model T Fords into the Western Desert. Bagnold's first expedition had been a short one in March 1926, a drive along the old caravan road from Cairo to Suez. A year later, Bagnold – by now a major in the Royal Corps of Signals – commanded a party from Suez to the southern Sinai. Then in October 1927 came his most ambitious expedition yet, penetrating 400 miles west from Cairo to the Siwa Oasis, where in 331 BC Alexander the Great had visited the Temple of the Oracle of Amun during his conquest of Egypt. Bagnold and his five companions (one of them a 26-year-old officer in the Royal Tank Corps called Guy Prendergast) set out in three Model T Fords, venturing onto an ocean of sand that was as merciless to the foolhardy and complacent as the Pacific or Atlantic oceans. In the account he wrote of the journey, Bagnold's prose ebbed and flowed with awe, astonishment and apprehension. He wrote of the 'terrible tract of white jagged rock' they encountered as they searched for the camel track that led towards Siwa; of the 'damp gardens of oranges and pomegranates' they drove through and of their sight of Siwa from a cliff-top 70 miles east, 'with its salty lakes and distant groves of palms dark green against a shining skyline of pale gold domes and sandy pinnacles'.[2]

On their return from Siwa the British explorers had come across a small Italian outpost, an incongruous reminder of the propensity of the human race to wage war even in the most remote corners of their planet. Bagnold tacitly supported the Arabs, who had been fighting a guerrilla war with the Italians since 1922, but it

This LRDG patrol has stopped to fill up with petrol. In the early days the petrol was carried in flimsy tins, packed in wooden casing, but these leaked so much that jerrycans soon replaced them. (Courtesy of the SAS Regimental Archive)

wasn't until the 1930s that tensions between Italy and Britain began to increase. Mussolini wanted control of the Mediterranean and that unsettled the British, who feared the dictator's ultimate aim in North Africa was the conquest of Egypt and the Sudan.

It was Bagnold's knowledge of the Western Desert that so interested Wavell. He knew that Italian spies had for some years been sending reports to their superiors about British defences and troop strengths in Egypt, and despite the signing in April 1938 of the Anglo-Italian Agreements, the aims of which were to keep the peace in Africa, Wavell didn't trust the Italians. They hadn't entered the war, but the presence in Benghazi, a Libyan port 675 miles west of Cairo, of a German military mission was proof of where Mussolini's sympathies lay.

CHAPTER 2

ONLY THE TOUGH NEED APPLY

On 16 October 1940 Bagnold wrote in his diary: 'Cable from WO [War Office] agreeing to my staying in Egypt. Posted to Armoured Divisions Signals, Matruh.'

Mersa Matruh, 135 miles west of Cairo, was situated halfway between the city of Alexandria and the Libyan border. It was also the HQ of the 7th Armoured Division. Bagnold knew the area well. The coastline west from Alexandria is flat, a chain of limestone reefs protecting the beach from waves. It was the limestone that lent the coastal dunes a 'dazzling whiteness, formed from the debris worn from the outer reefs'.[1] As Bagnold made his way west to Mersa Matruh he glimpsed some of the 70,000 people who were estimated in 1940 to inhabit the coast between Alexandria and Libya. They were composed almost 'entirely of nomadic, or semi-settled Bedouin, who raise camels and small cattle, and grow a little grain'.

Four thousand natives lived in Mersa Matruh, significant militarily because of its small harbour, but the most important person when Bagnold arrived was General Percy Hobart, commander of the 7th Armoured Division. Hobart's mind was more open than that of most senior British officers in North Africa and he agreed with Bagnold's suggestion that they should 'buy a small assortment of desert-worthy American vehicles and train a nucleus of officers and men in the art of cross-country driving'.[2] Nor was Hobart surprised when the suggestion was rejected by

OPPOSITE
Bill Kennedy Shaw, the LRDG intelligence officer, and (right) Shorty Barrett, the unit's quartermaster, who entered the church on his return to his native New Zealand. (Author's Collection)

his immediate superior, General Henry 'Jumbo' Wilson, a Luddite in the art of desert warfare. Bagnold was all the more appalled when he discovered that the only map the British had of the country west of Alexandria was dated 1915.

Bagnold's expertise at Mersa Matruh wasn't completely wasted, however, and he was able to demonstrate to the officers of the 7th Armoured Division some of the tricks he had picked up during his desert explorations a decade earlier. In his expedition into the Western Desert in 1927 Bagnold had dispensed with the unreliable magnetic compasses (because of all the metal in their vehicles) and used a sun compass instead. This was a variation on the sun dial, giving true bearings and not magnetic ones. On the rotating dial was a pointer that the driver lined up with an object on the horizon and then followed as he drove, keeping the pin's shadow on the pointer. It required patience, and one had to allow for the variation of the sun's azimuth but, by adjusting the bearing every 20 minutes, navigation became far more reliable.

Like a sailor on the high seas, Bagnold navigated at night with a theodolite and a knowledge of the stars, while the challenge of extracting a vehicle from sand was solved with the introduction of sand channels. These were sheets of perforated steel, 5 feet long and 11 inches wide, that were placed in front of the rear wheels of trucks and jeeps for support on the sand.

The last improvisation used by Bagnold was the most ingenious of the lot, although it wasn't his invention, as is often stated, but one he modified from an idea first introduced in World War I. It was a way of preserving that most precious of commodities in the desert – water. To reduce the amount of water lost during expeditions when radiators boiled over and blew water off through the overflow, Bagnold used a water condenser. 'Instead of having a free overflow pipe we led the water into a can half full of water on the side of the car so it would condense in the can,' he wrote. 'When that began to boil too it would spurt boiling water over the driver who would have to stop. All we had to do was turn into wind, wait for perhaps a minute, there would be a gurgling noise, and all the water would be sucked back into the radiator, which was full to the brim.'[3]

The longer Bagnold spent in Matruh, the more alarmed he grew that the British could be easily outmanoeuvred by the forces of Marshal Rodolfo Graziani, the 59-year-old

Sand Channels were five feet long and eleven inches wide and usually made of perforated steel. They were placed in front of the rear wheels of trucks and jeeps for support on the sand. (Courtesy of the SAS Regimental Archive)

Italian who had enjoyed a series of successes in the Abyssinian campaign of a few years earlier. Fortunately for the British, Graziani was as rigid in his thinking as General Jumbo Wilson, his British counterpart, and the two armies adopted an approach that was more akin to the battlefields of the Western Front in 1916 rather than the Western Desert of 1940. The Italians had erected a 400-mile barbed-wire line that ran south from the coast along the Libyan frontier with Egypt. The fence was 12 feet thick and 5 feet high in places, and consisted of a triple row of posts embedded in concrete. At intervals along the 400 miles of fence were outposts garrisoned by native troops, although opposite each of these outposts was a gap in the barbed wire big enough to allow a vehicle through.

The British had been working on defensive preparations of their own in and around Matruh, the Royal Engineers erecting a chain of concrete pill boxes, anti-tank ditches and minefields in anticipation of an Italian attack, as well as laying water pipes along the coast road back towards Alexandria.

The reason for this thoroughness was the importance of Egypt to the British. Control of the country meant one controlled the Suez Canal, the artery connecting the eastern oceans to the Mediterranean. To the north, in the Levant, Britain had the French forces in Syria to protect the canal from any German incursion, while to the south in Chad the French were also present to guard against any possible Italian attack from their base at Kufra in south-east Libya.

Bagnold was horrified by the blinkered vision of Wilson, an officer who was still in thrall to the static warfare of the Great War, a man lacking the imagination and

A distinctive feature and a boon for navigators, this was known as Chimney Rock and was located north of Kufra. (Courtesy of the SAS Regimental Archive)

intelligence to grasp how advances in transport, communication and weaponry made it possible to fight a more fluid, mobile and wide-ranging campaign.

Bagnold submitted a proposal a second time in January 1940 for the raising of a small reconnaissance force to patrol the 700-mile frontier with Libya, but again the idea was rebuffed by Jumbo Wilson. Irritated at the presumption of Bagnold, Wilson sent him to Turkey in February to idle his time away in a staff job. In April he flew to Khartoum to look up an old friend from his exploration days, Douglas Newbold, and he even found time to edit the proofs of the American edition of his book, *The Physics of Blown Sand*.

Then on 10 May there was another of Bagnold's laconic entries in his diary: 'Germans invade Holland and Belgium'. Bagnold had no way of knowing it at the time but the attack on the Low Countries by Nazi Germany would have far-reaching repercussions for him. 'Fall of Paris, French collapsing,' Bagnold told his diary on 15 June, and two days later Marshal Philippe Pétain, the hero of Verdun in the Great War, asked Germany for armistice terms. Britain's dismay turned to alarm when they learned that the French colonies in North Africa and the Middle East would not carry on the fight but would accede to the terms of the armistice agreed by Pétain, who became head of the Vichy government. Now Britain's position in Egypt, and its control of the Suez Canal, was threatened in the north, where French forces came under the command of the collaborationist Vichy government.

The situation was more stable in the south thanks to the decision of Félix Éboué, the governor of Chad, not to support the Vichy regime, but French forces in Morocco and Algeria were not so loyal. Their defection to Vichy meant that Italy, who had declared war on Britain on 10 June, no longer had to station a large proportion of its air and ground forces in western Libya in case of an attack from Morocco or Algeria. Instead these forces were released for use against the frontier of Egypt. With British troops in the Middle East cut off from their comrades in Europe because Italy controlled the Mediterranean and Red Sea routes, Bagnold thought it worth submitting his proposal for a light reconnaissance force once again. Third time lucky, he mused, as he updated his idea, explaining there would be three patrols heading deep into Libya to spy on the enemy's disposition:

Every vehicle of which, with a crew of three and a machine gun, was to carry its own supplies of food and water for 3 weeks, and its own petrol for 2,500 miles of travel across average soft desert surface – equivalent in petrol consumption to some 2,400 miles of road. By the use of 30-cwt [hundredweight] trucks there would be a small margin of load-carrying capacity in each. This margin, if multiplied by a large enough number of trucks would enable the patrol to carry a wireless set,

LRDG signallers used commercial procedure when communicating on their wireless so if the Germans intercepted the message they would believe it was an Egyptian company. (Courtesy of the SAS Regimental Archive)

navigating and other equipment, medical stores, spare parts and further tools, and would also allow extra petrol to be carried for another truck mounting a 2-pdr gun with its ammunition, and a light pilot car for the commander.[4]

Bagnold gave the proposal to an old friend, Brigadier Dick Baker, the pair having first met as officer cadets in the summer of 1914. Baker duly delivered the memo into the hands of Wavell, and as Bagnold recalled in an unpublished draft of his memoirs, written shortly after the end of the war:

> I had expected interest, a meeting perhaps, discussions as to whether the scheme was practicable, counter-proposals and considerable delay. But instead of this the whole scheme, just as it stood, had been strongly supported by the heads of both the operations and intelligence staffs, and had been read and approved by the C-in-C himself. I was to push on with it at once, under the aegis of Brigadier Shearer, the DMI [Director of Military Intelligence], without waiting for any formal authority.[5]

The previous complacency of the British high command had evaporated with Italy's declaration of war. Their position in Egypt was tenuous, and finally they appreciated it. The enemy's control of central Libya centred on what they called their Southern Territories Command, the headquarters of which was in Hon, in the north-west, one of five oases that also included Marada, Augila, Jalo and Jarabub. In the east of Libya (also known as Cyrenaica) the Italians were in possession of a chain of oases and wells that ran from the port of Benghazi 800 miles south into the heart of the desert. Therefore, when Italy entered the war, 'they had not only the means of reinforcing their aircraft in East Africa by flights from Kufra and Oweinat [also spelled Uweinat], but if they had so wished, they could have used Oweinat and Sarra as jumping-off places for raids by mechanised forces or by air on the Aswan Dan, our river port at Wadi Halfa, into Darfur or into the French possessions in the south-west'.[6]

In short, the British situation in Egypt in June 1940 was critical and Bagnold's proposition couldn't have been more opportune, hence the alacrity with which it was embraced by Wavell. There was just one thing – such was the pressing urgency Bagnold was instructed to raise his force within six weeks. He later described Wavell's decision to give him carte-blanche to put his idea into practice 'remarkable', adding: 'it was also astonishing that Wavell, on hearing my proposal for the first time, should have given me such a free hand seemingly without any pause for thought, specially when others had ridiculed any such idea as utterly impossible. He alone grasped the possibilities and implications.'[7]

'It was also astonishing that Wavell, on hearing my proposal for the first time, should have given me such a free hand seemingly without any pause for thought, specially when others had ridiculed any such idea as utterly impossible. He alone grasped the possibilities and implications.'

Ralph Bagnold

Bagnold wasted no time bringing his brainwave into life, cabling many of the men with whom he had explored the Libyan Desert in the inter-war years. These were members of the Zerzura Club, founded by Bagnold in November 1930 in the Greek bar of Wadi Halfa during his expedition into the desert that year. The club was named after the mythical oasis that had drawn many an adventurer into the desert. Among the six explorers present at the club's inaugural meeting were Guy Prendergast, Douglas Newbold and Bill Kennedy Shaw.

Prendergast, who had been on the 1927 expedition to Siwa, reluctantly declined the invitation to join Bagnold in Cairo. He was now a major in the Royal Tank Regiment and stationed in England. Similarly, Newbold was the political head of the Sudan government and obliged to fulfil his duties in Khartoum. One experienced explorer who did respond positively to Bagnold's telegram was 44-year-old Pat Clayton, who arrived in the Egyptian capital from Tanganyika where he had spent 18 years working for the Egyptian Survey Department.

Bagnold also approached Rupert Harding-Newman and Teddy Mitford, both of whom were serving army officers with experience of desert exploration. The former was stationed in Cairo, like Prendergast a tank officer, and while he wasn't given permission to join the new unit he was encouraged to offer logistical assistance in its formation.

A desert water hole from where artesian water could be drawn. (Courtesy of the SAS Regimental Archive)

Captain Mitford, a cousin of the notorious Mitford sisters, one of whom, Unity, was a friend of Adolf Hitler, was one of the few Europeans to have travelled by motor car across the desert to Kufra Oasis. He jumped at the chance to join Bagnold and his 'private army', and received permission to leave his regiment.

The other pre-war explorer recruited was 38-year-old Bill Kennedy Shaw, who was working for the Colonial Service in Jerusalem when Bagnold flew up to see him.

Some of the men from T Patrol, which was commanded by Pat Clayton until his capture in January 1941. (Courtesy of the SAS Regimental Archive)

Described by his contemporaries as 'utterly charming' with a 'tidy and academic mind', Kennedy Shaw spoke Arabic and was an expert in archaeology, botany, entomology and navigation.[8] Like Bagnold he had chafed at his contribution to the war effort in the first months of the conflict, but when he had written to Middle East Command offering his services as a desert explorer he had been told 'that it was considered inadvisable to take me off the job I was then doing – which was helping to censor the Palestine newspapers'.[9]

Kennedy Shaw couldn't believe his luck as Bagnold outlined his idea. 'Here was the army proposing to pay me to do what I had spent a lot of time and money doing for myself before the war,' he wrote later in his war memoir, *Long Range Desert Group*. 'This was a chance which comes only once in a lifetime … in two weeks I was out of the Colonial Service and into the army.'

Between them, Bagnold and his coterie of desert explorers called up old contacts and cajoled new ones in their quest to have the unit ready within the six weeks demanded by Wavell. Harding-Newman 'wangled' a quantity of sun compasses from the Egyptian Army; maps were printed at the Cairo Survey Department; theodolites were charmed from the Physical Department and field glasses were donated by race enthusiasts from the Gezira Sporting Club. Among other items obtained during this period were nautical almanacs (for use with the theodolites), logarithmic tables and trouser clips (to keep maps on their boards). All the while, recalled Kennedy Shaw, 'in half-forgotten shops in the back streets of Cairo we searched for a hundred and one (to the Army) unorthodox needs'.

After the capture of Clayton, T Patrol was led by the highly regarded New Zealand officer, Bruce Ballantyne. (Courtesy of the SAS Regimental Archive)

The biggest challenge was the vehicles, or at least it would have been had not Harding-Newman been in Cairo to help. Bagnold described Harding-Newman's contribution to the formation of his unit as 'invaluable' and within 24 hours of being asked, he had four types of truck for Bagnold to test. 'We took them out for test runs over rocks and through soft sand,' remembered Bagnold. 'I decided there and then upon an ordinary commercial pattern of 30-cwt Chevrolet, fast, simple and easy to handle.' Mitford recalled that Bagnold 'produced a camouflage pattern of very broad dark and light stripes, different for each truck, which would help in areas of rock and scrub'. Additionally, the 7th Armoured Division's red rat insignia was painted on each vehicle to further conceal the unit's 'real purpose'.[10]

An immaculate T2 Patrol, commanded by Second Lt Saunders, pose for the camera. (Courtesy of the SAS Regimental Archive)

Harding-Newman also charmed the Egyptian government into loaning Bagnold 19 trucks from their fleet, with a further 14 supplied by General Motors in Alexandria. These were then delivered to the Army Ordnance workshops where Harding-Newman oversaw their adaptation to off-road desert travel – including the attachment of water condensers to radiators, the raising of the sides of the normal box body in order to carry the required loads, mountings for machine guns and brackets for compasses.

Bagnold was delighted, all the more so because he found it onerous to go cap in hand to organizations and companies in search of equipment. A shy and introverted man by nature, with a stammer to boot, Bagnold wasn't a man who exuded effortless bonhomie. An officer who joined the unit a few months later described its commanding officer as a 'small wizened figure with piercing eyes and an abrupt manner',[11] while David Lloyd Owen, who ended the war as CO (commanding officer) of the LRDG (Long Range Desert Group) said of his predecessor, 'He was not particularly ebullient nor forthcoming with pleasantries. He was not that kind of man; there was never any time to waste over trivialities in his life. He lived it to a plan, which was worked out in every detail of efficiency and purpose'.[12]

Bagnold had his vehicles and equipment, now he just had to find the men to fill the ranks of his new unit. His first choice were Australians, conscious that in World War I they had manned the Light Car Patrols (LCP), the motorized unit formed in 1916 to patrol the Egyptian border against attack from the Senussi forces led by Sayed Ahmed esh Sherif, an ally of the Turks. It was the LCP who, according to Bill Kennedy Shaw, had invented the sun compasses and the water condensers, although

David Lloyd Owen (standing far left) with members of his Y Patrol. The sergeant on the right of the photo is the highly respected Jock Carningham, who was captured on Leros in 1943. (Author's Collection)

they had to make do with tyres that were just 3½ inches in diameter, thin and fragile compared to the 10-inch sand tyres on the 30cwt Chevrolets.

Lieutenant General Thomas Blamey, in command of Australian forces in the Middle East, refused to release any of its men to serve under British command on the orders of his government, so a despondent Bagnold returned to Cairo and approached Brigadier Edward Puttick, temporary commander of the New Zealand forces in Egypt in the absence of Major-General Bernard Freyberg, who was in England with the second infantry brigade of the NZ division. Puttick acceded to Bagnold's request and 80 officers, non-commissioned officers and men from the New Zealand Divisional Cavalry Regiment and Machine Gun Battalion were selected from the volunteers who answered the call for 'men who possess stamina and initiative'.[13]

Bill Kennedy Shaw was impressed when the New Zealanders arrived in Cairo to begin their training. He had never encountered any before. 'All the knowledge I had of them were my father's words of the last war – that they were the finest troops from the Dominions. Closer acquaintance showed that one should always believe one's father.'[14] Bagnold described the Kiwi volunteers as a 'sturdy basis of sheep-farmers, leavened by technicians, property-owners and professional men, and including a few Maoris. Shrewd, dry-humoured, curious of every new thing, and quietly thrilled when I told them what we were to do.'[15] Kennedy Shaw shared his commander's assessment, adding that: 'Physically their own fine country had made them on the average fitter than us, and they had that inherent superiority which in most of a man's qualities the countryman will always have over the townsman.'[16]

Bagnold explained to the New Zealanders that the unit to which they now belonged was concerned primarily with reconnaissance; that they were to discover what the Italians were up to in the interior of the Libyan Desert 600 miles west of the Suez Canal. To reach the enemy's positions they would have to cross the Great Sand Sea, the vast protective barrier roughly the size of Ireland that stretches from Siwa Oasis, in the north-west of Egypt, almost as far south as Sudan. In total, the Libyan Desert is the size of India, 1,200 miles by 1,000, composed of limestone to the north and sandstone to the south. The terrain varies enormously, from the treacherous sand seas to the 6,000ft massif of the Jebel Uweinat, and temperatures were similarly inconsistent, sometimes reaching 120°F in the shade in the summer and plummeting to several degrees below freezing in the winter. The landscape was also one of sharp contrasts. The gravel desert was called in Arabic *serir*, the stony

New Zealanders, like these men of T Patrol, were the first recruits to the LRDG and their initiative and endurance were highly valued by Ralph Bagnold. (Courtesy of the SAS Regimental Archive)

areas known as *hammada*. Both, in general, were good to travel on because the wind had removed the sand, a process known as 'deflation'. At other times they would encounter a bed of powdered clay, which enveloped intruders with choking, billowing clouds of white dust that were visible for miles around.

Bagnold explained that reconnaissance wasn't possible by air, because what long-range aircraft were at their disposal were required for other purposes, 'and in any case would have been of little avail for patrolling such an enormous area without an elaborate system of landing grounds and petrol supplies, neither of which existed'.[17] It would have to be done by motor vehicle, manned by a small band of intrepid men who respected but weren't cowed by the immensity of the desert. Bagnold, Kennedy Shaw and the other middle-aged desert explorers spent several weeks schooling the New Zealanders in desert travel and navigation, vehicle maintenance and the conservation of food and water. Kennedy Shaw was impressed with the 'speed and thoroughness' with which the New Zealanders absorbed all the instructions. 'For it is not enough to have learned how to operate, in the military sense, in the desert … the problem is to make yourself so much master over the appalling difficulties of Nature – heat, thirst, cold, rain, fatigue – that, overcoming these, you yet have physical energy and mental resilience to deal with the greater object, the winning of the war.'[18]

———————

The landscape could change rapidly from flat, hard gravel surface into broken, hilly country. (Courtesy of the SAS Regimental Archive)

Bagnold had his unit ready for action within the six weeks allotted by General Wavell. The officer afforded the privilege of leading the inaugural patrol was Pat Clayton, who drove out of Cairo on 7 August in two Chevrolet trucks with a hand-picked party of seven. They journeyed west, motoring across the Italian routes leading from the coast to Kufra and the south, and returned to the Egyptian capital without mishap 12 days later, having travelled 1,600 miles in 13 days. 'We had, as hoped and intended, not fired a shot or seen the enemy,' reflected Clayton. 'But we had proved that [we] could go and come back to a strict timetable.'[19] The patrol had also discovered a hitherto unmapped strip of sand sea, 100km wide, immediately east of the Jalo–Kufra road.

The next day, 20 August, Clayton and Bagnold briefed General Wavell on the first sortie of the unit – provisionally designated the Long Range Patrol – and such was his admiration for their achievements Wavell 'made up his mind then and there to give us his strongest backing'.[20]

CHAPTER 3

INTO ACTION

Bagnold divided his unit into three patrols, assigning to each a letter of no particular significance. W Patrol was commanded by Captain Teddy Mitford, captains Pat Clayton and Bruce Ballantyne (a New Zealander) were the officers in charge of T Patrol, and Captain Don Steele, a farmer from Wellington, led R Patrol. Each patrol consisted of two officers, around 30 other ranks, transported in 11 30cwt Chevrolet trucks and a light 15cwt Ford V8 pilot car. Each patrol was armed with a 37mm Bofors anti-tank gun, four Boys anti-tank rifles and 11 Lewis guns, the gas-operated weapon from World War I.

Rations (which were packed in wood petrol cases when the LRDG was on a patrol) were of particular concern to Bagnold, based on his own experience, and Kennedy Shaw was responsible for devising the unit's diet while 'up the blue', army slang for on operations in the desert. 'Knowing that we should often get no fresh meat or bread or vegetables for weeks or months on end, we needed a special ration scale,' he said. Tracking down back issues of *Geographical Journal*, Kennedy Shaw used the scales listed in the magazine by Harding-Newman in his accounts of his desert expeditions in the 1930s. 'Using these and the kinds of food provided by the Army in the Middle East, I increased the amounts of some, reduced others, and sent the result to the medical people,' explained Kennedy Shaw.[1] The scale was approved and a sample menu drawn up that became the template for all British special forces units for the rest of the war. It comprised:

Major Don Steele, left, the New Zealand officer who commanded R Patrol, and Colonel Guy Prendergast, who replaced Bagnold as the LRDG CO in August 1941. (Courtesy of the SAS Regimental Archive)

Breakfast suggestions
Porridge (no milk or sugar)
Fried bacon with oatmeal fritter
Bacon and oatmeal cake
Bacon stuffed with cooked oatmeal
Bacon with oatmeal chappatties [sic]
Tiffin
Lentil soup
Various sandwich spreads on biscuits
Cheese and oatmeal savoury
Cheese and oatmeal cake
Oatmeal and date cookies
Dinner
Stewed mutton with dumplings
Meat pudding

The water ration was then six pints a day, wrote Kennedy Shaw, 'one in tea at breakfast, two in tea in the evening, one in lime-juice at lunch, and two in your water-bottle to be drunk at will'. The ration was sufficient in winter but a test of discipline in the summer. There were times, when the sun was at its fiercest, when water was the only topic of conversation. The men talked about the best way to conserve their six pints: some recommended small sips at regular intervals, others said large gulps less frequently worked best. One or two men liked to damp a handkerchief with a few drops of water and press it to their forehead or neck. The more elaborately minded left their water in a thermos overnight so the water was cool in the morning.

In the first week of September, Bagnold and his unit embarked on their first operation. The Italians, after three months of inactivity, had finally advanced east, crossing the Egyptian frontier as far as Sidi Barrani, approximately 45 miles west of the British position at Mersa Matruh. Bagnold decided to head into the Libyan Desert to discover if the enemy was on the move towards Kufra and a possible strike into Egypt from the south. It was just the sort of reconnaissance that Wavell had in mind when he authorized the formation of the Long Range Patrol. On 5 September, Bagnold, Kennedy Shaw and a small HQ patrol left Cairo in the company of Mitford's W Patrol, comprised entirely of Kiwis. Pat Clayton's T Patrol, also containing New Zealanders, included among its ranks trooper Frank Jopling, an English-born 28-year-old farmhand from Auckland.

On Clayton's first short reconnaissance of the desert the previous month, he had been a little perturbed to discover that several of the New Zealanders had brought cameras with them, as if they were tourists on a jolly excursion. Subsequently an order had been issued by Bagnold that cameras and diaries were strictly forbidden on any operation into enemy territory. Jopling ignored the command, commencing a journal from the first day that he entitled, 'Our First Trip Into Action'. As he recorded, it wasn't the most auspicious of debuts:

An early LRDG patrol with the lead vehicle an American Chevrolet. Note the windshields and what appears to be the pith helmet worn by the soldier. (Courtesy of Jack Valenti)

35

5th Sept. 1940: Well, well, well, what organisation!! and what a start for a history-making trip. We were all lined up and all ready to move off when they suddenly decided that the 15cwt V8s were no good the way they were as when they loaded them up, the tyres hit the mudguards so they decided that they would have to take them to Ordnance and get them altered. So we were told that we wouldn't be leaving until 4.0 p.m.[2]

The V8s were the Ford pilot cars that by the end of the year had been largely discarded because they lacked durability and their engines frequently clogged with sand. On this afternoon, however, the first ones to be repaired belonged to HQ and W Patrol, and they moved off at 2pm. Jopling's T Patrol followed a short while later, the soldiers grouching at the delay. 'Not necessarily because we want to have a go at the Italians,' wrote Jopling, 'but more for the adventure and the excitement of the trip. We are going where no trucks have ever been before over country that has never been mapped, we will probably see things that have never been seen by white men.'[3]

The vehicles drove through the afternoon and into the early evening, the men transfixed by the changing colours of the desert as the sun began its descent. They stopped for the night at 7.30pm having covered 123km, R, T and W patrols camping in different spots among the dunes. They then embarked on what would become in time an all-too-familiar routine. Two of the patrol began to cook supper, or 'tea' as Jopling called it, and as the smells began to waft tantalizingly around the vehicles the navigator finished plotting the dead reckoning of their day's travel and then confirmed their position by taking a snap shot of the stars with his theodolite. The gunners examined their weapons and cleaned them if necessary, and the drivers and fitters (Jopling's role) checked the tyre pressures, lubricating oil, petrol and water. They would also check for any signs of wear and tear to the vehicle and any damage would be reported to the navigator, who in turn would brief the patrol commander. The most important item was water, because if it was ever found that there was shortage – leaky jerrycans, for example – then the patrol would have to be closed down and returned to base. Only when all the tasks had been accomplished to the commander's satisfaction could the men tuck into their food. On the evening of 5 September, Jopling and his comrades were treated to 'bully beef, spuds, onions and peas and curry, all made into a stew'.

An LRDG patrol traverses the Libyan Desert. The vehicles kept a good distance between each other in case of aircraft attack. (Author's Collection)

Captioned originally 'Stuck on a razorback', this photo shows three LRDG soldiers discussing the best method to extricate their vehicle from the crest of the sand dune. (Author's Collection)

The night passed uneventfully, as did the following day, as Jopling described in his diary.

6th Sept. 40

12-0 noon.★

I am afraid I have had neither the time nor opportunity to write this sooner. We got up at 6-0 a.m and set off at 8-0 a.m. We couldn't very well start earlier as clouds hid the sun and it is very slow going without the sun compass. We have now done 134 kilos [sic] over very rough going. I hope it is better this afternoon. They are putting the scrim and nets over the trucks now and they look very effective. 'W', 'R' and ourselves are all here but we will be parting from the 'W' Patrol any time now. We are having sardines and tinned fruit for lunch, which sounds all right to me just at present.

6-0 p.m. We have again stopped for the night near some sand dunes after having travelled 257 kilos since breakfast, which is the biggest mileage we have put up in one day since there was such a force as an LRP [Long Range Patrol].

It has been very rough and soft all day except the last 20 kilos which has been very good. The poor old truck has had to work hard today and has been boiling most of the time.

There is another stew on tonight but I like them very much.

Well, I must stop now before I get caught.[4]

★ Patrols always stopped for lunch at midday because this was the hour that the sun was directly overhead and cast no shadow, and so rendered the sun compass ineffective.

In the days that followed, the three patrols laid petrol and supply dumps along the Libyan frontier so that they would be able to operate in and around Kufra and Uweinat without having to return to Egypt for a resupply. T and R patrols transported 7,000 gallons of petrol across the hardest tract of the Sand Sea from Siwa Oasis to a pre-war landmark called Big Cairn on the western fringe. The Cairn was five feet high, the only feature in a flat monotonous gravel plain between two sand seas. It had been built by Pat Clayton in 1932 and now it was used as a beacon for a supply dump of petrol and water.

Meanwhile Kennedy Shaw oversaw the laying of a petrol dump beyond 'Ain Dalla, on the eastern edge of the Sand Sea. He had last visited 'Ain Dalla in 1930 and it hadn't changed in the intervening decade. The stunted palms, the decrepit wooden hut and the refreshing waters of its spring. The route to 'Ain Dalla was what Kennedy Shaw called the 'underground road to Libya', allowing those daring enough to travel on it to enter Libya from Cairo without being spotted because it was 'guarded by the sand sea which the Italians would never expect us to cross'.

Once all the supply dumps were in place, the patrols split up. Clayton headed south towards the French frontier in Tekro, 600 miles south, Steele returned to Siwa to ferry more supplies to the Big Cairn, and Mitford and Kennedy Shaw drove east towards the Kalansho Sand Sea in the direction of Kufra.

En route they were confronted by dunes as high as 300 feet in a range that stretched for 20km. Kennedy Shaw and Mitford led by example, demonstrating to the Kiwis the safest way to surmount a dune – by accelerating up the slope, then slowing near the top and stopping on the crest with all four wheels in line. Then it was a question of toppling the truck gently over the edge of the precipice, so the vehicle sailed down the sand axle-deep in first gear to the bottom. Never, warned the two explorers, accelerate over a dune, because 'in a flying leap from the crest the car turns over and over'.*

On September 16 a *qibli* descended on Mitford's patrol, the Libyan name for the hot wind peculiar to the region. Kennedy Shaw had experienced the Egyptian *khamsin*, but that seemed mild compared to the suffocating heat of the *qibli*. 'You don't merely feel hot,' he recalled. 'You don't merely feel tired, you feel as if every bit of energy had left you, as if your brain was thrusting its way through the top of your head and you want to lie down in a stupor till the accursed sun has gone down.'[5] Often men were sick after supper because of the effects of a *qibli*, their digestion in turmoil. It was the Rhodesians who eventually discovered what came

---

* In the three years the LRDG operated in the desert they suffered one death and one broken back as a result of vehicles taking dunes too fast.

to be known as the 'anti-*qibli* pick-me-up'. It consisted of equal parts of rum and lime-juice, and the men swore by its medicinal powers.

The *qibli* lasted three days and it wasn't until 20 September that the men began to breathe freely once more. On the same day they ran into their first Italians. 'While we were following the track to Kufra near the LG [Landing Ground No. 7] there appeared, churning slowly through the soft sand, two six-ton lorries of the Italian firm of Trucci and Monti, the fortnightly convoy to Kufra,' said Kennedy Shaw.[6] Mitford ordered his men to fire a burst from the machine gun over the lead truck, thus giving W Patrol the honour of firing the unit's first shots in anger. But that was the extent of the 'battle'. The two vehicles braked hard and out stumbled two Italians and four native troops, and a goat. Mitford dismounted and he and his men took stock of their prisoners. They were a sorry-looking bunch. One of the Italian drivers spoke English, the rest just grinned nervously. It was hard not to feel a smidgen of sympathy for the native soldiers, caught up in a European war and armed with hopelessly inadequate weapons. One complained that his wife wouldn't be happy to hear he'd been captured. Mitford reassured the soldier 'that he will be allowed to write and explain his absence to his wife'.[7] Inside the trucks the New Zealanders discovered 2,500 gallons of petrol, a lot of medical supplies, a quantity of shirts and mats and, most importantly, a bag of official mail. That provided useful information, as did the prisoners, who informed their captors that the Italians had recently despatched 6,250 soldiers to Uweinat.

Mitford's patrol reached Cairo on 4 October. Bagnold described them as 'bearded, unwashed but exultant ruffians', the stench from their ragged uniforms so overpowering that most had to be peeled off their bodies and burned.

Pat Clayton's T Patrol had also sported extravagant beards on arriving back at Abbassia Barracks on 1 October. In the three weeks since they had parted company with the other two patrols, Frank Jopling had stayed faithful to his diary, recording their adventure daily.

13th Sept. 40.
We are 347 kilos South of SIWA now. We are all enjoying this trip and not one of us would change places with any man in any army. I have since found out that the first 60 kilos from SIWA as far as is known, have never been crossed by white men.

14th Sept. 40.
10-0 a.m. This morning I started doing maintenance on the truck but the wind got up and started a sand storm. This sand is a sort of fine pebbles, and believe me, when it is travelling at 30 or 40 MPH it can sting. However, we had to give up

the maintenance and we have rigged up as good a shelter as possible and we are now going to have a spell. The sand still seems to come through but it is better than nothing.[8]

On 15 September, T Patrol crossed the Egyptian border and by the end of the day they were some 100km inside Libya. Jopling stood guard from 9pm to 10pm and passed some of the time listening to Lord Haw-Haw on the wireless.* The next day, 16 September, the patrol encountered the *qibli* that had so enervated Bill Kennedy Shaw and his men. Jopling judged the temperature to be 'at least 130° in the shade', but noted in his diary that everyone remained in good spirits.

They set off early the following day before the desert became too great a furnace and by 9am had covered nearly 100km. Double tyre tracks were spotted and followed, leading to what Jopling described as an outpost. Clayton instructed the men to prepare for action and the patrol then charged the target as if they were a band of marauding tribesmen on camels. But the target never defended itself and when they got closer, Clayton saw it was an emergency landing ground for Italian aircraft. There was a palpable sense of anti-climax among the New Zealanders. 'We were all keyed up now,' recorded Jopling, 'and were scanning the horizon for anything that may come over the top.' But nothing appeared and the men drove off in frustration. Over lunch Clayton told the men to cheer up; tomorrow they would make for Naarten Bisciara, a well that was guarded by Italians. They'd have their chance for a scrap then.

---

* AKA William Joyce, the American-born Irish fascist who fled to Germany in 1939 and spent the war broadcasting Nazi propaganda in English. He was hanged for treason in January 1946.

An LRDG patrol in late 1940, again, thought to be en route to Murzuk in January 1941. (Courtesy of Jack Valenti)

But once again the enemy proved elusive. 'We made a spectacular charge only to find that there was no one there and we had the well to ourselves,' wrote Jopling in his diary. This time the disappointment was diminished by the urge to draw water from the well. It was a challenge. The water, Jopling estimated, was 180ft below the lid of the well, but there was a pulley, to which the New Zealanders attached the bottom half of a jerrycan. Slowly, carefully, the men hauled up the first bucket of water. It tasted 'beautiful', and there was even enough with which to have a good wash.[9]★

Reinvigorated, Jopling was better able to appreciate the desolation of their location. Few men of their civilization had ever stood in such a remote spot. Siwa was 800 miles distant. Scattered around the well was a carpet of bones. Clayton explained to the men that some were the carcasses of sheep and goats, killed by nomads for food as they camped at the well; other bones belonged to camels that were too weak to continue and had therefore also been sacrificed for food.

The next day, 19 September, they launched a third fruitless attack on a target that turned out to be a shelter for nomadic camel trains. There was another well, one which was measured at 500 feet deep. 'It makes one wonder how it was ever made,' wrote Jopling, who discovered a dead snake close to the well. He showed it to Clayton, who identified it as a horned viper. 'Is it poisonous?' asked the Kiwi. 'Deadly,' replied the officer.

The New Zealanders liked what they saw of Clayton. He knew his stuff all right and, while he respected the desert, he was at ease in its vastness. He seemed impervious to panic, and that could only rub off on his men. 'There is no doubt the captain has got a lot of confidence in himself or perhaps I should say contempt for the enemy,' Jopling confided to his diary on the evening of 18 September.

Every night so far we have been allowed to light fires to boil up and make tea, etc, and last night, being only about 15 miles off the well, we thought we certainly wouldn't be allowed to light a fire. But he came along and said we could light a fire providing we didn't take too long. So tonight with the danger of aircraft following our tracks we certainly wouldn't be allowed to light a fire but sure enough he comes along and says we can light as many fires as we like as he wants to attract attention of anyone round here. He also said tonight that there are only about two pilots in Libya that they would send down here and he didn't think they would bother.[10]

★ It is worth noting that water rations usually forbade men from washing. One LRDG veteran, Les Sullivan, recalled after the war that Bagnold taught them how to wash using sand. 'He said that washing does not get you clean because we don't normally get dirty. He reckoned you washed and bathed to get rid of dead cells of skin. So in deep desert we bathed in the sand.'

Word had by now reached T patrol that Captain Mitford's W Patrol had had a brush with the enemy, claiming first blood for the LRP. The two patrols were making for a rendezvous close to Uweinat, and Clayton's men were 'quite keen' to find some Italians to fight so that they wouldn't be subjected to ribbing from their compatriots. They saw no Italians, but shortly after lunch on 25 September, just as Jopling was finishing a cigarette in a nice shady spot, he was ambushed by an enemy far more feared. 'I saw a movement in a bush about a yard from me,' he wrote. 'I looked up and there was a snake coming towards us.' Jopling shouted a warning and the man next to him, Fred Kendell, grabbed a shovel and with one well-aimed blow decapitated the serpent. They measured it. It was 4ft 6in. in length and 2in. wide. 'Is it poisonous?' they asked Clayton. He picked up the head and saw the two fangs. Yes. 'No one could sleep on the ground after that,' said Jopling.

The patrols rendezvoused not far from Uweinat on 26 September. The original intention had been to meet at Uweinat, but the intelligence provided to Mitford by the captured native troops of 6,250 reinforcements recently arriving there had necessitated a change of plan.

The patrols soon separated, Bagnold having informed Clayton and Mitford that they would return to Cairo, refit, and seek permission from Wavell to launch a series

Some of the LRDG shot gazelles to supplement their rations although not all soldiers approved of killing the local wildlife. (Courtesy of the SAS Regimental Archive)

of ambushes against Italian convoys heading north from Uweinat and Kufra. R and W patrols left first for Cairo, and Clayton led his T Patrol in the direction of Abbassia on the morning of 27 September. The going was good and at dusk on 28 September, Jopling proudly noted in his diary that they had covered 336km that day, a record for the patrol. At lunch on 1 October, the patrol gazed at the three pyramids in the distance as they ate their rations. They were almost close enough to smell the soap waiting for them back at base. They finally rolled into Abbassia in mid-afternoon, requiring directions to their new barracks in an isolation hospital. Once there, the quartermaster escorted them to the store rooms where they were reunited with their kit bags. Then came the mail. Jopling had 19 letters. It was like being a little boy at Christmas once more. He was hot, tired and dirty, but he spent four hours reading his mail, digesting each word. Only then, as he explained to his diary, did he turn to his appearance. 'Well, I am going to have a hot bath which we can get here and then to go to the barber to get a haircut, shave and shampoo, after which I will probably feel a lot better.'

Jopling paid for his ablutions from the £1 given to each soldier at the orderly room, along with a word of thanks from Ralph Bagnold for their efforts during

This gazelle, shot in March 1942, was cut up and turned into a stew. (Courtesy of the SAS Regimental Archive)

what he acknowledged as a punishing operation deep behind enemy lines. He said that General Wavell had promised to express his gratitude to the unit in a letter which would be pinned to the notice board. Wavell fulfilled his promise, and the letter was duly exhibited:

I should like to convey to the officers and other ranks under your command my congratulations and appreciation of the successful results of the recent patrols carried out by your unit in central Libya.

I am aware of the extreme physical difficulties which had to be overcome, particularly the intense heat. That your operation, involving as it did 150,000 track miles, has been brought to so successful a conclusion indicates a standard of efficiency in preparation and execution, of which you, your officers and men may justly be proud.

A full report of your exploits has already been telegraphed to the War Office and I wish you all the best of luck in your continued operations in which you will

This LRDG soldier sits behind a Vickers K gas-operated machine gun, capable of firing up to 1,200 rounds per minute. (Getty)

be making an important contribution towards keeping Italian forces in back areas on the alert and adding to the anxieties and difficulties of our enemy.[11]

Bagnold referred to the 'letter of appreciation' in his diary on 2 October, and three days later he recorded that he'd submitted an official request to reconstitute the Long Range Patrol as the Long Range Desert Group (LRDG), which was 'to consist of 2 squadrons of 3 patrols each. More officers to be asked for'. The new name would, Bagnold hoped, reflect that his force was more than just a small reconnaissance patrol.

On 17 October, Anthony Eden, Minister of State for War, visited Abbassia Barracks to inspect the LRP. Jopling was impressed with the British politician, a man who in his own war had been awarded a Military Cross in 1916. Eden was 'informal and chatted with the men very well', and they made a similar impression on the minister. The following month the War Office authorized the expansion of the unit to comprise two squadrons each of three patrols, each patrol consisting of two officers and 28 other ranks. Bagnold was promoted to acting lieutenant colonel, Don Steele rose from a lieutenant to acting captain and Captain Mitford replaced his three pips with a crown as he became a major. Finally, the War Office agreed that in future the unit would be known as the Long Range Desert Group.

While the officers of the LRDG enjoyed all the privileges in Cairo that came with their rank, the men had to make do with the more insalubrious establishments. Not that they didn't try their luck in the more 'swanky' places. Jopling took his pay into town with the objective of living it up for a couple of days. 'I decided I would like to stay at an expensive hotel for a couple of nights to see if I would still be a "gentleman", so I enquired at 3 hotels and they all said that no soldiers were allowed, only Officers. When I asked them why, they said "because they [soldiers] drink too much and make too much noise!" ' Jopling protested that he was teetotal but the hoteliers laughed in his face. 'I suppose they couldn't believe that a man could be a soldier and not drink,' he muttered to his diary.

CHAPTER 4

EXPANSION AND EXCITEMENT

The LRDG was expanding, but with British soldiers and not New Zealanders. General Freyberg, upon returning to the Middle East from England, was as 'wild as anything'[1] when he discovered some of his finest troops had been purloined by the British. Storming into Wavell's office, the New Zealander was told that the men were making his country proud 'and would stay'. A furious Freyberg cabled the New Zealand government in protest and eventually a compromise was agreed whereby the New Zealanders would be 'replaced gradually' by British soldiers. But nonetheless Bagnold was now faced with the problem of recruiting soldiers able to withstand the demands of the LRDG. As he noted in the war diary: 'Owing to chronic shortages in officers and other ranks in the Middle East, unit and formation commanders were very loath to part with men of the high standard required for the peculiar and exacting work which the Long Range Patrols existed to do.'

While Bagnold and Kennedy Shaw embarked on a recruitment campaign among the infantry depots of the Middle East, W, T and R Patrols sortied once more into the desert to conduct operations between Kufra and Jalo, approximately 300 miles to the north. A force of some 700 Italians had been garrisoned at Jalo for a number of years, their HQ in the oasis's fort, outside which was a native village. The water in Jalo was brackish and unlike other desert oases there were no pools in

OPPOSITE
Benny Watson brews up using a 'Benghazi burner', a fuel can filled with sand and petrol. (Courtesy of the SAS Regimental Archive)

47

which to bathe. Additionally, the air was not just fetid, it was black with the flies attracted by the latrine pits and, in some cases, the human faeces that lay uncovered in the hot sun.

Frank Jopling had trouble getting to grips with their destination, describing the places to his diary as 'Koofra' and 'Jarlow'. He was more sure of their mission, once Captain Clayton had briefed the patrol. 'We are going to find a narrow part of the road and put some mines down and we are going to look for the most likely alternative route where they would most likely go after they found out that the road was mined, and lay some more there,' he wrote.[2]

Jopling sensed there was a 'bit of excitement' as the patrol headed into the desert. It would be a short mission — Clayton promised they would be back on 7 November — and this time they had orders to actively seek out and engage the enemy. T Patrol was accompanied by Captain Steele's R Patrol, along with an undesignated patrol of four trucks commanded by Bill Kennedy Shaw, but Teddy Mitford's W Patrol had been disbanded, with the men returned to their New Zealand regiments.

In recognition of the more aggressive nature of the operation, Clayton's truck was armed with a Vickers K machine gun, a gas-operated weapon that could fire up to 1,200 rounds a minute. It was far superior to the obsolescent Lewis Gun and gave the patrol confidence.

Lt Cecil 'Jacko' Jackson, right, was the Rhodesian officer responsible for taking many of the photos in this book. (Courtesy of the SAS Regimental Archive)

The going was variable as they headed west. They covered 120km in two hours on the morning of 28 October over what Clayton described as 'the best going God made'. The next day they spent wearying hours digging out vehicles from the hot, liquid sand, but on All Hallows' Eve they were chilled by 'a strong icy wind'. To make life more uncomfortable, Clayton for the first time forbade the lighting of fires because they were very near Italian positions. Jopling and his pals rigged up a tarpaulin as a wind breaker and huddled together for warmth round the primus stove.

The men were up early the next morning, 1 November, sheathed in their greatcoats and cap comforters. The bitter cold followed them north, and by 7am they were only 60 miles from the Libyan coast. Clayton considered it a good place

to sew some mines on the road. Transport travelled frequently along this route, and
what's more, Clayton told the men, the Italians would likely think the mines had
been laid by a raiding party that had arrived by boat and struck inland.

With the mines concealed in the road, the LRDG headed west, then turned
south, towards the oasis at Aujila. The men were on a heightened state of alert as
they began to see more and more tyre tracks. There was a fort as well as an oasis at
Aujila but they did not know the strength of the garrison. They mined the approach
to the oasis, recorded Jopling in his diary:

An LRDG vehicle is
bogged down in the
mud after a desert
storm. (Courtesy of
the SAS Regimental
Archive)

It didn't rain often in
the desert but when it
did the terrain could
quickly become a sea
of mud. (Courtesy of
the SAS Regimental
Archive)

And the captain, having given the signal to start up, had just started to move forward, when a Native soldier came over the ridge giving the Italian salute, thinking we were an Italian colonel and his escort, or something. As soon as he got close to the truck, Clarrie Roderick who was on the truck fixed his bayonet and jumped off the truck, pointing rifle and bayonet at the soldier, who nearly dropped with fright, but managed to raise his hands above his head.

The captain first put him on his truck but afterwards put him on mine. He informed us that there were five men in the fort but only two soldiers, both Italian Sgts.[3]

Furnished with the information, Clayton led his patrol to the top of the rise overlooking the fort and on his signal, the LRDG blazed away with rifles, Vickers, Bofors and Boys anti-tank rifles. 'Believe me,' reflected Jopling, 'I wouldn't care to have been in the Fort while the bombardment was on. We fired 7 shells with the Bofors gun and every one was a hit.'★

Captioned 'With our prisoners', this photo was taken in September 1941. (Courtesy of the SAS Regimental Archive)

★ The 37mm Bofors was mounted on a turntable at the back of a truck, and came to be disliked by the LRDG because of its weight.

Ron Low and Ken
Low around a campfire,
somewhere in Libya,
October 1941.
(Courtesy of the SAS
Regimental Archive)

As the intensity of the fire eased, the fort gates were flung open and out ran five
terrified figures in the direction of the native village situated nearby. Clayton didn't
pursue them; he had the prisoner requested by Bagnold, and he was anxious not to
dawdle in an enemy location. He did, however, allow his men a few minutes to look
inside the fort, where the LRDG discovered a couple of machine guns and a
number of swords, two of which were seized as souvenirs.

R Patrol, meanwhile, under the command of Don Steele, had also been busy
mining roads, in their case in the vicinity of Uweinat. On 31 October they had come
across an Italian dump containing 75 18kg bombs, 640 2kg bombs and ten drums of
petrol, each one with 44 gallons of precious fuel. Kennedy Shaw recalled that Steele,
'who always liked playing with explosives, had a day out'. And his day wasn't finished.
Later in the afternoon, on a landing ground west of Ain Zuwaia, R Patrol destroyed
an Italian Savoia-Marchetti, a three-engined bomber, along with 160 drums of petrol.

As well as the destruction of the bomb dump and aircraft, and the sacking of the
fort, the LRDG patrol was notable for its co-operation with the Royal Air Force
(RAF). From 28 October to 4 November, a Vickers-Valentia from No. 216
Squadron, crewed by six airmen and also carrying Captain Mitford and Captain
Frank Edmondson, the medical officer, was at their disposal. It was fitted with long-
range tanks and fuel had been cached by the LRDG at three dumps prior to its first
flight, which, as Jopling proudly told his diary, was the first time an aircraft had
flown over the Great Sand Sea. Disconcertingly, however, added the New Zealander,
'the plane followed our tracks at an altitude of 600ft and spotted our trucks 15 miles
away, which shows that our camouflage isn't very effective'.

Two LRDG soldiers prepare to get a small fire going at the end of a day's patrolling. (Courtesy of the SAS Regimental Archive)

Watson and Noble of S1 Patrol on the road from Hon to Misurata, September 1941. Note that Noble is wearing the Arab headdress, *Kafiya* which, while it kept out sand, was prone to getting entangled in equipment. (Courtesy of the SAS Regimental Archive)

However, overall the experiment achieved mixed results. Resupply by air had proved useful materially and psychologically to the LRDG, but the aircrew had been dependent on the patrol for water as there hadn't been space in the aircraft for their own supply. Additionally, the fuel dumped by the LRDG prior to the mission had only just proved sufficient. When the Vickers-Valentia touched down at Heliopolis on 4 November, after flying a total of 1,900 miles in 24 hours and 40 minutes of flying time, the aircraft had one hour's fuel left in the tank. Nonetheless Bagnold, ever the innovator in desert travel, believed air transport had great potential for the LRDG.

T Patrol arrived back on 6 November, having covered 2,100 miles in total, 24 hours earlier than Clayton had promised before they set out on their mission. Once more the men were a sight for sore eyes as they drove into their barracks at Abbassia. 'A stranger meeting a LRDG patrol returning … would have been hard put to decide to what race or army, let alone to what unit, they belonged,' wrote Kennedy Shaw. 'In winter the use of battledress made for some uniformity, but in summer, with a month-old beard thick with sand, with a month's dirt, skin burnt to the colour of coffee, and clad in nothing but a pair of torn shorts and chapplies, a man looked like a creature from some other world.'[4]

Chapplies were the sandals adopted by the British Army on the North West frontier, and which proved far more practical in the desert for everyday living than boots, which quickly filled with sand. As for headgear, the LRDG had experimented first with the topee (also called a pith helmet) and then the Arab headdress, or *kafiya*. Both proved impractical, the topee because so many were crushed 'beneath a case of rations or a gun magazine and were reduced to pulp' and the *kafiya* because, though it was excellent at keeping out sand, it was uncomfortable in hot weather and prone to get tangled in the engine or the weapons. Instead, the men of the LRDG found that what was most practical and also offered the best protection was the cap comforter, a garment which looked like a short scarf but could be worn as woollen hat. Then later on in the war the peaked cap of the Afrika Korps, complete with neck shield, became a firm favourite.

Five days after T Patrol returned, Wavell, having pored over the intelligence reports, wrote to Bagnold telling him the LRDG's work 'is most valuable and shows skill and enterprise of a high order'. Wavell had already sent the intelligence to London, explaining that owing to the LRDG's information the Italians were compelled to divert troops and vehicles from the main battlefield in the north to deal with the guerrilla attacks in the south. He had also highlighted that, because of the LRDG's aggressive patrolling between Kufra and Uweinat, the Italians would be increasingly unlikely to launch an attack on the Nile from this area.

Goggles, such as this pair worn by John Kroeger, were vital for drivers on desert patrols. (Courtesy of the SAS Regimental Archive)

Members of G Patrol shortly after their formation in late 1940, possibly on their way to attack Murzuk with Captain Pat Clayton in January 1941. (Courtesy of Jack Valenti)

CHAPTER 5

FIGHT AT THE FORT

With the Long Range Desert Group undergoing an expansion, Bagnold required a more spacious barracks for the unit, and he found one within the walls of the Citadel, an imposing edifice built by Saladin in 1166 using stone brought from the small pyramids of Gizeh. The LRDG moved into their new home in the first week of December, a relocation that, as their official war diarist noted, coincided with the cessation of the unit as 'a purely New Zealand family and [it] began to assume a new character with the arrival on December 5th of British personnel to fill the establishment of Unit HQ and one complete squadron'.

One of the unit's unofficial diarists, Frank Jopling, expressed his reservations about the upheaval. 'They are going to make the LRDG a lot bigger with the inclusion of Tommies,' he wrote on 5 December. 'We don't like the sound of it much as we think that after we have trained all these Tommies we may be sent back to our Units.' Jopling's mood darkened further when he arrived at the Citadel. 'I went in the new barracks this morning to cart biscuits but we couldn't even get them in the morning so I had to go down again in the afternoon and even then we couldn't get them until 5 p.m.,' he complained to his diary. 'I don't like the look of the barracks in comparison with the place we are in now.'

Jopling and his comrades moved into their new abode on 7 December, and two days later he was one of several New Zealanders sent on 'a three day trip with the

OPPOSITE
Tom Merrick was one of the LRDG's best navigators and helped train other members of the unit in the art of finding their way across the desert using the sun. (Courtesy of the SAS Regimental Archive)

In between patrols there was usually time for a spot of sightseeing in Egypt for the LRDG. This photo of the Sphinx was taken in September 1942. (Courtesy of the SAS Regimental Archive)

Scotch Guards to teach them a little about desert driving'. The guardsmen were among the 36 selected from the 3rd Battalion The Coldstream Guards and the 2nd Battalion The Scots Guards. Designated G [Guards] Patrol, they were commanded by 25-year-old Captain Michael Crichton-Stuart of the Scots Guards with Lieutenant Martin Gibbs, a Coldstreamer, his second-in-command.

Crichton-Stuart was a blue-blood. The grandson of the 3rd Marquess of Bute, his father was Lieutenant Colonel Lord Ninian Edward Crichton-Stuart, killed fighting on the Western Front in 1915 while the sitting Member of Parliament for the united boroughs of Cardiff, Cowbridge and Llantrisant. Educated at Eton and Cambridge, Crichton-Stuart's lineage was impressive, though first impressions didn't go down well with the New Zealanders. 'The O.C. of G3 Patrol is Capt. Crichton-Stuart and the 2/IC is Lt Gibbs of Gibbs Dentrifice,'★ wrote Jopling. 'We don't like either of them but don't have anything to do with them so it doesn't matter much.'

As the guardsmen were instructed in the ways of the desert, the LRDG commander was in the throes of planning his boldest operation yet. It had been hatched in November and entailed an attack against Murzuk, a well-defended Italian fort in south-western Libya set among palm trees with an airfield close by, approximately 1,000 miles west of Cairo as the crow flies. As Bagnold recorded, the fort 'was far beyond our self-contained range but a raid on it seemed possible geographically if we could get some extra supplies from the French Army in Chad'. The aim of the attack wasn't just to harass the enemy deep inside their lines, but to send a clear message to the Free French that they were a valued and valuable ally in the North African campaign.

Bagnold flew to Chad at the start of November and met the commander of the French troops, Colonel Jean Colonna d'Ornano, a tall red-headed officer in his mid-forties. The Frenchman agreed to the request to supply the LRDG on one condition: that he and his men participate in the assault on the fort. Bagnold agreed.

As G Patrol readied itself for its inaugural operation, the desert war swung spectacularly the way of the British. In mid-September six divisions of Italian troops had advanced cautiously into the Western Desert, covering 60 miles before calling a halt at Sidi Barrani, some 80-odd miles west of the British positions at Mersah Matruh. Their commander, Marshal Rodolfo Graziani, ordered the construction of

---

★ Gibbs Dentrifice, or toothpaste, was the leading company of its type in Britain at this time, and in 1955 it was the first product to be promoted on UK television.

a series of fortified camps that were spaced too far apart to support one another. For nearly two months the desert war was in abeyance until Wavell 'decided that, as the Italians did not come on, he would sally forth and strike at them'. The attack was launched by General Richard O'Connor's Western Desert Force early on 9 December, and it caught the Italians completely off-guard. The British force of 30,000 – compared to the 80,000 enemy troops – captured thousands of prisoners and 400 guns in the first three days of the assault. The Italians fled in panic to the coastal fortress of Bardia, their rout so complete that if Wavell had pressed the attack he could have advanced into Libya. Instead he stuck to the original plan, which was to recall the 4th Indian Division as soon as Sidi Barrani had fallen and transfer it to the Sudan. In the meantime, the British dug in and waited for the arrival from Palestine of the 6th Australian Division before continuing the offensive against the demoralized Italians.

The success of the British strike at Sidi Barrani almost led to a change of role for the LRDG, 'in which we were to cut the enemy's lines of communication along the coast'. To Crichton-Stuart's relief, the operation was cancelled and G Patrol continued preparing for the raid on Murzuk.

Now that the guardsmen no longer needed their hands held, Frank Jopling made the most of this quiet period. On 20 December he enjoyed a game of billiards

Tom Merrick uses his theodolite to shoot the sun, and at night it would be used for an astrofix. (Courtesy of the SAS Regimental Archive)

and in the evening watched *Pirates of the Air*, a 1916 propaganda film about World War I aerial warfare. Jopling didn't much appreciate the outdated and jingoistic film but the following evening he found Lana Turner's performance in *These Glamour Girls* much more to his liking.

Jopling began Christmas Day with a game of billiards before joining his comrades in the canteen. 'For Xmas dinner we had roast turkey, Xmas pudding, which was very good,' he recorded in his diary. 'The sergeants waited on us at the table and the officers shouted us a bottle of beer each. After dinner I played more billiards.'

Two days later, on 27 December, the LRDG departed Cairo. They had been briefed on Boxing Day with Clayton – recently promoted to major – telling

T Patrol that they could be away as long as three months. They would also be accompanied by two Arabs, one of whom, said Jopling, 'is sort of a prince among the Arabs and they are going to be used partly as interpreters and partly as inducement for the Libyans to surrender'.

In fact, the 'prince' was Sheikh 'Abd el Gelil Sief Al Nasr, chosen personally to accompany the LRDG by Sayed Idris, the Senussi leader. The second Arab mentioned by Jopling was the sheikh's personal slave, and Crichton-Stuart recalled that the former 'had welcomed this opportunity of a trip to his old tribal lands, so long as he got a chance to shoot an Italian or two'.[1] In total there were 76 raiders in 23 vehicles, comprising T and G patrols under the overall command of Major Clayton.

They made good progress across the desert and spent New Year's Eve camped in the middle of the Great Sand Sea.,' wrote Crichton-Stuart in his operational report. 'Withal it is utterly lifeless and dead, without a blade of grass or a stone to break the monotony of sky and sand.'

'Packed and shaped by the prevailing wind over thousands of years, this Sand Sea compares in shape and form with a great Atlantic swell, of long rollers, crested here and there, with great troughs between'

Michael Crichton-Stuart

New Year's Eve was a rather melancholic affair for the men, an unwanted opportunity to dwell on sweethearts, mothers, fathers, siblings, thousands of miles away. Jopling wondered how his sweetheart, Irene, whose letters were so priceless, was spending the final day of 1940. The men had a brief sing-song round the campfire but none of them stayed up to usher in the first day of 1941.

The patrols split on the approach to the border, travelling independently into Libya and rendezvousing near Tazerbo, 350 miles east of Murzuk, on 4 January 1941. The day was notable for a discovery made by Bill Kennedy Shaw, who had a nose for such things. 'The country was as featureless and barren as could be,' wrote Crichton-Stuart, 'but when we stopped on rock once, to pump up our tyres again after deflating for the soft sand, Shaw discovered flint instruments of some bygone civilization.'[2]

On that same day Clayton left with four trucks to collect the French contingent from Chad, and Bill Kennedy Shaw took three trucks to see whether Tereneghei Pass was negotiable by vehicle and therefore viable as a possible escape route after the attack on the fort. 'It was a good trip,' recalled Kennedy Shaw, thrilled with the

opportunity to fill in a blank map as he blazed a trail on a hitherto unexplored route. They weaved a path over the Eghei Mountains, 'a jumble of sandstone, basalt and granite' and 'saw no sign of life, even the Tibbu [also spelled 'Toubou', herders and nomads originating in northern Chad] seldom visit these barren hills'.[3]

While Kennedy Shaw was exploring the Tereneghei Pass, Jopling was reforming his opinion of Captain Michael Crichton-Stuart. Despite his background as a Guards' officer, he was broad-minded and approachable, with an intellectual suppleness that absorbed swiftly the nuances of guerrilla warfare. On seeing Jopling studying G Patrol's map, Crichton-Stuart wandered over and explained to the New Zealander the plan of attack on Murzuk and of the withdrawal. 'It sounds as though it is going to be a great trip,' wrote Jopling. After his talk with Crichton-Stuart, Jopling fell into conversation with the man he'd described with mild disdain a few days earlier as a prince – Sheikh 'Abd el Gelil Sief Al Nasr. 'He is a far more important man than I at first thought,' Jopling recorded in his diary. 'His people are around Murzuk and Kufra, etc. He is also a Bey, which is a high sort of knighthood conferred on him by King Farouk [king of Egypt from 1936 to 1952]. He reckons he would like to get into Murzuk before us and have a talk with the population and he reckons he could get the people to rise up against the Italians and then we come in. However, just what we do remains to be seen.'[4]

Clayton returned with the French contingent on 7 January. Colonel d'Ornano brought with him supplies and also two junior officers, two sergeants and five

Before settling down to supper after a day's operations, the LRDG patrol checked their weapons, water and vehicle and reported any problems to the patrol commander. (Courtesy of the SAS Regimental Archive)

native soldiers. None of the Frenchmen spoke English, but one of the New Zealander navigators, Terry Brown, had spent most of his childhood in Morocco and was fluent in French. Colonel d'Ornano made an impression on Crichton-Stuart, who noted in his report that the Frenchman 'was a magnificent figure of a man, very tall, in native uniform, complete with *burnous* [a long cloak of coarse woollen fabric with a hood] and a monocle'.

That night Sheikh 'Abd el Gelil Sief Al Nasr joined what Crichton-Stuart described as 'an international council of war', in which representatives from France, Britain, New Zealand and Libya discussed the impending attack on Murzuk. The sheikh revealed that several years ago he and his men had laid siege to the fort, an account which was treated with more respect than the 'wireless message from Cairo giving fearsome and rather incredible details of the defences of Murzuk from a document captured at Sidi Barrani'.[5]

The 23-vehicle raiding party set off on the 350 miles to Murzuk at 6am on 8 January and the featureless plain was soon supplanted by a bewildering array of terrain, from dark volcanic rocks to sharp-cornered boulders half buried in the ground.

At least their progress was unimpeded by any sight of the enemy, and early on 11 January they were ten miles north of the target, having covered 1,333 miles in 18 days. Clayton sent a reconnaissance party towards the fort and they returned reporting 'not a soul was in sight'. The raiders sat down to luncheon and later made their final preparations for the attack. Kennedy Shaw constructed a sand-plan of Murzuk, using it for the final briefing, which was précised by Crichton-Stuart.

An LRDG vehicle enters a *wadi* (a dry river bed) in search of a suitable spot to camp for the night. (Courtesy of the SAS Regimental Archive)

Having first explained that the natives inhabited a string of small oases to the north and east of Murzuk, Kennedy Shaw said that Murzuk itself 'sported an aerodrome and a large, modern stone fort with a considerable garrison and a wireless station. There had been stationed there the "Auto-Saharan Company", the Italian equivalent of our Long Range Patrol, well equipped but absurdly used'.[6] He ended his talk with a quote from Machiavelli: 'Those enterprises are best which can be concealed up to the moment of their fulfilment.'

Then they set off to the target.

On the road leading to the fort the raiders drove past a huddle of natives. Almost as one they clicked to attention, giving the fascist salute and shouting 'Bongiorno'. A grin spread across the grimy faces of the LRDG, broadening as they spotted up ahead a plump figure cycling towards the fort. Clayton pulled over and invited the postmaster, Signor Colicchia, to hop on board. The 'terrified official' accepted the invitation and acted as their guide on the final approach to the target. 'Ahead I could now see the fort, partly hidden by trees,' recalled Kennedy Shaw, 'and with some after-lunch strollers around it. The surprise was complete.'[7]

The plan, finalized with the help of Kennedy Shaw's sand-plan, was straightforward: Clayton's T Patrol would attack the airfield that lay in close proximity to the fort while G Patrol targeted the actual garrison, situated in the fort south-east of the town. The LRDG didn't have the firepower to destroy the thick walls of the fort, but they hoped to 'frighten or surprise the garrison' into surrendering. As to what could go wrong, though the LRDG didn't fear the garrison itself, they did worry about the main Italian air base at Fezzan, 250 miles north, and what it might do on receiving a radio message requesting aerial assistance.

The closer one got to the Libyan coast the greener the landscape became. (Courtesy of the SAS Regimental Archive)

When the convoy was 150 yards from Murzuk, close enough to see the Italian flag fluttering above the main central tower, the gates of the fort opened and out turned the guard, ready to welcome in what they imagined was an Italian relief force. That was the cue for Clayton's patrol of six trucks to head towards the airstrip, while Crichton-Stuart's force targeted their weapons at the guard outside the fort and 'let them have it'. As he later admitted, 'we were rather sorry for them, but they probably never knew what hit them'.[8]

In the official report of the attack on the fort, built by the Ottomans during their occupation of Libya, Crichton-Stuart described the subsequent chain of events: 'All [LRDG] positions were from 250 yards to 500 yards from the fort, the broken ground, scrub, and a few native huts affording considerable cover,' he wrote. 'Effective resistance, however, began at once. The fort was engaged by G Patrol, half of T Patrol and the French, with one 37mm Bofors and two 2in. mortars, and with rifle and M.G. [machine gun] fire.'

The mortars were under the direction of Lieutenant Martin Gibbs, who was concentrating his fire on the western wall of the fort. They scored an early success when a bomb hit the main tower, sending a thick cloud of black smoke billowing into the air, and within a few minutes the tower was ablaze.

What Crichton-Stuart's report omitted was the unfortunate incident that occurred midway through the attack. Kennedy Shaw, who was engaged with Clayton's force on the airfield, subsequently gave a second-hand account in his war memoirs, describing how 'in the middle of the attack a touring car drove up to the gate. In it was the Italian commander, who had probably been out to lunch, and also as some said afterwards, a woman and child. One shell from the Guards' Bofors put an end to them.'[9]

The 'effective resistance' mentioned by Crichton-Stuart soon had the LRDG pinned down and 'any movement brought down heavy fire'. The slave of Sheikh 'Abd el Gelil Sief Al Nasr didn't endear himself to his British allies by standing up after each shot with his old rifle and shouting a stream of abuse at the Italians. The LRDG had no idea what he was saying, and probably nor did the enemy, but nothing was lost in translation with the ferocity of the response from the fort.

On the airfield, meanwhile, the other half of T Patrol was also encountering some resistance, as Jopling described in his diary.

We stopped about 700 yards from the hangar and there were quite a few soldiers running about and quite a few pillboxes scattered about so we got behind a rise and opened up on them. After quite a few had fallen and a few Bofors shells

Some of John Olivey's men pose for the camera en route to attack an Italian fort at El Gtafia in December 1941. (Courtesy of the SAS Regimental Archive)

Ron Low proudly
displays the Italian
sword liberated from
El Gtafia during the
successful raid.
(Courtesy of the SAS
Regimental Archive)

had gone into the hangar, we advanced to another rise just in time to prevent
some soldiers from entering an anti-aircraft pit. Then the skipper [Clayton] came
past from the fort and went to circle the hangar, and just as he turned a corner of
the hangar a machine-gun opened up on them at only 20 yards away, so the
skipper jammed on the brakes and put it in reverse. How the skipper, Wink Adams
and Clarrie Roderick escaped, goodness knows.[10]

But Colonel d'Ornano didn't. Sitting in the back of Clayton's vehicle, the
Frenchman was killed instantly by a bullet to his throat. The Bofors was brought to
bear on the gun emplacement, and it was destroyed. As the LRDG concentrated
their fire now on the hangar and the defenders inside, Kennedy Shaw watched in
amazement as 'shuffling with half-bent knees across the landing ground … a string
of old women carrying firewood bundles on their heads'.

There was a brief lull in the shooting, long enough for the raiders on the airfield
to turn their gaze towards the fort in response to the explosion caused by the
mortar shell hitting the central tower. 'All the time there were snipers,' recalled
Jopling. 'But we couldn't find out where the bullets were coming from.'

For close on two hours the firefight with the Italians inside the hangar continued.
Then a white flag was waved from the one of the windows. Clayton sent one of the
prisoners taken early on in the raid to parley with the bearer of the flag. Soon
around 20 men of the Italian Air Force emerged with their hands in the air. Clayton
placed them under guard, and then the LRDG delved inside the hangar. 'There

Two men from Olivey's S2 Patrol, Watson and Simpson, stage a mock sword fight after the raid on El Gtafia. (Courtesy of the SAS Regimental Archive)

were three beautiful Gibley bombers costing about £15,000 each,' wrote Jopling. 'And a beautiful sending and receiving wireless set and many bombs, parachutes and other valuable equipment. Of course, all the boys were in for a bit of looting and while that was going on, the planes and building were soaked in benzine and the wireless set smashed, and after taking thousands of rounds of .303 ammunition and many rifles we left a trail of benzine and set a match to it. What a waste. But I suppose that is what war is, a war of destruction.'[11]

The LRDG selected two prisoners from among their considerable haul – the ones they considered best placed to answer an interrogator's questions – and left the remainder behind. Clayton, having fired a white flare as the signal for the withdrawal, waited for Crichton-Stuart and G Patrol to arrive, but the wind had got up during the attack and they hadn't seen the flare. Eventually Clayton drove to the fort and rounded up his men 'and the whole Patrol withdrew in a thick sandstorm to the aerodrome'. As the column moved off, the jolt unbalanced one of the prisoners, who fell from the back of the truck. Rather than seize the moment to escape, the terrified Italian 'dutifully started running after the truck to avoid being left behind'.

The LRDG paused to bury d'Ornano and Sergeant Cyril Hewson, the only other fatality of the attack, five miles to the north of Murzuk. It was a sobering ceremony, laying to rest two of their own in a spot so remote and so far from their homeland. 'We dug a wide grave and after wrapping each of them in their respective blankets, laid them side by side in the grave,' noted Jopling. Major Clayton conducted the funeral service as the sun set and some of the men contemplated their own mortality. One of the New Zealanders had a bullet graze his hand without it breaking the skin; another was hit in the foot, the bullet lodging in his leather boot (the LRDG changed footwear prior to raids). Such were the fortunes of war.

Having departed the graves, the LRDG had a brief diversion when they overran a small outpost at the town of Traghen, whose 50 inhabitants 'marched out en masse to surrender with drums beating and banners flying'. All but two of the prisoners were native troops under the command of a pair of Italian carabinieri.

On 13 January, the LRDG were feeling pleased with life. The mission had been a resounding success – they now had four prisoners – and soon it would be time to return to Cairo. Then in the late afternoon up went the cry of 'aircraft'.

'In this outfit we don't mind how many machine guns are firing at us or how many rifles but one thing we do not like is bombers,' wrote Jopling. It was the sensation of utter helplessness that unnerved them, and the worst moments were when the aircraft swooped down out of the sky like a giant metal bird of prey. 'When they pass straight over head you wonder if they have let go of their bombs, and if so, will they land anywhere near you,' reflected Jopling. 'Then you see them pass on and you think "well, if they had let their bombs go they would have dropped by now". But even then you are not sure and by the time you are sure, the plane is on its way back again and you go through the same sensation all over again.'[12]

Camouflage netting conceals the LRDG vehicles from any passing enemy aircraft. (Courtesy of the SAS Regimental Archive)

Unless a vehicle was moving it was very hard for even the sharpest-eyed pilot to spot it from the air. (Courtesy of the SAS Regimental Archive)

On this occasion the bomber came in low, the pilot peering down to check that they were indeed the raiders who had wreaked havoc at Murzuk. Beneath him he saw several figures, including Jopling, dash across the desert to the nearest cover behind a small hillock. Meanwhile the gunners fitted a drum of tracer bullets to their weapons and began firing. The bomber made a second pass and this time released his load, two bombs exploding with a 'boom' that shook the sand on which Jopling lay. But the bombs fell far wide and the Italian flew off into the twilight having expended his weapons.

The LRDG continued south for the next week, heading towards the French-occupied town of Zouar in northern Chad. That entailed negotiating a way through the Tibesti Mountains, which they successfully did on 19 January. That evening Jopling told his diary about the experience:

> I reckon I have just seen the 8th wonder of the world, and that was the road we have just come over. It is really beyond description. The country is just a mass of mountains of one solid piece of rock and we came along a road made through these mountains for about 40km. It is very steep in places and has great corners on it, but the surface, considering the country it had to go through and considering that there are only a few trucks going through a year, is nothing short of marvellous.[13]

Crichton-Stuart called it the 'worst country we ever experienced' and described it in his report thus: 'From broken rocky plateau we dropped steeply into rock bound valleys, only finding a way out with great difficulty, by putting flat stones over the soft, sandy patches between the stony going, and charging the trucks up the escarpments one by one. Somehow the tow kept up, by masterly driving, even over giant sand dunes which checked the way between great black brags with vertical cliffs.'[14]

Colonel Bagnold was waiting to greet Clayton and his men at Zouar, which in the words of the French was situated in '*beau pays*' [beautiful country] of a '*wadi* [dry river bed] thick with trees and beyond it rocky grey-black hills and gazelle grazing in twos and threes'. Once in Zouar, Bagnold and Clayton discussed the operation while the men washed with water drawn from the well by Senegalese soldiers. It had been nearly a month since the men had last bathed and, as Jopling discovered, removing several layers of dirt was no easy matter. 'After 3 lots of water we began to look more like our old selves again,' he wrote. 'And after giving ourselves a good final soaping all over we got the prisoners to pour a watering can of water over us for a shower. It was great.'

The LRDG didn't stay long in Zouar. They were soon on the move once more, heading south-east under Bagnold's navigation to Faya to discuss with the French the impending attack on Kufra. Six days later, Clayton's T Patrol crossed back into Libya and they were only 70 miles south of Kufra when they were attacked by an Italian motorized patrol on Gebel Sherif on 31 January. Three of the LRDG's 11 vehicles were destroyed and Corporal Rex Beech was killed.N.B The British explorer, John Blashford-Snell, was leading a desert trek in 1963 when by pure

This patrol has been travelling on gravel desert, known in Arabic as *serir*, which makes for good going because the wind has removed the sand, a process known as 'deflation'. (Courtesy of the SAS Regimental Archive)

chance he camped for the night in the Gebel Sherif, and discovered Beech's grave with its rough wooden cross. He reported the find to the Imperial War Graves Commission and Beech's remains were re-interred in Knightsbridge War Cemetery, just south of the main road from Benghazi to Tobruk. Clayton ordered the rest of the patrol to withdraw from the valley. 'I was shepherding them away to the south and being the last car got full attention from the planes,' wrote Clayton in a letter to his sister-in-law on 10 February. 'The neighbouring trucks failed to see we were hit by the planes' machine guns.'[15]

One Italian bullet had pierced the radiator, two more had blown out the front tyres. Clayton had also suffered a cut to his head caused by a slither of shrapnel. Ignoring the gushing blood, Clayton and one of his two comrades, Lance Corporal 'Wink' Adams, jumped out of the vehicle and set about repairing the damage. The other crew member, Clarrie Roderick, kept the aircraft at bay with the Vickers. 'They kept circling and gunning us while we changed wheels and mounted tyres,' recalled Clayton. One enemy bullet hit the pump connection, causing a further delay, but over the noise of battle, Clayton heard a triumphant yell from Roderick as his bullets shattered the cockpit of one plane. 'We poured in water and started again and did 3 or 4 kilos until the engine dried up,' said Clayton. They jumped out, replenished the water and set off again. But the Italian pilots were in no mood to break off the attack. Another aircraft came in low, its guns raking the ground all around the fleeing vehicle. A bullet ripped through Clayton's forearm and another shattered the engine. The three men dived from the truck, but this time they knew there was no chance to make running repairs. Approaching through a cloud of dust they saw two Italian trucks. Further resistance was futile.

The next morning, 1 February, Captain Crichton-Stuart and his men of G Patrol had their breakfast interrupted by a dust cloud approaching from the north. Abandoning the food for their weapons, the guardsmen waited for the vehicles to emerge from the dust. When they did they recognized four vehicles of T Patrol. The survivors, Frank Jopling among them, recounted the previous day's attack, listing the eight men missing.★ Led by New Zealander Ronald Moore, the quartet decided against walking the 70 miles to Kufra to surrender to the Italians, and instead set off south in the hope of reaching Free French lines. In what became an epic tale of endurance and fortitude, three of the men (the fourth died from wounds sustained in the initial ambush) walked for 200 miles before being found by the French. and warning that Clayton's papers and code books had been in his truck when he was captured. There were tales of great gallantry, too, notably that

---

★ In fact four of these men had evaded capture by hiding among the rocks until the Italians had departed.

of Corporal Tony Browne, who despite having been wounded in the foot during the attack at Murzuk was at the heart of the resistance in the Gebel Sherif, courage that was recognized with a Distinguished Conduct Medal. 'His coolness,' ran the citation, 'was instrumental in saving his vehicle and crew when subjected to a determined low-flying bombing and M.G. attack by an enemy aircraft.'

There was an urgency therefore for Crichton-Stuart to inform the French not to continue with their planned attack on Kufra, as the Italians would be waiting. A message was passed to a grateful General Philippe Leclerc, commander of the Free French troops (he would eventually capture Kufra on 1 March) and, once done, G Patrol began their 1,200-mile journey back to Cairo. They arrived at 8.30 on the morning of 9 February, having covered 4,300 miles and totted up six weeks' pay and five days' leave. 'After making my preliminary report, I took a taxi to Shepheard's Hotel, went to the hairdresser's and said "Shave and haircut, please",' recalled Crichton-Stuart. 'I gave him a ten-piastre tip for not even flinching.'

After his interrogation Clayton was sent to a prisoner-of-war camp, from where he wrote to his sister-in-law in Cairo. He asked her to pass a message to the LRDG asking them to send a note to the families of Roderick and Adams, reassuring them of their well-being. Clayton had obviously spent the past ten days turning over events in his head, wondering if he could have avoided such a fate. 'I don't feel I did at all well,' he told his sister-in-law. 'But every chance we took turned wrong that day and after 36 days' travel men and vehicles were a long way below par.'[16]

Clayton clung to the comforting thought that at least his good friend, Kennedy Shaw had not been with them. And on further reflection, perhaps he need not be too downcast. 'I had a good run and cannot complain,' he concluded. 'After all, I took two forts and an aerodrome and burnt Murzuk fort and blew up lorries north of Aujila – not bad for 44.'

The Italians were delighted. Finally, they had scored a victory against the British guerrillas, and more to the point they had captured 'Major Klayton [sic] … well-known explorer of the desert'. The unit that surprised the British was the Auto-Saharan Company, the nearest force the Italians had to the LRDG. Most of the men were experienced desert travellers and most knew of Clayton's formidable reputation.

CHAPTER 6

THE AFRIKA KORPS ARRIVE

W hen Crichton-Stuart and G Patrol arrived back at the Citadel, they were met by many new faces. Major Guy Prendergast had arrived from England at last[*] as the unit's second-in-command, and the second Patrol recruited from British soldiers had nearly reached its full complement. Designated Y Patrol, so-called because its members had been drawn from the Yeomanry regiments comprising the 1st Cavalry Division in Palestine, 32 recruits had reported to Bagnold in late January having been selected by Captain Pat McCraith, the officer in charge of Y Patrol. Bagnold was not impressed by what he encountered. 'It was found that many of the personnel were unsuitable,' commented the LRDG war diary, 'being ex-cavalry reservists of bad character whom their units wanted to get rid of.'

Of the 32 recruits, 24 were soon on their way back to their regiments. Among the eight who remained were Stuart Carr and Anthony Cave. More than a foot separated the pair in height, with the 6ft 4in Carr known as 'Lofty' to his pals and the 5ft 2in. Cave answering to 'Tich'. Cave had enlisted in the Wiltshire Yeomanry in 1935 aged 16, and then applied to the LRDG when he spotted a notice in

OPPOSITE
Recently returned to their base at Kufra, this LRDG patrol receives a much-needed short back and sides. (Courtesy of the SAS Regimental Archive)

---

[*] Contrary to some sources, which state that Prendergast was a direct replacement for Pat Clayton, Bill Kennedy Shaw confirmed in his memoirs that Bagnold had already procured his former fellow explorer from England before the capture of Clayton.

Following the sacking of the Italian fort at El Gtafia in December 1941, Benny Watson, Ginger Low, Ron Low and Tiny Simpson of S2 Patrol display their booty. (Author's Collection)

January 1941 seeking men of 'initiative and integrity'. It had been harder to prise the 20-year-old Carr from the Staffordshire Yeomanry, but prise him Bagnold did, having heard stories of the brilliant navigator idling away his days in Palestine with a regiment that was stagnating in a quiet backwater. 'He called us Bagnold's Blue-eyed Boys,' recalled Carr. 'And he also told us to forget everything we had learnt up to now because we were no longer in the regular army.'[1]

Having kept just eight of the original batch of recruits, Captain Pat McCraith went off in search of more men with the qualities to impress Bagnold. He eventually found them, one of whom was a young Mancunian called Ron Hill. He was 'suffering the indignity' of being on anti-parachute duty in the Canal Zone, serving in a force that was an amalgam of the Gloucestershire Hussars, the Wiltshire Yeomanry and the County of London Yeomanry. A diphtheria epidemic had just swept through the force and Hill was desperate for a change. 'During this enforced activity volunteers were called for to join the Long Range Desert Group, about which little was known except that it operated deep down in the desert,' he recalled.[2] 'As I was interested in seeing the really true desert (the coastal fringe where most of the battles had been was hardly that), I put myself up as a volunteer.'[3]

Hill was one of three men chosen by McCraith, who in due course told him he had 'interviewed over 500 volunteers in order to select 20 men'. The men chosen for Y Patrol were ordered to report to the Citadal and Hill's eyes widened when he entered the old Ottoman fort. The inside of the Citadal was a treasure trove of 'unorthodox items required for clandestine operations', the likes of which Hill had never encountered in the Hussars. There were sheepskin coats, chapplies, kafiyas, sand mats, theodolites, 'and the thousand and one other vital pieces of equipment such as guns and bullets'.

The new recruits met some of the 'rum sort of chaps' already in the unit, marvelling at the diversity of accents that stretched from Exeter to Edinburgh to Auckland. They were shown to their billets but it wasn't until sundown that the Citadel's other inhabitants emerged. 'I remember being dossed down on my blankets and soon became aware of being attacked,' said Hill. 'Nasty, vicious bed bugs streaming out of the cracks of the walls at night … fortunately for me, I seemed to be immune to the worst of their depredations and remember, in my half-sleep, picking them off my body and tossing them on to the other sleeping forms alongside, who awakened at sun-up covered with bumps and blood stains from the bug bites.'[4]

As Y Patrol Patrol took shape, it did so amid a blaze of publicity for the LRDG. The attack on Murzuk had caused something of a stir in the Allied media and on 14 February the *Times* of London published a lengthy article on page 4 that was one of many in a similar vein. 'A remarkable story of exploits in the vast Libyan Desert during the last six months by a small body of motor commandos, known as "the Long Range Desert Group" has just been revealed,' began the article. 'Going out in small patrols, usually of three cars, they have consistently and successfully harassed Italian outposts, reduced isolated forts, interrupted communications and generally kept the Italians guessing, playing a small but important part in the eventual sweep to Benghazi.' According to Crichton-Stuart, 'overnight we all developed glamour and Bagnold became a "Modern Lawrence" [of Arabia]: I raised no protest when a charming old lady called me "intrepid".'

A group of LRDG Rhodesian soldiers celebrate the start of their leave in January 1942. (Author's Collection)

The 'sweep to Benghazi' referred to by the *Times* had brought the first phase of the war in North Africa to a conclusion. In two months General Richard O'Connor's Western Desert Force (which subsequently became the Eighth Army) had advanced 500 miles and 'beaten and destroyed an Italian army of four corps, comprising nine divisions and part of a tenth. It had captured 13,000 prisoners, 400 tanks and 1,290 guns, beside vast quantities of other material.'[5] The Allies advanced west along the coast, seizing Bardia (4 January), Tobruk (22 January) and Benghazi (5–6 February). The enemy retreated to El Agheila, a bottleneck where they hoped to block an advance from Cyrenaica into Tripolitania (the western region of Libya). O'Connor wanted to press the attack and throw the Italians out of North Africa once and for all, but on 12 February Winston Churchill sent a telegram to Wavell, congratulating General Richard O'Connor's Western Desert Force in capturing Benghazi 'three weeks ahead of expectation'. Believing that their advances in North Africa were irreversible, Churchill instructed Wavell to transfer the bulk of his troops to Greece (under the command of Jumbo Wilson) in readiness for a German invasion. The Desert Air Force was removed almost entirely en masse, to the consternation of the Long Range Desert Group. 'Our armoured division at Agheila was left with 40 obsolete tanks and 40 captured Italian tanks,' commented Crichton-Stuart. 'While the 11th Hussars had been relieved by another regiment in ancient Marmon Harrington armoured cars … shortage of armoured cars and anxiety about his southern flank led General Neame of CYRCOM [Land and Air Forces in Cyrenaica] to ask Middle East Headquarters for assistance from the LRDG in the middle of March 1941.'[6]

A plan was agreed whereby the Long Range Desert Group would operate in the El Agheila area, harassing the Italians to make them believe there was still a large-scale Allied presence in Cyrenaica. As for what Crichton-Stuart described as the 'rumours and signs' of the arrival of a significant German presence in North Africa, the British high command appeared blasé in the early spring of 1941. British complacency was soon to be punished. In the same week in February that Churchill cabled Wavell, instructing him to transfer the bulk of his troops to Greece, the vanguard of the Afrika Korps arrived in Libya.

When Adolf Hitler learned of Italy's humiliation he was initially indifferent. North Africa was a sideshow, inconsequential in comparison to his ambitions in the Balkans and Russia. It was Grand Admiral Erich Raeder, head of the German navy, who did most to turn Hitler's attention towards events in the region. What, Raeder asked of his Führer, would happen to Germany if the British maintained their iron grip on the Mediterranean? It would seriously jeopardize Hitler's plans for conquest in the East. Nonetheless, it was with reluctance that on 11 January 1941 Hitler issued 'Führer Directive No. 22', authorizing the raising of a force to be sent to

The arrival in Libya in February 1941 of Rommel and his Afrika Korps presented a far greater challenge to the LRDG than the Italian army. (Author's Collection)

North Africa to support Germany's Italian allies. Codenamed Operation *Sunflower*, the force was designated 5 Light Division, though it was not until 6 February that Hitler appointed Erwin Rommel as the unit commander, a dashing 49-year-old general who had led the 7th Panzer Division, 'The Ghost Division', during the invasion of the Low Countries the previous year.

In late February 1941 Rommel ordered the Afrika Korps to the front, augmenting their strength with a number of dummy tanks mounted on Volkswagens. The Germans dug in around the El Agheila bottleneck and, with just one squadron of RAF fighters ranged against them, the Luftwaffe controlled the sky in North Africa, exploiting their numerical advantage to prevent the British discovering how few troops they actually had on the ground. Other factors worked in Rommel's favour: not only had the battle-hardened 6th Australian Division been sent to Greece, but the 7th Armoured Division was back in Egypt resting and refitting. Their replacements, the British 2nd Armoured Division and 9th Australian Division, were inexperienced and under-equipped and their commander, General Philip Neame, was callow in desert warfare compared to his predecessor, O'Connor.

By March the training of Y Patrol was complete, and so Bagnold paired them with G Patrol to form A Squadron under the command of Major Mitford, with an additional patrol, S, formed of soldiers from Southern Rhodesia. B Squadron consisted of two New Zealand patrols, T and R, after General Freyberg had relented and allowed the LRDG to continue employing his soldiers.

A Squadron was instructed to attack the Italians around El Agheila, while in early April Bagnold led B Squadron to Kufra to replace the Free French forces as garrison troops (the Sudan Defence Force had agreed to fulfil this role but they couldn't arrive until July). Bagnold became in effect the king of Kufra, no easy reign given that three languages were spoken in the town and a similar number of currencies were in circulation. In an attempt to bring some kind of harmony to Kufra, Bagnold issued a proclamation 'Under British Military Government' upon arriving in the oasis. There were five articles in all, each one a series of dos and don'ts. He also promulgated a series of instructions to the LRDG to reduce the likelihood of any cultural misunderstandings. Entitled 'Some Points on Conduct When Meeting the Arabs in the Desert', it read:

> Remove footwear upon entering their tents. Completely ignore their women. If thirsty drink the water they offer but DO NOT fill your waterbottle from their personal supply. Go to their well and fetch what you want … do not expect breakfast if you sleep the night. Arabs will give you a midday or evening meal.[7]

Each officer was also given a note in Arabic, to be handed to the natives if they ever found themselves lost in the desert. 'To all Arab peoples – greetings and peace be upon you', the note began. 'The bearer of this letter is an officer of the British Government and a friend to all Arabs. Treat him well, guard him from harm, give him food and drink, help him to return to the nearest British soldiers and you will be rewarded. Peace and Mercy of God upon you.'[8]

The LRDG moved into Kufra following the Italian flight in March 1941 and here they are salvaging one of their enemy's petrol pumps. (Courtesy of the SAS Regimental Archive)

The arrival in North Africa of Guy Prendergast eased some of the administrative pressure on Bagnold, and the tank officer quickly saw how best to develop the earlier experiment with aircraft as a means of supply and communication. Prendergast had learned to fly in the 1930s while serving in Sudan with the Western Arab Corps, purchasing a de Havilland Puss Moth and on one or two occasions flying it to England. The RAF had refused to loan any of their own aircraft to the LRDG so, recalled Prendergast, Bagnold 'asked General Wavell if he would cough up enough money from Army funds for the LRDG to buy its own aircraft. To our surprise the answer was "yes".'[9] Prendergast 'nosed about' in Cairo's Almaza airport and discovered two WACO aircraft that belonged to wealthy locals.★ The RAF refused to help Prendergast find replacements so 'I got my chaps to do a midnight raid on an army dump at Cairo, where I had spotted some crates containing new Continental engines for American [Sherman] with which the British army was equipped.' Enquires were made, prices agreed and soon the LRDG were in possession of the two aircraft, having paid £3,000 for the pair. WACOs were biplanes whose names derived from the original American manufacturer, the Weaver Aircraft Company of Ohio. The more powerful of the two had a Jacobs 285hp engine and was nicknamed 'Big Waco', while 'Small Waco' possessed a Jacobs 225hp engine. Once Prendergast had recruited Trevor Barker, who had been taught to fly by the celebrated Australian

★ Later in the desert the two WACOs began to lose power due to the effect of sand on the pistons and cylinders.

It was the brainchild of Guy Prendergast, seen here unloading stores, to obtain two aircraft to maintain a link between Cairo and their remote desert bases in Kufra and Siwa. The man leaning on the wing is Trevor Barker, who along with Prendergast piloted the WACOS. (Author's Collection)

aviator Charles Kingsford Smith, famed in 1928 for making the first transpacific flight from the USA to Australia, the pair familiarized themselves with the machine at Almaza. Prendergast then removed the back seats and installed a fold-up canvas seat so that wounded men could be transported and supplies carried.

The crucial skill required was navigation, as Prendergast appreciated. 'We had good compasses and drift indicators and I had taught myself how to find my position on the ground by means of position lines from shots of the sun taken by a sextant,' he remembered. 'We carried an RAF bubble sextant that we had "liberated" somehow and a yachtsman's sextant with an artificial horizon.'[10] They also carried a chronometer and tables, and most importantly one of the LRDG trained navigators. 'Their job,' explained Prendergast, 'was to take accurate drift readings and plot our progress on a map, also to help with refuelling at our dumps and to help with the astro-nav if we had to land to fix our position.'[11]

Prendergast was punctilious to the point of obsession about logistics – one of the reasons Bagnold had been so eager to bring him to North Africa – and before the WACOs began traversing the desert, he sent out LRDG patrols to prepare a series of landing grounds on routes they would fly over. 'These were stocked with petrol and every 15 miles on the route was a small dump of food and water in case we, or any patrol men who had their vehicles burnt up, should have to walk home,' said Prendergast.

Prendergast took off on his inaugural flight in a WACO on 24 March, flying 'as high as possible to get out of the bumpy air'. The aircraft reached maximum speeds of around 140mph and in a short space of time was providing a valuable link between Cairo and Kufra in the late spring of 1941.

Garrisoning the oasis was not what Bagnold had in mind when he'd raised the LRDG nine months earlier, and patrolling was the only way to break the tedium. Even that distraction became scarce as petrol supplies began dwindling in April. The nearest petrol dump was in Wadi Halfa, 650 miles east, a journey that took the 10-ton lorries a week at best to make.

While B Squadron were stuck in Kufra, A Squadron under Captain Teddy Mitford, comprising G and Y Patrol, drove out of the

Three Rhodesian soldiers, Scott, Massey and Kroeger, show off their tans at Kufra Oasis, which was captured from the Italians in March 1941. (Courtesy of the SAS Regimental Archive)

Citadel on 25 March and turned west along the coast road, passing through Mersa Matruh and past Sidi Barrani, 80 miles west, where the previous December General O'Connor had captured 39,000 Italian prisoners in three days. They crossed into Libya at Fort Capuzzo and continued west through the ports of Bardia and Tobruk. No enemy was seen and the only casualty was Sergeant Jack Dennis, stung by a scorpion. Scorpions, like vipers, were an occupational hazard in the desert and the creatures would often seek out the soldiers at night for warmth. One officer in G patrol, Captain Alastair Timpson, recalled 'getting out of my sleeping bag one morning when one of the black variety [of scorpions] popped out from under my chin and scuttled away'.[12] In the Guards Patrol, 'Pongo' Reid held the record for scorpion stings – six, though none caused him much discomfort.

Once or twice desert cheetahs were spotted by the LRDG on patrol, but the creature that they detested the most was also the smallest. 'The fly of Africa is intent on nosing its way into the eyes, ears and nose,' recalled Timpson. 'In swarms, as they were here, the flies were as powerfully obnoxious as Gulliver's multitudes of Lilliputians, but far more evil. It was impossible for any man to be on sentry for more than half an hour without risk of his becoming unreliable, if not mad.'

'In swarms, as they were here, the flies were as powerfully obnoxious as Gulliver's multitudes of Lilliputians, but far more evil. It was impossible for any man to be on sentry for more than half an hour without risk of his becoming unreliable, if not mad.'

Alastair Timpson

When A Squadron reached Derna, they headed up into the Jebel [sometimes spelled Gebel] Akhdar, the 'Green Mountains'. For the uninitiated, it was an extraordinary transformation, exchanging the hot, dusty desert roads for what Crichton-Stuart described as the Jebel's 'trees, lush grass and cattle'. On the other side of the Jebel the LRDG camped on the night of 30 March just outside CYRCOM headquarters at Barce. Mitford went into the town to report to General Neame, receiving instructions to reconnoitre Marada Oasis, approximately 250 miles south. Neame was concerned that German troops were planning to outflank the British position at Barce towards the end of April.

Mitford detailed Crichton-Stuart for the reconnaissance, and he left Barce early on 31 March with five trucks. The LRDG were no longer using the 30cwt Chevrolets, which were unfit for purpose after thousands of miles of tough desert travel.

Unfortunately, it had not been possible to replace like with like, so Bagnold reluctantly took ownership of a consignment of Ford 30cwt four-wheel drive trucks. Seventy of these vehicles were given to the LRDG in February, and it took nearly a month of modification (notably camouflaging them in colours that included pink – effective because it blended in with the haze of the sun at dawn and dusk) before they were considered desert-worthy. Even then, Bagnold harboured doubts as to the Fords' suitability because of 'their greater weight … and the complications introduced by the front wheel drive'. Nearly all the men preferred the Chevrolets because they were easier to handle and because they had a bonnet. The Fords didn't, and hot air from the engines was a constant irritation to the men on patrol.

As Crichton-Stuart and his patrol headed south, the going grew worse and 'the heavier new trucks, sticking and grinding away despite their four-wheel drive, gave a lot of mechanical trouble'. The vehicles weren't the only source of anxiety for the LRDG. On tuning into the BBC news on the evening of 1 April, Crichton-Stuart heard that 'the enemy had broken through at Agheila and were approaching Agedabia'.[13] Agedabia was south of Barce, effectively cutting Crichton-Stuart and his men off from Barce. Unfortunately, when he tried to contact CYRCOM on the radio he couldn't get through, so Crichton-Stuart pressed on with his mission. 'Each evening the operator tried in vain to contact the squadron, while the BBC news became ominously vaguer,' he said.

As the five LRDG vehicles were swallowed by the vast dunes of the interior of the Libyan Desert, in their rear the British were retreating in the face of Rommel's offensive, launched on 31 March. The German armour – many of the tanks Mark III and Mark IV Panzers – were far superior in firepower to the British Crusader tanks and the captured Italian M13 tanks that Neame's men were also using. But what put the fear of God into the British armour more than any tank were the 88mm anti-aircraft guns that could disable a tank from the distance of a mile.

By sundown on 1 April, the British had been pushed back in disarray and in the days that followed hundreds of their soldiers were captured as Rommel sent a battle-group ahead of his armour in a hook that entrapped the enemy east of Derna, close to the point where the coastal road rose into the Jebel Akhdar.

By now General O'Connor, still recuperating from a stomach ulcer, had arrived in the front line from Egypt. On the evening of 6 April, Neame, O'Connor and Brigadier John Combe, commanding the armoured cars of the 11th Hussars, got lost in the darkness on their way to their new battlefield HQ. They were eventually found, by the Germans.

Within a fortnight of launching his offensive Rommel had swept the British out of Cyrenaica, captured thousands of prisoners, and restored the confidence of

A group of LRDG soldiers outside the mess room in Kufra Oasis in September1941. (Courtesy of the SAS Regimental Archive)

his Italian ally. All that remained of the British in Libya was a small besieged garrison in the port of Tobruk, and Bagnold and B Squadron of the LRDG at Kufra, 500 miles south. Somewhere in between those points in early April was Crichton-Stuart and his small patrol.

Rommel's offensive had rendered their mission to reconnoitre Marada irrelevant, but it had taken until the late afternoon of 5 April before Crichton-Stuart's signaller finally raised Mitford on the radio, which was a pre-war No.11 set that was carried by every patrol. The standard operational procedure for radio communication required the patrol's signaller to contact the wireless room in the Citadel (in Cairo) at a specific time each evening. Since British signallers had replaced New Zealand ones in November 1940, they had been taught to imitate code messages sent between Egyptian inspectors of state wireless. This, recalled Lofty Carr, was because the 'LRDG's cover was as an Egyptian company ... on the radio we used commercial procedure not military procedure, which is completely different, so that if Jerry was listening he would believe it was an Egyptian company and not us'.[14]

Mitford told Crichton-Stuart he was in Mekili and advised G Patrol to head to Jarabub, 215 miles to the east. The news dismayed Crichton-Stuart. 'It was an ugly situation, for Mekili was the last stop before Tobruk, and it meant that not only it and Bardia were threatened, but also Jarabub and Siwa.' G Patrol arrived at Jarabub on the morning of 10 April and were welcomed at the town's fort by a 'platoon of Senussi Arabs recruited in Egypt and commanded by a Frenchman'.[15] Living up to the reputation of his countrymen, the French officer treated Crichton-Stuart's patrol to a lavish meal, but towards its end the alarm was sounded. 'Seizing our weapons we rushed to man the battlements in the best Western style and grimly covered a number of vehicles approaching from the north,' recalled Crichton-Stuart. 'The strength of my field glasses alone prevented internecine warfare, as just in time I identified the remainder of A Squadron.'

Mitford and his squadron, consisting of Y Patrol and the other half of G Patrol, were tired, grimy and hungry when they drove into Jarabub. Crichton-Stuart said the squadron 'celebrated our reunion in Chianti', before listening to an account of their operation.

They had left Barce on 1 April, heading south towards Msus, approximately 60 miles inland from the coast. The terrain was rough and progress slow, and along the way they strayed into a minefield. Captain Pat McCraith's V8 car drove over one ordnance, leaving him with a broken arm, shattered teeth and a body pock-marked by shrapnel, and one of Y Patrol's most effective operators, Anthony 'Tich' Cave was captured as the LRDG skirmished with the Italians on the outskirts of Mekili. Then at dawn on 8 April the Germans attacked the town in force from the south, east and north, and only the dexterous leadership of Mitford, allied to the dust storm, enabled the LRDG to withdraw without being detected. Mitford led his men towards the south-east, pausing at first light on 9 April to attack a column of German artillery at rest in a gully. 'He hid us down behind a ridge and then moved us very cleverly off the ridge and we got behind a number of German artillery pieces with their backs and guns to us,' recalled Lofty Carr.[16] The LRDG moved noiselessly into position and on a hand signal from Mitford opened fire. 'We obliterated these Germans,' remembered Carr, 'and then hopped it.'

On 10 April they arrived at Jarabub, where Crichton-Stuart was waiting with the bottles of Chianti, but within 48 hours the squadron was on the move again, this time to Siwa. Here they found Guy Prendergast. He had no wine to offer them, only a reorganization of the squadron into three patrols, led by Mitford, Crichton-Stuart and Martin Gibbs.

'During the month that followed the operational employment of G Patrol could be summed up as a) passive misuse and b) active misuse,' reflected Crichton-Stuart, who took his patrol west in an attempt to salvage some of the vehicles abandoned in the British withdrawal. He was too late, however, and aborted the mission because of the large enemy presence in the area. Next Crichton-Stuart's patrol spent a week observing enemy movements on the track that led from Aujilawjila to Jarabub. The men suffered from heat and tedium, their surveillance 'enlivened only by a football'.

Gibbs' patrol, meanwhile, comprising an equal number of guardsmen and yeomanry, was maintaining a similar watch on the northern approach to Jarabub.

The two patrols returned to Siwa in late April, around the time Rommel's Afrika Korps seized the coastal town of Sollum, just inside the Egyptian border and approximately 130 miles north of Jarabub.

Gibbs was therefore detailed to take his patrol and guard 'the immediate approaches to Jarabub'. This mission coincided with what Bill Kennedy Shaw described as the 'worst *qibli* in LRDG history', a heat storm far more merciless than the one his patrol had endured the previous September. For Gibbs and his patrol it was made all the worse by the fact there was no water to be had from the wells around Jarabub: they had been polluted by the Italians during their occupation.

With inadequate water, Gibbs and his men began to suffer the effects of extreme thirst and dehydration. They couldn't sleep and argued among each other, until eventually Gibbs radioed Crichton-Stuart and requested permission to abort the patrol. When they arrived at Jarabub Crichton-Stuart was shocked by their state. He oversaw their evacuation to Siwa, and Gibbs, after six weeks convalescing, returned to the Guards.

To their relief, the LRDG were ordered in mid-May to embark on a more aggressive patrol, in tandem with a British offensive to try and retake Bardia. Crichton-Stuart's instructions were to protect the southern flank of the 11th Hussars as they advanced west across the Egyptian frontier into Libya. On 14 May G Patrol arrived at the rendezvous point close to the Libyan side of the frontier fence. 'I saw a number of armoured cars and at least two tanks which looked like our cruisers,' Crichton-Stuart wrote later in his patrol report. Peering through his field glasses, Crichton-Stuart was unable to discern any markings on the vehicles because of dust and camouflage. Taking guardsman William Fraser in his truck, Crichton-Stuart advanced towards the vehicles. 'At about 250 yards one M.G. [machine gun] opened fire at, but over, me,' he wrote. 'The next moment they opened up with a number of M.G.s, both heavy and light, with plenty of tracer, and a few shots from a tank gun. Their shooting was very poor, and my truck was the only one hit.'[17]

Crichton-Stuart swung his vehicle round and drove manically over the desert to escape the hostile fire. Beside him, Fraser tried to stem the flow of blood from two bullet wounds to his arm. The sluggish response of the truck

A desert latrine, like this one at Kufra, wasn't the height of sophistication. (Courtesy of the SAS Regimental Archive)

indicated that a bullet had also punctured a tyre. Ordering three trucks to continue south, Crichton-Stuart stopped his vehicle out of sight of the enemy and with the help of men from the fourth lorry began changing the wheel. 'We failed to get the tyre changed,' he explained in his report, 'for we heard the enemy coming and all got on to the other truck and away with enemy armoured cars 300 yards behind.'[18]

There now began a frantic pursuit south across the desert, the LRDG vehicles travelling at 45mph and their hunters matching their speed. The British glanced back, checking the distance; after a few miles, there was no doubt that the enemy was closing. Faster, faster, urged Crichton-Stuart, and the trucks shook and rattled as their drivers neared their maximum speed of 50mph. 'An unlucky shot got another truck's tyre,' said Crichton-Stuart, 'and I transferred their crew on to mine, which now had nine on board. We only just got away in time. After this, firing back and cracking up to 50 again, we gradually drew away, and about five miles south of Fort Maddalena, having been chased for over 30 miles, I halted.'[19]

Crichton-Stuart couldn't even say for certain in his report if their assailants had been German; they may have been British. But whoever they were, it was fortunate their shooting was wayward. Apart from the minor wound to Fraser, no other soldier had been hit, although when Crichton-Stuart prepared for bed that evening he discovered that one bullet had shattered the toothbrush in his kit bag and another holed his tin mug.

G Patrol was ordered to Siwa, 350 miles north-east of Kufra, where it spent the rest of May. Prendergast had established his HQ in a stone building built on a rocky outcrop close to the oasis's landing strip – a levelled area of sand strong enough to withstand light aircraft. Though the men of G and Y Patrol were dispersed throughout Siwa, a communal meeting place was one of the oasis's many pools. 'Out of their dark green depths cool water bubbled,' recalled Crichton-Stuart, 'and Cleopatra's Bath, in particular, close-shadowed by palms, made the midsummer heat of Siwa easy to bear.'[20]

Crichton-Stuart was less enamoured with the locals. In his view they were 'degenerate and diseased [and] lived in a honeycomb of mud huts built on top of one another like a playing-card castle'. Not all the men shared this narrow-minded opinion, and Bill Kennedy Shaw took a great interest in the natives. ★ In Tripolitania, through which the Eighth Army swept in four months, there was less opportunity for the Arabs to aid us, but many of them did so: one Arab of my

---

★ On 18 September 1945, the *Times* of London published a letter written by Kennedy Shaw entitled 'Arab Helpers', in which he stated: 'Twice the British advanced into Cyrenaica and twice withdrew from it, and at each retreat the Italians took vengeance, sometimes with great severity, on those Arabs whom they suspected of having helped us.'

acquaintance hid two airmen for some months in his house in the centre of Tripoli city. It is to be hoped that the Council of Foreign Ministers will bear these facts in mind when planning the future of the former Italian colonies in North Africa.' The LRDG intelligence officer was fascinated by the practicality of the locals in exploiting the natural resources of Siwa: olives, dates, grapes and pomegranates. Writing in a 1944 issue of the *Geographical Magazine*, Kennedy Shaw explained: 'The date palm in fact supplies almost all simple human needs – food for men and animals, palm wine, fuel, building timber, leaves for thatch, baskets, mats, sandals and fibres for ropes.'[21]

Captain Richard Lawson, who became the LRDG's medical officer in December 1941, appraised Siwa shortly after his first visit to the oasis. Of the '200 pools of deep clean water', he wrote, 'all are suitable for drinking and many have an output of several thousand gallons daily. Two pools, one by the rest house and one at the foot of the Jebel Takrur, were used for drinking water only and were already fenced and concreted. There is little or no dysentery or typhoid among the natives.'[22] The doctor also noted that half a dozen of the pools were reserved for bathing or washing and in this way avoided contamination.

Drawing water at Kufra in the summer of 1941 when, to their frustration, the LRDG were deployed as garrison troops. (Courtesy of the SAS Regimental Archive)

CHAPTER 7

MISUSE AND
MALARIA

ay had been a trying month for the LRDG, as it had been for the Allied army as a whole. On 27 May three Afrika Korps assault groups had driven the British out of the Halfaya Pass, the strategically important escarpment just inside the Egyptian border with Libya. The enemy, noted General Rommel, 'fled in panic to the east, leaving considerable booty and material of all kinds in our hands'.[1] The next day, 28 May, a gloomy General Wavell lamented the fact that his 'infantry tanks are really too slow for a battle in the desert'. Easy prey for the German 88mm anti-tank guns, the British armoured corps had suffered heavy casualties since the arrival of the Afrika Korps, but Wavell nonetheless retained his belief that he would 'succeed in driving the enemy west of Tobruk'.

As Wavell prepared to launch Operation *Battleaxe* in mid-June, he received a complaint from Ralph Bagnold 'as to the misuse of the LRDG Patrols' in the preceding weeks. Teddy Mitford in particular had agitated for a more 'active employment' rather than acting as garrison troops and fetching and carrying supplies to Mersa Matruh. Additionally, an outbreak of sickness at Siwa had decimated G patrol. 'Men started going down with a fever which the medical officer attached to the squadron diagnosed as malaria,' recorded Crichton-Stuart. 'When he sent to Mersa Matruh for supplies of quinine and other appropriate medicines he got the curatives he asked for, but the authorities refused to send him

OPPOSITE
(left to right) David Lloyd Owen, Jake Easonsmith and Gus Holliman, three LRDG officers sporting a variety of headwear. Only Lloyd Owen survived the war. (Author's Collection)

The Irrigation Pools at Siwa

ABOVE
The irrigation pools at Siwa were the perfect way to cool off at the end of a long patrol, or even a long day. (Courtesy of the SAS Regimental Archive)

OPPOSITE TOP
There were many of the pools at Siwa and while some were used solely for bathing, others were reserved for washing laundry. (Courtesy of the SAS Regimental Archive)

OPPOSITE BOTTOM
Captain Michael Crichton-Stuart recalled: 'Out of their dark green depths cool water bubbled ... they made the midsummer heat of Siwa easy to bear.' (Courtesy of the SAS Regimental Archive)

the necessary preventatives, curtly informing him that Siwa was NOT [they repeated NOT] malarial.'[2] Eventually an expert in tropical diseases was despatched to Siwa from Cairo and within 24 hours he confirmed that 'the oasis was swarming with anopheles mosquitoes'.

On 6 June Captain Pat McCraith rejoined the LRDG at Siwa, arriving from Cairo with a batch of new trucks to replace the ones lost in recent patrols. The following day Y Patrol returned from Jarabub and the unit underwent another reorganization: Y, G and a new temporary patrol, H, were formed, with McCraith leading Y, Crichton-Stuart G and Jake Easonsmith H. All three patrols comprised six trucks and were issued with similar instructions, 'the conveyance of agents to the interior of Cyrenaica and the collection of their reports, and with gathering geographical information about the country south of the Jebel-el-Akhdar'.[3] Also formed in June 1941 was the unit's Survey Section, under the eye of Bill Kennedy Shaw.

The day before Crichton-Stuart was scheduled to lead his patrol on a surveillance of enemy traffic on the main road through the lush countryside of the Jebel Akhdar, he succumbed to malaria. Reluctantly he handed over command to Jake Easonsmith, of Y Patrol, who took with him a recently arrived G Patrol officer called Anthony Hay, erstwhile of the Coldstream Guards. Hay was to replace Crichton-Stuart, who

The exploits of the LRDG captured the media's imagination and they appeared in newspapers, magazines and even gave radio interviews during the desert campaign. (Getty)

had been summoned back to the Scots Guards, and although he had persuaded his CO to allow him three months to school Hay in the work of an LRDG officer, Crichton-Stuart's remaining time in the unit was bedevilled by recurrent malaria. Throughout the summer he spent a lot of time in Mersa Matruh, grouching at the misuse of the LRDG and of another special forces unit called Layforce. Formed in the summer of 1940, just as the LRDG came into being, Layforce was commanded by Colonel Robert Laycock and comprised three commando troops – Nos. 7, 8 and 11. No. 8 Commando was also known as Guards Commando, and among its ranks when it sailed from Britain on the last day of January 1941 were Randolph Churchill, the prime minister's son, George Jellicoe, son of the famous World War I admiral, and a 25-year-old Scots Guards lieutenant called David Stirling. Crichton-Stuart wrote:

> The frustration felt by the LRDG during this season was shared and even exceeded by a commando force under Colonel Laycock … They spent the summer in abortive attempts at harassing the enemy's rear by sea landings. At the end of the summer the force was disbanded, defeated by the difficulties of a rocky coast and the unreliable sea. It was simply not yet realised that the desert approach was incomparably easier and safer, for there you could hide from the air.[4]

Most of Layforce were returned to their parent units, but not David Stirling. Crichton-Stuart met him several times in Cairo and Mersa Matruh and the former was keen to pump the LRDG officer for information on their operations. Together the pair 'discussed … at length' the advantages of a desert approach to enemy targets rather than a seaborne approach. Crichton-Stuart, of course, was thinking solely of using vehicles. Stirling, however, had another method in mind, one that in the course of that summer started to take shape.

CHAPTER 8

HEAVY LOSSES AND A NEW LEADER

G eneral Wavell launched his offensive, Operation *Battleaxe*, on 15 June, the intention of which was to sweep the Axis forces out of Cyrenaica and relieve the pressure on the besieged port of Tobruk. The assault failed, the British armour being destroyed by the German 88mm guns in Halfaya Pass, renamed 'Hellfire Pass' by the Allies. 'The three-day battle has ended in complete victory,' wrote Rommel to his wife on 18 June. 'I'm going to go round the troops today to thank them and issue orders.'[1]

Despite his success at repelling the British attack, Rommel was unable to capitalize on his triumph by pushing into Egypt. His lines of supply and communication were now stretched precariously thin, and the defiant Allied defenders in Tobruk – to his rear – caused him consternation. Nevertheless, at the end of June Rommel wrote again to his wife, declaring the 'joy of the Afrika troops over this latest victory is tremendous … now the enemy can come, he'll get an even bigger beating.'[2]

The failure of Operation *Battleaxe* cost General Wavell his job. The LRDG's principal champion was replaced as commander-in-chief by Claude Auchinleck with Lieutenant General William Gott succeeding O'Creagh as commander of the 7th Armoured Division. With Wavell gone, and the Allies reeling from their losses, the LRDG had lost, for the time being at least, some of its clout. Not only was

OPPOSITE
An LRDG observation post in the Libyan Desert. Look carefully for the lookout! (Courtesy of the SAS Regimental Archive)

Michael Crichton-Stuart recalled to his regiment, but Major Teddy Mitford was summoned back to the 1st Battalion Royal Tank Regiment and Pat McCraith was returned to the Sherwood Rangers Yeomanry (although their losses had been sustained during the battle for Crete in late May). His loss was a particular blow for Y Patrol, recalled Lofty Carr, the navigator. 'A lot of officers in the army were resentful of soldiers who displayed any intelligence or initiative, but not McCraith,' reflected Carr. 'He was a fussy fellow, a solicitor before the war, who would spend the whole night before any operation checking every item personally so that the QM [quartermaster] would be at his wit's end.'[3]

If losing Crichton-Stuart, Mitford and McCraith wasn't bad enough for the LRDG, they also had to cope with the loss of their commanding officer. Twelve months after raising the unit, Ralph Bagnold decided in June 1941 that it was time to hand the baton of command to a younger and more active man – Guy Prendergast. Bagnold – 'Baggers' to the men – expanded on his decision to resign in an editorial published in *Tracks*,★ the first and only issue of the LRDG magazine, published in June 1941. Reflecting on the work of the LRDG, Bagnold wrote proudly:

> The unit has more than achieved the purpose for which it was designed. It has in
> fact become famous, not only for the exploits of individual patrols but for its ability
> to exist and to move about over a desert and in a climate both of which had been
> thought impossible for any military force … I now leave the LRDG with the

---

★ On the front cover was the LRDG badge, a scorpion with the words beneath *Non Vi Sed Arte* (Not by Strength but by Guile). The badge was the brainchild of Teddy Mitford, who during a pre-war expedition to Kufra had been impressed by the insignia of an Italian air force squadron of a black scorpion within a blue wheel.

Where the enemy was known to be close the LRDG would double back on themselves to confuse aircraft who might spot their tyre tracks. (Courtesy of the SAS Regimental Archive)

It wasn't just sand that posed a problem for the LRDG in the desert, as this patrol discovered when they became bogged down in a salt marsh. (Courtesy of the SAS Regimental Archive)

knowledge that it has more action and useful work in front of it, against an enemy for whom new methods must be evolved. May I thank all ranks for their hard work and ready cooperation, and wish the unit the best of luck for the future.[4]

What Bagnold didn't divulge was the toil taken on his health over the last 12 months. He was now 45 and the pressure of command, of raising and leading a reconnaissance force, combined with the brutal environment of the Libyan Desert, had left him

Bill Kennedy Shaw wrote of traversing a salt marsh: 'Drive your truck two yards from the beaten track and it will be sunk to its axles in the quicksands.' (Courtesy of the SAS Regimental Archive)

exhausted. To only his close associates did he confess that his health 'was beginning to suffer, so I thought it was time to quit'.

His departure wasn't, however, immediate. It was agreed that he would hand over command to Prendergast officially on 1 August, allowing the latter time to familiarize himself with his new role, and also oversee the recruitment of new officers and men to the LRDG. Together with Bagnold, Prendergast toured transit camps and infantry depots in search of fresh blood.

Alexander Stewart was a bored 21-year-old in the Armoured Troops Workshop of the Royal Army Ordnance Corps when Bagnold and Prendergast arrived one morning at his depot. 'As we listened in a big marquee the bulk of the troops walked out,' recalled Stewart, a Scot from Banffshire. But he was attracted to what he heard and what he envisaged. 'It would be a minimum of discipline, army discipline, and free from parades and drills and so on.'[5]

Guardsman Spencer Seadon was recovering from a leg infection at a Left Out of Battle camp when Bagnold arrived in search of recruits. 'A notice came up asking for volunteers,' recalled Seadon, who shared a ridge tent with eight other convalescing soldiers. 'So we said we would all join the LRDG [because] we were fed up in this camp, there was nothing much to do … we went up and one by one they came out and they said, "Blimey Spence, we're not joining that mob, they're a suicide squad".'[6]

Bill 'Smudger' Smith, a signaller, encountered a similar response when he answered the call for volunteers. 'My sergeant did his best to dissuade me,' he recalled. 'He sincerely believed I was courting certain death. "They're a suicide

squad, Smudge." What little I had heard about the LRDG suggested the suicide was reserved for the enemy so I did my utmost to calm the good sergeant's fears.'[7]

Archie Gibson jumped at the chance to escape the Scots Guards, where he 'felt stifled by the discipline'. He told Prendergast and Bagnold he was a skilled driver who could handle any vehicle in any terrain. 'From what I'd heard of the Long Range Desert Group it was definitely my type of operation,' he reflected. 'I liked the whole mystique of the desert, and the fact that we'd be moving in small parties using our own initiative.'[8]

The 'mystique' was also the attraction for a 23-year-old officer called David Lloyd Owen, who had commanded a company of the Queen's Royal Regiment

An LRDG patrol
prepares for a
roadwatch near the
Arco dei Mileni', better
known to the Allies
Marble Arch because
the Italian monument
resembled the famous
London landmark.
(Courtesy of the SAS
Regimental Archive)

during the rout of the Italian Army in December 1940. Subsequently, and for reasons that eluded Lloyd Owen, he had been posted to the Officer Cadet Training Unit (OCTU) in Cairo in charge of administration. 'I was about at my wits' end and loathing every minute of it all,' recalled Lloyd Owen. Admitting that he 'had always been a bit of a dreamer' with a love for 'Beau Geste and other tales of the French North African Empire', Lloyd Owen applied for the LRDG and was accepted after a rigorous interview by Bagnold.[9]

One or two men volunteered simply because they were the volunteering kind. 'One morning a little officer turned up on the parade and said he was calling for volunteers for the LRDG,' remembered Jim Patch, a 21-year-old signaller from London. 'We'd never heard of but it sounded all right so my friend, Bill Morrison and I, volunteered.'[10]

With its ranks replenished, the LRDG was placed under the command of Lieutenant General Sir Alan Cunningham, recently appointed commander of the reconstituted Western Desert Force, henceforth known as the Eighth Army.

On the same day that the Eighth Army came into being, Bagnold wrote from Cairo to Prendergast, whose headquarters were at Kufra. He began by reassuring his successor that the transfer of the LRDG to the Eighth Army 'is quite all right as far as you are concerned'. Bagnold then offered his thoughts on what Prendergast should do about administration, supplies, the mobile medical unit and the signal section. He cautioned that there were problems once more with General Freyberg, commander of the New Zealand forces in Egypt, and Bagnold informed Prendergast that 'things are such in a muddle with the NZ people between what they say and what they write that I really think you should never rely or act on any more verbal arrangements with them'.[11]

Five days later, on 29 September, a conference was held at Eighth Army HQ, attended by both Prendergast and Bagnold, in which the role of the LRDG was discussed. A major operation was brewing, and the LRDG were told they would have a small but significant part to play. Their tasks, as laid out in the conference minutes, would be as follows:

a. To obtain information as to enemy movements on certain tracks, and in certain areas, and to watch his reactions to any offensive by us.

b. To provide further information of the state of going in certain areas.

c. At all times the LRDG should try and harass the enemy as far as possible, and in any way they liked provided they did not get too involved themselves. The army commander realized that the LRDG should not deliberately court trouble, and was in no way armoured.

d. Any tactical information obtained would be required as early as possible. During and before offensive operations, LRDG would be justified in taking more risks than usual in order to send back up to date information.[12]

CHAPTER 9

THE SAVIOURS OF
THE SAS

By mid-October 1941, the LRDG was at Kufra in its entirety. David Lloyd Owen was delighted with what he found, the oasis living up to the idyll he imagined when reading stories of the desert as a young boy. 'It was so unbelievably peaceful,' he wrote. 'The Arabs with their donkeys padded silently across the sand and only the slight rustle of the palm trees in the breeze would disturb the silence.'[1]

Lloyd Owen's Y Patrol parked their trucks in the shade of some palm trees, and while his men bathed in the two salt lakes close by, where it was possible 'to lie floating on your back and contemplate the perfection of the blue sky above', the officers assembled before Prendergast. There were several introductions to be made: not only Lloyd Owen was new to the unit, but so too were Frank Simms, also recruited to Y Patrol, and Alastair Timpson of G Patrol. Timpson was 26, a product of privilege, having been educated at Eton and Cambridge. Upon leaving university he had entered the gold mining business in South Africa, but he returned to Britain on the outbreak of war and received a commission in the Scots Guards.

The LRDG weren't long at Kufra, although long enough to enjoy a duck shoot or two around the salt lakes, and in November they moved 350 miles north-east to Siwa. 'It was common knowledge that something was simmering up north,' recalled Timpson.[2] On the 13th of that month Prendergast briefed his men on the offensive

OPPOSITE
Captain Crosby 'Bing' Morris, was older than most LRDG officers but the New Zealander proved a brave and resourceful soldier. (Courtesy of the SAS Regimental Archive)

that was to begin five days hence and the role that the LRDG would play. Most of the talking was done by Bill Kennedy Shaw. He explained that their job was purely reconnaissance, and to each officer he allotted an area in which to operate and 'report in detail on what the enemy does behind his front line'. On no account, emphasized Kennedy Shaw, was any patrol to go looking for trouble. 'It will only give the game away if you do,' he said. 'Your job is to watch and tell me what you see and you can't do that if you are seen yourselves.'[3]

The SAS became self-sufficient in the summer of 1942 and in the opinion of David Lloyd Owen lost some of their effectiveness. Captain Malcolm Pleydell, their medical officer, is standing second from right in the middle row. (Author's Collection)

One initiative of Prendergast's since assuming command had been to reorganize the patrols, dividing them into two, because he felt a ten vehicle patrol was too conspicuous. In future a patrol such as Y Patrol would be split into Y1 and Y2, each comprising five 30cwt trucks with one smaller pick-up truck.

The four Guards and Yeomanry patrols, along with a New Zealand patrol under Bruce Ballantyne, left Siwa on the morning of 15 November 1941, three days before General Claude Auchinleck launched his grand offensive codenamed

A group of Rhodesian LRDG soldiers, including Jacko Jackson (second left) and Stan Eastwood (far right) enjoying the shade offered by Kufra's palm trees in September 1941. (Courtesy of the SAS Regimental Archive)

Operation *Crusader*. Its aim was to retake Cyrenaica and seize the Libyan airfields from the enemy, thereby enabling the RAF to increase their supplies to Malta, the Mediterranean island that was of such strategic importance to the British.

To achieve these aims, Auchinleck intended his 13 Corps to launch a frontal attack on a 65-mile front against the Axis forces holding the front line, while the 30th Corps would swing round the flanks and annihilate Rommel's armoured force of 174 tanks, markedly inferior in number to the 710 tanks at Auchinleck's disposal. Meanwhile the besieged garrison at Tobruk, 70 miles behind the German front line, would break out and meet the 30th Corps as they advanced west across Cyrenaica.

The LRDG's role was observing and reporting enemy troop movements, alerting GHQ to what Rommel might be planning in response to the offensive. They did have an additional responsibility, however, one that entailed Captain Jake Easonsmith's R1 Patrol collecting a party of 55 paratroopers – 'Parashots', as the LRDG called them – once they had carried out a daring raid on a string of enemy airfields at Gazala and Tmimi.

It was no coincidence that Prendergast detailed Easonsmith to collect the paratroopers, who in fact were David Stirling and his recently formed Special Air Service Brigade.* Henceforth, for the sake of clarity, I will refer to them as the SAS. A wine merchant before the war, Easonsmith was a man able to adapt to any given situation with an infectious good humour. Unorthodox and unflappable, the 32-year-old was by far and away the most popular officer in the LRDG. Timpson was beguiled by Easonsmith's 'calm and kindly judgement', while Lloyd Owen said of him: 'Not only was he a natural leader of men, because he understood men in the kind of way which few others have done, but he was also a master at the art of craft and guile.'[4]

Easonsmith left Siwa at 0530 hours on 17 November and travelled north in seven LRDG trucks and two Bedford lorries belonging to the SAS. The first rendezvous was reached two days later, and there the patrol left the two SAS vehicles. Pushing north–north-east towards the second RV (rendezvous) at the Gadd-el-Ahmar crossroads, Easonsmith encountered Lloyd Owen and Y2 Patrol. They had spent the last few days in a *wadi* (a dry river bed) observing a track along which it was presumed the enemy would move. They hadn't, however, and a frustrated Lloyd Owen gladly accepted Easonsmith's instructions to help him in the collection of SAS raiders.

---

* The actual designation of Stirling's 60-strong force was L Detachment, Special Air Service Brigade, a deliberate attempt by MEHQ [Middle East Headquarters] to fool the Germans into believing – through one of their many spies in Egypt – that an airborne brigade had arrived from Britain.

Paddy Mayne, who succeeded David Stirling in early 1943, as commanding officer of the SAS. He finished the war with the DSO and three bars. (Author's Collection)

During the evening of 19 November, Easonsmith reached the first RV and a few hours later Captain Jock Lewes, the second-in-command of the SAS, appeared with nine of his men. In the early hours of the following morning David Stirling arrived with only his sergeant, Bob Tait, and not long after dawn Paddy Mayne and eight exhausted men showed up.

Mayne's subsequent report of the inaugural SAS raid encapsulated the wretched failure of the operation. In the laconic manner for which he was famous, the former Ireland rugby international described an 'unpleasant' landing on ground studded with thorn bushes and with the parachutists buffeted by winds of 25mph. Two men were injured and several of the SAS containers lost, but nonetheless Mayne led his men towards the target, an airfield on which he counted 17 aircraft. Their reconnaissance completed, Mayne and his men laid up in a *wadi* and waited for nightfall. Mayne wrote in his report:

> It had rained occasionally during the day and at 1730 hours it commenced to rain heavily. … After about half an hour the *wadi* became a river, and as the men were lying concealed in the middle of bushes it took them some time getting to higher ground. It kept on raining and we were unable to find shelter. An hour later I tried two of the time pencils N.B A time pencil resembled in shape and size a biro pen. It was a glass tube with a spring-loaded striker held in place by a strip of copper wire. At the top was a glass phial containing acid which broke when squeezed. The acid then ate through the wire and released the striker. The thicker the wire

the longer the delay before the striker was triggered (the pencils were colour coded according to the length of fuse). The time pencil was part of the 'Lewes Bomb', invented by Jock Lewes, an SAS officer, and was placed in a small cotton bag containing plastic explosive coated with petroland they did not work. Even if we had been able to keep them dry, it would not, in my opinion [have] been practicable to have used them, as during the half-hour delay on the plane the rain would have rendered them useless.[5]

To his consternation, Mayne discovered that the instantaneous fuses did not work, either, and despite waiting overnight in the hope they would dry out, he aborted the attack on the aerodrome the following day when it became apparent the fuses were useless. 'I withdrew that night, 18/11/41, some twenty miles on a bearing of 185 degrees,' wrote Mayne. 'The next night I did a further five miles on that bearing and then turned due west for approximately three miles where we contacted the LRDG.'[6]

Though Mayne was disconsolate at having to scrub the operation within sight of the target, Stirling was more sanguine about the failure of the first SAS raid, even though 34 of the 55 men who had parachuted into Libya had been killed or captured. 'David told me the story of his drop and of all that had gone wrong,' recalled Lloyd Owen, who had first made Stirling a mug of tea fortified with whisky. 'He had had rotten bad luck and any lesser man would have had his ardour completely damped. Not so David. He was already trying to analyse what had gone wrong and deciding how it would go right next time.'[7]

'He had had rotten bad luck and any lesser man would have had his ardour completely damped. Not so David. He was already trying to analyse what had gone wrong and deciding how it would go right next time.'

As Stirling and his 20 SAS survivors were transported by the LRDG to Jarabub, further north the Germans were fighting back after their initial surprise at the British offensive. The launch of Operation *Crusader* over a 65-mile front from Sollum to Jarabub had gone as well as Auchinleck had hoped. Armoured troops made steady progress, reaching the escarpment at Sidi Eezegh (32 miles south-east of Tobruk) and capturing its airfield on 19 November. However, the next day Rommel launched a fierce, fast counter-thrust that caught the Allies off-guard.

Tanks fought a series of 'long and confused' engagements, neither side capable of landing the knockout blow. But learning of the Allied breakout at Tobruk, Rommel struck south-east into his enemy's rear at Sidi Omar in an audacious manoeuvre that outfoxed the Allies and cost General Cunningham his job (he was replaced by Neil Ritchie).

Rommel's thrust towards Sidi Omar also led to a change in the LRDG's role, with Lieutenant Colonel Prendergast receiving fresh instructions from Eighth Army HQ on 24 November. No longer were they to be passive observers; instead the LRDG were told to 'act with the utmost vigour offensively against any enemy targets or communications within reach'. In particular, the patrols were ordered to focus on Mekili, Gadd-el-Ahmar and the coastal road in the vicinity of Jedabia.

Prendergast and Bill Kennedy Shaw studied the map and then directed each patrol to an area within the target zone. David Lloyd Owen's Y2 Patrol headed off towards El Ezzeiat, capturing a small Italian fort and its garrison of ten Italians and two Libyans. The prisoners were only too willing to provide information on enemy troop dispositions in Derna and Mekili.

Meanwhile the 11 men of Y1 Patrol, under the command of Captain Frank Simms, were instructed to attack convoys travelling between Mekili and Derna. For the first couple of days they saw no suitable targets, but on the late afternoon of 1 December the patrol located a large camp at a road junction 20 miles south-west of Derna. Simms and his navigator, Lofty Carr, reconnoitred the camp and discovered it was a motor transport park of 30 vehicles approximately 800 yards off the main road to Gazala. In his subsequent report recounting the attack, Simms kept his description to a minimum, simply writing that he had split his force into two raiding parties and that 15 vehicles were damaged before the patrol withdrew.

On returning to the RV, however, Simms discovered that Carr was missing. They waited an hour but when the navigator failed to show Simms concluded that he had been captured. But Carr hadn't been captured, and on finding himself left behind in the darkness he kept calm and set off on foot for where he hoped the patrol would lie up when dawn broke. At first light he was 2 miles from his destination and close to a main road used by the enemy. 'I heard noises of animals which I associated with a Senussi settlement,' Carr wrote in a report. 'With due caution [I] approached, and finding it to be indeed a Bedouin camp, I asked for food and water and was provided with camel's milk, macaroni and coffee by the natives.'[8]

Carr remained a guest of the Senussi for more than a week. It was imprudent to leave, as their camp was on the periphery of the offensive and Axis troops were visible in the distance. On a couple of occasions Carr was ushered by the Senussi to a cave in a *wadi* as German patrols approached the village. His narrowest escape was on 12 December. 'I was lying under some camel saddles when six tanks came into the village,' recalled Carr. 'I wasn't sure whose they were so I started walking towards them. On their forage caps the soldiers had a roundel like the RAF. I remember thinking "I didn't know the British tanks had those". They were German. Fortunately I was dressed as an Arab so I very quietly turned round and ducked into a tent'.[9]

Realizing he was stuck in the village for the foreseeable future, Carr began noting down information that might prove useful upon his liberation.

> December 13: Was taken to cave early. Artillery and auto cannon active all day. 30 enemy motor cycle combinations passed through village.
>
> December 14: Cave at dawn. Artillery, bombs and auto cannon. Senussi shepherd [Mohamed] brought news of crashed RAAF [Royal Australian Air Force] officer.
>
> December 15: Wounded RAAF officer arrived. Goat ate my map.
>
> December 16: Patrols around and artillery and small arms fire to east.
>
> December 17: Note reached 31st regt (Field) RA and was acknowledged. RAAF officer and self went on donkeys and were picked up in truck and taken forward.[10]

Carr eventually reached the HQ of the 4th Indian Division on 20 December, where he was 'suspected of being a fifth columnist'. Confirmation of his identity was provided by Lieutenant Colonel Prendergast and Carr was back with the LRDG two days before Christmas. He swapped tales with his comrades, furnishing them with details of his escapade with the Senussi, while they in turn enlightened him with accounts of their successful operations in conjunction with the SAS.

Jalo Oasis in December 1941. Neither the LRDG nor the SAS liked the oasis, which was plagued by flies and where the water was brackish. (Courtesy of the SAS Regimental Archive)

Since the start of December the LRDG had transported SAS raiding parties to a series of targets, including an attack by Paddy Mayne on Tamet airfield that destroyed 24 aircraft. More recently, Lieutenant Bill Fraser and five men had blown up 37 aircraft at Agedabia with help from the LRDG, who for their efforts had earned the affectionate nickname 'The Libyan Taxi Service'.

Prendergast had visited Eighth Army headquarters in Tmimi, Derna on 21 December to receive fresh instructions, orders he passed on to his men when he returned to Jalo in time for Christmas. As well as observing the enemy's movements and recording topographical details in Tripolitania, the LRDG were to 'carry out offensive patrols as far behind the enemy's lines as possible, and act aggressively against his L. of C. [Lines of Communication] in areas where such action was unlikely to be expected'.

Not stated explicitly in the orders received by Prendergast, but taken as read, was a desire on the part of Eighth Army for the LRDG to continue providing assistance to the SAS, who were now inflicting as much material damage on the Luftwaffe as the RAF. One such collaboration commenced on Christmas Day when a 15-strong T2 Patrol, under the command of 2nd Lieutenant Crosby 'Bing' Morris, left Jalo with two SAS parties to attack two airstrips, one at Arco dei Mileni (known to the British as Marble Arch because the Italian monument resembled the famous London landmark), and the second 60 miles further west along the coast at Nofilia.

At 38, Morris was a good deal older than most of the ten SAS men he was transporting to their targets, and had it not been for his mother he would have

This photo was taken at Jalo in December 1941, at the time when David Stirling's SAS based themselves at the oasis and drew heavily on the expertise of the LRDG. (Courtesy of the SAS Regimental Archive)

fought in World War I. As a 15-year-old in 1918 he had been queuing at the recruitment office in Fairlie, Canterbury, New Zealand, when his mother 'grabbed him by the scruff of his neck' and hauled him home. A farmer, Morris was an excellent rower and had been selected to compete for New Zealand in the 1928 Olympic Games in Amsterdam. But Morris and the rest of the rowing team never made it to Holland because of a shortage of funds to cover their passage to Europe.

The patrol reached the target area without mishap and on 27 December the LRDG dropped Fraser and his four men about 6 miles from the aerodrome at Marble Arch. On the afternoon of the following day Lieutenant Jock Lewes and four men were deposited close to Nofilia. With the first stage of their mission accomplished, Morris and T2 Patrol headed 10 miles south and lay up to await the return of the SAS raiding parties.

Lewes and his men reached the target and spent several hours observing the activity. They counted 43 aircraft, several fuel and ammunition dumps, and made a note of the enemy dispositions. They had neither the men nor the explosives to destroy all the aircraft, so Lewes drew up a plan of attack in a sector containing 18 planes. At nightfall they moved in. It was surprisingly easy to infiltrate the airfield and the SAS had soon placed a bomb on the first aircraft, where the port wing joined the fuselage. They moved onto the second aircraft, then the … But there was no third. To the dismay and bemusement of the SAS, they realized after a brief search in the darkness that the rest of the aircraft had gone. Hurrying off the airfield, Lewes led his men towards the rendezvous, each man wondering why he had not heard the

Robert 'Ginger' Riggs, seen here at Siwa in October 1941, was killed two months later when his patrol was mistakenly attacked by an RAF fighter as they escorted an SAS raiding party to their target. (Courtesy of the SAS Regimental Archive)

The graves of Robert Riggs and Laurence Ashby, killed in a friendly fire incident on 22 December 1941, as they escorted an SAS raiding party. (Courtesy of the SAS Regimental Archive)

departure of the aircraft in the preceding hours. At sundown on 30 December Lewes's party were picked up by Morris, who described subsequent events in his operational report.

> 31.12.41. This morning we proceeded back to Marble Arch to pick up Lt Fraser's party. During the past three days many enemy planes were sighted flying up and down the coast road. At about 10.00 hours in open country we were sighted by a *Messerschmitt* [110 fighter], who immediately attacked us with M.G. fire from a height of about 60 feet. We dispersed as quickly as we could.[11]

There was little cover for the vehicles as the aircraft came in for a second attack. One of the SAS men valiantly fired at their assailant with a Bren gun, but it had no effect as cannon fire erupted around the helpless patrol. The ME 110 broke off the attack after its second pass. Out of ammo, guessed the men on the ground. But there was no time to lose. Other aircraft would surely have been summoned by the pilot on his radio. Morris spotted some large rocks a couple of miles to the north and led his men towards them. Barely had they the time to camouflage the vehicles before they heard the sound of more aircraft. 'The planes flew low and followed our tracks,' wrote Morris, adding that there were two Stuka dive bombers and a Storch reconnaissance aircraft.

> Incendiary bullets were used and also cannon … my own truck was the first to go, catching fire. Hand grenades, belts of ammunition and petrol then blew up, completely wrecking the vehicle. Another truck was destroyed by a bomb shortly

afterwards. From where I was at this time I could see two large columns of smoke from my own and the bombed truck and after a second bomb had been dropped a third lot of smoke was seen in the direction a truck had taken when disappearing.[12]

When the Stukas eventually broke off the attack they left behind a scene of death and destruction. Three of the LRDG's five vehicles had been destroyed and a fourth was missing. Miraculously, there was only one fatality, although the death of Jock Lewes was a heavy blow to the SAS, and particularly to David Stirling, who in the raising of the force had leaned heavily on his friend's orderly intelligence. Once Lewes had been buried, the nine survivors set off on the 200 miles to Jalo in the one serviceable truck, Morris anxiously scanning the desert, not just for more aircraft but also signs of the missing truck. He saw nothing, and at 1700 hours on New Year's Day they reached Jalo where Morris informed Prendergast of the attack, the death of Lewes and the probable death of eight members of the LRDG and Corporal 'Chalky' White of the SAS.N.B Unfortunately little information exists as to either the full name of White (not to be confused with another 'Chalky' White, who served with 1SAS later in the war) or his definitive fate.

Then, on 9 January, a native from the British-controlled oasis at Augila arrived at Jalo with a message. Some soldiers, more skeletons than men, had been found in the desert. They claimed they were 'Inglizi', although they were in fact all New Zealanders bar one who was indeed English.

Gunner Edward Stutterd was later debriefed by Bill Kennedy Shaw, relating to the LRDG intelligence officer a tale of incredible endurance. In the initial attack, explained the 32-year-old Stutterd, his truck had not been hit and they had sought shelter in a shallow *wadi*. When the Messerschmitt had expended its ammunition, they started to drive north, then veering east until they spotted a salt marsh. 'By this time we were running south-west, skirting the marsh and ahead about three miles to the west sighted the only cover for miles so headed for it with the almost certain knowledge that we would be chased,' recounted Stutterd. 'On arrival at the cover, which proved to be only low rolling hills, we hid the cars as well as we could. Brown and I started to get the camouflage net out and our truck covered up while Garven went on look-out. Immediately he told us that there were two aircraft circling our tracks a couple of miles away. They were Stukas and wasted no time in "giving us the works".'

Stutterd told Kennedy Shaw how he and his comrades had fled from their truck as the Stukas swooped, diving among scrub and pressing themselves against the hard desert gravel. None of the nine LRDG soldiers, nor White, the SAS raider, were hit, though the truck was destroyed. Once the aircraft had left, the four had a discussion in which they agreed that their best course of action was to head to Augila, the nearest British-occupied oasis. The ten men pooled their rations and counted three gallons of water, one packet of nine biscuits and a tin of emergency chocolate rations.

Shortly after midday on New Year's Eve, 1941, the men set off on foot for Augila, travelling in two parties of five, each man taking his turn to carry the water drum for 12-minute stretches. Their intention was to cross the Marada to Agheila road before darkness descended. 'We travelled in spells of an hour with quarter-hour rests,' said Stutterd.

> At midnight we celebrated the New Year with our first ration of water, a quarter of a pint, and a half-hour spell, to the accompaniment of dropping flares and ack-ack fire in the direction of Agheila. The R.A.F. were on the job. We marched on until the sun rose and decided to have a break in a *wadi*. The weather was bitterly cold and I climbed to the top of the ridge to look for signs of the road. Three-quarters of the way up I heard aircraft again so went to ground. Two Stukas approached from the direction of Marada and flew north across our tracks of the previous night. Ten minutes later they flew south on the east side of us. These were the last aircraft to worry us.[13]

The men huddled together for warmth, but the cold was so great it was impossible to sleep. They let a few hours pass to see if any more aircraft arrived, but none did. Stutterd used the time to fashion a pair of moccasins from his greatcoat because his sandals had by now fallen to bits.

S Patrol spent December 1941 escorting SAS raiding parties to Libyan airfields but in January 1942 they were able to pose for the camera. This photo shows (left to right) Maxfield, Merrick, McKay and Massey. (Courtesy of the SAS Regimental Archive)

Judging that the Germans had called off the chase, the ten men set off at 1400 hours on New Year's Day and marched across the desert for long, cheerless hours. They paused for a rest the following morning and some of the men breakfasted on desert snails. 'I made a half-hearted suck at one in the shell which turned out to be more obstinate than my hunger and so I desisted,' explained Stutterd. 'In the mid-afternoon we decided to get going again. Here White, the [SAS] parachutist, left us. He had had the long march to the landing ground at Nofilia and back and his feet were almost raw. He said he would go towards Marada and try to seize a truck and get home that way. Actually we thought he meant to give himself up so as not to hinder the rest of the party. We gave him some water and did not see him again.'[14]

By now the men's bodies were racked by hunger and exhaustion, their minds clawed by doubt. There were few words exchanged as they tramped across the desert; each man preferred to be alone with his own thoughts, fighting the gathering fear that assailed every one – the fear of a wretched, slow, agonizing death. They were down to three-eighths of a pint of water each. 'At dawn the next morning we sighted a fire which seemed to be about seven or eight miles away,' said Stutterd. 'We reasoned that where there was fire there were Arabs and where there were Arabs there was water and perhaps food.' The men agreed to head towards the fire, but after marching for several hours the fire was no nearer. The trickery was too much for five of the party, who laid down to rest. Stutterd and three other men – Garven, Martin and Brown – pressed on, determined to find this fire. Stutterd told Kennedy Shaw:

We marched for an hour or so and came to some very moist ground in the marsh. Our thirst by this time was getting very bad and we dug a small well, hoping for water. Brown carried on towards the fire, saying that he 'would fire a shot if he found anything'. After a while we struck water at about three feet, but it was far too salt to drink. We baled it out for a while with a tin hat, trying to clear it up, but it was no good. Then I thought I heard a shot and we headed for the sound. After an hour's walking we found Brown with four Arabs and it was not long before we were gargling the small drop of water they had with them and eating a few dates.[15]

The Arabs then led the four LRDG men to a spring 6 miles away, and by nightfall the rest of the party arrived and they were asleep round a large fire started by the Arabs. Their water supply replenished and their hunger marginally eased by the dates, the soldiers bade farewell to their hosts the following day and set off with a full drum of water.

A Desert Sandstorm

ABOVE
The approach of a sandstorm was never welcomed with the wind throwing fine gravel into the faces of the men at a speed of 30 or 40 mph. (Courtesy of the SAS Regimental Archive)

OPPOSITE TOP
If the LRDG had time, and it was possible in the terrain, they would dig shallow holes and take refuge as the storm passed over. (Courtesy of the SAS Regimental Archive)

OPPOSITE BOTTOM
The worse sort of sandstorm was a *qibli*, which not only whipped up a huge cloud of dust but also brought unbearable heat. (Courtesy of the SAS Regimental Archive)

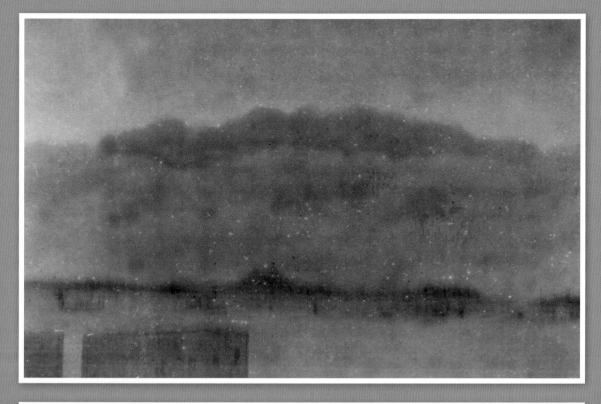

It soon became apparent that the march was taking a toll on their bodies. They had barely enough strength to carry their precious supply of water, and the cold now cut through their emaciated bodies with cruel relentlessness. 'We were making fairly slow progress now, being very tired,' admitted Stutterd. 'The weather also was very threatening. About 3.30pm it began to rain, and judging our distance from Augila to be about twenty-five miles, we decided to drink as much as we could, leave the water and make all speed for the oasis. We moved off but after a couple of hours had to stop for a rest: sleep was overpowering.'[16]

They attempted to move off at 0730 hours on 7 January, but a dust storm suddenly blew up and they were forced to dig shallow holes in the ground with what remained of their strength.

By mid-morning they were on their way, doubled up against a punishing head wind. They kept going for most of the daylight hours, but that evening there was a tacit acknowledgement among the men that they were down to the last dregs of their endurance. 'The next morning spirits were getting fairly low,' said Stutterd. 'Thirst was troubling us badly and our feet were getting almost unbearably sore. Our marching spells were cut to a fraction and every one was getting very tired. About 11 a.m. we sighted a *wadi* to the left of the road and as the sun was the warmest we had felt it for the whole journey we got down for a two hours' sleep.'[17]

It required all of their energy and willpower to rise themselves from their slumber and continue their slow plodding march. It would have been so easy to stay where they were, and carry on sleeping. But the men cajoled and encouraged each other, and they were soon on their way. They hadn't been travelling long when Stutterd thought he saw some palm trees in the distance. 'I hesitated to say anything about it. Our eyes were sore and by this time we were seeing things. However, they became so distinct that I mentioned it and we decided that they were palm trees. We headed off the road for the oasis which was about five miles away at that stage.'[18]

Hardly allowing themselves to believe they may have reached Augila, the men agreed to cover the distance in intervals of half a mile, resting their weary bodies in between. But excitement overcame them, the adrenalin giving them an impetus. Just before sundown on 8 January they stumbled into Augila. 'I found an empty Arab garden and a hut which we appropriated for the night,' recounted Stutterd. 'We lit a good fire, boiled some turnips and onions and had a glorious drink out of the well. After the most comfortable night since December 30th (it was now January 8th) we cooked more turnips and onions, made some date tea and set off for the fort. On the way we met two Arab policemen who took charge of us and led us to their barracks. Too much praise cannot be given to those Arabs for the way they treated us.'[19] When word reached the LRDG of the arrival of the nine men, a delighted Major Don Steele jumped in a truck and drove the 20 miles to Augila. 'Never have I enjoyed the sound of a motor more than the one that took us back to Jalo and safety,' reflected Stutterd.

The nine LRDG men had to be helped from the truck by their comrades and each then received an examination from Captain Richard Lawson, the medical officer, who had joined the unit the previous month. 'Their ankles were painful and swollen, as were their knees, and their feet were oedematous,' he wrote.[20]* The men also had severe indigestion, which in some cases was to last for several days.

Kennedy Shaw was also there to welcome the men home, marvelling at their accomplishment of covering 200 miles on foot with the bare minimum of food and clothing, faced with extreme cold and heat. The intelligence officer was struck by the wild staring eyes of the men and searched his mind for where he had seen such a look before. Then it came to him. 'In the second volume of [Captain] Scott's Last Expedition, the official account of his explorations in the Antarctic before the Great War, there is a photograph of Wilson, Bowers and Cherry Garrard taken a few minutes after they had arrived back from their winter journey to Gape Crozier … It was twenty years since I had read Scott's book but I had never forgotten the look in the eyes of those three men in the photograph. I saw the T2 men the day after they reached Jalo. I remembered where I had seen that look before.'[21]

---

* Oedema is frequently caused by famine and leads to swelling and discolouration of the skin, often turning it black.

CHAPTER 10

ON THE BACK FOOT

The return of the nine men was a rare bit of good news for the LRDG in the winter of 1941–42. Captains Frank Simms of Y Patrol and Tony Hay of G Patrol were both captured on operations, and on 24 January the Afrika Korps advanced, forcing the LRDG to withdraw from Jalo to Siwa.

By the start of February the Germans had reoccupied Cyrenaica as far east as the line Bir Hakim to Gazala (known as the Gazala Line), and Eighth Army instructed the LRDG to ascertain to what degree the enemy was using the main coastal roads, and if fuel and supply dumps were being stockpiled in the area north-east of Jedabia, which might suggest Rommel's intention to advance on Tobruk.

Rommel was not gathering himself for any more offensives, having already overstretched his supply lines in his advance of the previous month. He was now urging Berlin to provide him with the men and machines to finish off the British in North Africa, but to his frustration his requests were stone-walled. 'Our demands for additional formations were refused on the grounds that with the huge demand for transport which the Eastern Front [Russia] was making on Germany's limited productive capacity, the creation of further motorized units for Africa was out of the question,' he wrote in his journal, adding that it was 'a sadly short-sighted and misguided view'.[1] In March 1942 the Afrika Korps received 18,000 tons of supplies, 42,000 tons fewer than Rommel calculated his army required for victory in North Africa.

OPPOSITE
A folboat (collapsible canoe) such as this one was used by the SAS during raids against shipping in Benghazi harbour in the spring of 1942. (Courtesy of the SAS Regimental Archive)

An LRDG patrol enjoy a cup of tea at Siwa in March 1942. (Courtesy of the SAS Regimental Archive)

He also received a few thousand additional men to augment his three German divisions 'whose fighting strength was often ludicrously small'. Rommel resigned himself to taking on his enemy with far inferior resources.

Auchinleck, meanwhile, was consolidating his defensive positions and would not be ready to launch a fresh offensive for several more months. Throughout March the LRDG gathered intelligence on the enemy's movements and supplies, information gratefully received at MEHQ (Middle East Headquarters). 'The commander-in-chief directs me to say how impressed he is with the work of the LRDG in the carrying out of their deep reconnaissance along the Tripoli–Benghazi road, and elsewhere,' cabled Lieutenant General Thomas Corbett, chief of the general staff, to Prendergast on 7 April. 'The information which they are producing is of the utmost value to us at the present.'[2]

Despite the glowing praise from MEHQ, Prendergast was becoming ever more exasperated with what was being asked of the LRDG. Keeping enemy traffic under surveillance – what was known as 'road watching' – was of course an integral part of their work, but it was playing what Prendergast described as 'universal aunt' to the SAS, stranded aviators and secret agents that grated. 'These demands have usually been met,' he wrote, 'but not without straining the unit's own resources and personnel.'[3]

Then on 23 April 1942 the LRDG received fresh instructions from Eighth Army HQ. With estimates stating that more than half the enemy's maintenance tonnage for Cyrenaica was being transported on the road from Tripoli to Benghazi, the LRDG were ordered to step up their road watches both west of Cyrenaica but also inside its boundaries as well. In addition, where possible they were to conduct offensive operations, the main targets designated as petrol motor transport and armour. The two types of operation didn't complement one another, and waging a guerrilla war deep behind enemy lines would only increase the chances of discovery for those LRDG covertly conducting a road watch.

By now there had been several changes within the LRDG. Captain Jake Easonsmith was second-in-command, Lieutenant Robin Gurdon had replaced Tony Hay as commander of G2 Patrol and Captain Bing Morris had taken over command of A Squadron in light of Don Steele's return to the New Zealand Expeditionary Force.

Gurdon was unique among the LRDG. Not only was he 38, married with three children, but he was an aristocrat, the son of Sir Bertram Francis Gurdon, 2nd Baron Cranworth of Letton and Cranworth. He had no need to volunteer for service, being above military age, but he stepped down from his directorship of Imperial Airways and enlisted in the Coldstream Guards before joining the LRDG in February 1942. 'Practically all situations were natural to him, though he injected a good deal of his own preferences into what he did and whom he did it with,' recalled Alastair Timpson, who commanded G1 Patrol. 'He hated the war but he was determined to take an active and effective part in trying to win it.'[4]

In an attempt to reconcile the LRDG's conflicting tasks, Alastair Timpson and his Guards Patrol began experimenting on how 'to devise a method of destroying enemy vehicles without the enemy finding out how the destruction was done, or at least the areas where the aggressors operated'.[5] If successful, hoped Timpson, the enemy wouldn't suspect enemy guerrillas but believe that their depots had been infiltrated by fifth columnists.

After a week at Siwa practising different methods, it was agreed that the only really effective way to plant a bomb on a moving vehicle was first to make it slow down. But how to achieve this without causing suspicion? Set up a fake maintenance warning on the road, someone suggested. A couple of hurricane lamps on top of two oil drums with a pole stretched between, alongside which would be a large sign in German 'Achtung! Strassenbau' (Road under Repair). The drivers, seeing the sign looming out of the darkness, would slow down, at which point the LRDG would leap up from the side of the road and gently drop over the tailgate of the vehicle a haversack inside which was a 2lb bomb, similar to the ones used by the SAS during their airfield raids. Timpson approved of the plan. 'When the explosion came, half an hour or an hour to two hours later, depending on which type of time-pencil we employed, it would be a shattering surprise and an insoluble riddle for those who investigated the disaster.'[6]

Timpson's G1 Patrol left Siwa on 8 May and headed for the stretch of coastal road between Marble Arch and Sirte. They selected for the first attack an area about 20 miles north-west of Marble Arch and on the night of 14 May Timpson and six of his men concealed themselves by the side of the road with 25 bombs between them. The rest of the patrol remained in the vehicles, only 150 yards away, machine gunners behind their weapons and drivers behind their wheels, all ready for a rapid withdrawal if things didn't go to plan.

There was plenty of traffic on the road, but to Timpson's chagrin the drivers blithely ignored the warning signs and carried on without slowing. Waiting for a lull in the traffic, the men pulled the barrier further out into the road so that drivers would be obliged to decelerate. They did, but only momentarily, giving the LRDG raiders only a brief window in which to emerge from the roadside and drop their lethal haversacks into the back of the trucks. Additionally, the tailgates of the enemy vehicles were higher than the ones that the LRDG had practised on and entailed throwing the haversacks rather than dropping them, adding precious seconds to their task. Eventually, by 0200 hours, Timpson had had enough and announced they were changing tactics. They would cruise the highway in their trucks and attack any lone targets. Timpson had travelled three miles when one of the tyres on his truck burst. The spare wheel was also found to have a puncture. It was not their night. By the time a fresh tyre had been obtained from another vehicle, dawn was nearly upon them, and Timpson led his men off the road and into Wadi Cahela. They breakfasted, slept, and then lunched. Timpson was just putting a spoonful of tinned peaches to his mouth when the sentry came tearing down the *wadi*. Enemy transport, he panted, following our tracks. 'I ordered the gunners to stand to just as the enemy opened fire,' recalled Timpson. George Matthews, a 25-year-old from Leicester who had joined the LRDG from the Coldstream Guards, clambered up on top of his truck to where his machine gun was positioned. He was killed by a bullet to his forehead. Timpson remembered the incoming fire as 'brisk', and said vital seconds were lost in responding to the enemy attack because of the camouflage nets that had to be dragged off their vehicles. Timpson scanned the *wadi* for signs of the enemy and saw several soldiers crawling across the desert floor 150 yards away. 'They were attacking us from the top of the *wadi* and closing in on the hillsides around us,' he said. 'I felled one with a rifle as he approached with a bunch of others on the hillside.'[7]

By the time Timpson had identified the enemy as Italian, the LRDG's guns were in action. Their two Vickers 'kept up a good steady patter' and the double Browning 'poured out streams of lead', while Timpson and a couple of other men grabbed some hand grenades and readied themselves for an assault on their left. After 20 minutes the Italians began to pull back, and Timpson hurriedly ordered the three trucks at the bottom of the *wadi* – furthest away from the enemy – 'to leave by our only remaining line of retreat, up a small subsidiary river bed'. The LRDG extracted themselves from the *wadi* without sustaining further casualties, and the only opposition they encountered was a section of Italians endeavouring to work their way round the rear of the British. A long burst from the Browning scattered them and G Patrol were out of the *wadi* and out of immediate danger. Nonetheless, Timpson appreciated they were still in grave danger. The main road was just a few hundred yards away and it was of course inevitable that the Italians had radioed for reinforcements, probably on the ground and in the air. 'They would expect us to make off in a south-easterly direction,' said Timpson. 'We therefore set off towards the south-west, changing our course frequently in an attempt to lose our tracks, in very open formation and going as fast as we could.'

> *'They would expect us to make off in a south-easterly direction. We therefore set off towards the south-west, changing our course frequently in an attempt to lose our tracks, in very open formation and going as fast as we could.'*
>
> **Alastair Timpson**

But on this occasion their luck was in. At breakneck speed they covered 65 miles without molestation and finally Timpson called a halt 'among some small dunes and scrub in the middle of a large open plain'.[8] They buried Matthews and marked the spot in anticipation of retrieving his body at a later stage.★

Throughout the spring of 1942, General Auchinleck had come under increasing pressure from Winston Churchill to break the stalemate in the Western Desert. The British prime minister believed Malta was in danger of falling into German hands: something that, as he emphasized in a wire he sent to Auchinleck at the end of April, would be 'a disaster of the first magnitude for the British Empire'. Auchinleck retorted that he must have more time to build up his reserves, but when Churchill was told a large convoy would sail for Malta during a moonless period in June he issued Auchinleck with an ultimatum: either launch an offensive against the Axis forces before the middle of June or be relieved of your command. But before

---

★ George Matthews' remains were never found and he is commemorated on panel 54 of the Alamein Memorial.

123

Auchinleck had time to respond to the PM's threats, Rommel launched his own offensive against the Allies' left flank.

Leading his troops in a right hook, Rommel's intention was to sweep past the French garrison in Bir Hakim and attack the British behind the Gazala Line. While this audacious outflanking manoeuvre was performed, the Italian X and XXI Corps launched a diversionary frontal assault on the line. The fighting was intense and for three days the Axis and Allied armour fought while the First Free French Brigade offered heroic resistance at Bir Hakim. Rommel's supply line was stretched perilously thin, so he pulled the Afrika Korps back and formed a defensive position called 'The Cauldron'. The British advanced, confident that victory was within their grasp, with the Afrika Korps having lost nearly 200 of its 320 tanks in four days of fighting. But the 21st Panzer Division countered and the German anti-tank guns took a heavy toll on the British armour. Slowly Rommel began to gain the upper hand. On 10 June Bir Hakim was finally taken by the Germans, and three days later the British armour was decimated in what became known as 'Black Saturday'. The Eighth Army pulled back from the Gazala Line and, in what was subsequently dubbed the 'Gazala Gallop', withdrew all the way to El Alamein. On 21 June Tobruk finally fell, along with 50,000 British and Commonwealth troops.

The disastrous events had bitter consequences for the LRDG. They were forced to abandon Siwa, the oasis that had been one of their bases for more than a year. The rear party left the oasis on 28 June and established a new base at Fayoum, a town 62 miles south-west of Cairo. Nonetheless, reflected Timpson, every cloud has a silver lining. 'Fayoum was healthier than Siwa and pleasantly close to Cairo, in fact one hour's jeep ride away, as was frequently proved.' Captain Richard 'Doc' Lawson was certainly relieved to evacuate Siwa; in the first three weeks of June he had recorded 26 cases of malaria among the LRDG, as well as an increase in the number of men suffering from lumbago and mysositis, muscle inflammation that can cause weakness and pain. This, he believed, was due 'to the clothes soaking in sweat during the day and when the sun goes down and they go on driving, they cool off too rapidly'.[9]

The arrival of Lawson in the LRDG led to a sharp improvement in the treatment of the sick and wounded. As he himself noted in writing a brief history of his role within the unit, 'in the early stages it was difficult to persuade patrol commanders to take on an extra man to an already heavily loaded patrol'.[10] Consequently, patrols embarked on operations miles behind enemy lines without any soldier possessing anything more than a basic knowledge of first aid. That complacent attitude underwent a fundamental shift in the course of the desert war, and Lawson wrote that 'it was satisfying to find in the later stages that whoever else was left behind the orderlies were always sure of one of the coveted places in the patrol'.[11] When he joined the unit one of his first innovations was 'to build a truck which would carry all M.I. [medical inspection] room drugs and equipment above the standard load, i.e. 28 gallons of water and 16 jerrycans of petrol'. Acquiring a 15cwt Indian pattern Chevrolet, Lawson built the vehicle up to 4ft 6in. from the floor with wood and canvas, and an iron superstructure was added so that when on patrol its height was 4ft 9in. and when required as an M.I. room this increased to 6ft. 'The floor area is 6 foot square,' added Lawson, 'and all drugs and equipment were fitted into solo padded boxes, keeping them firm while moving. When stationary these boxes could be unbolted and moved into permanent buildings.'[12]

In the 15 months that Lawson served as the LRDG's medical officer on combat operations in North Africa, from January 1942 to April 1943, he kept a detailed record of his work, noting that 'the sickness rate was not high'. Gunshot wounds were also uncommon, with just 41 cases in 15 months, and almost entirely from aircraft and with the odd one a result of driving over a mine. 'Bacillary dysentery, V.D., jaundice were rare and nearly always followed leave or coastal visits for supplies,' he wrote. 'There was no amoebic dysentery; malaria highest in May and June. Diphtheria was treacherous in that sore throats on patrol developed paresis [slight or partial paralysis] on return to camp or even on the next patrol.'[13]

If malaria was at its most prevalent in the early summer, desert sores were most common in the autumn, the cases decreasing by Christmas, with only two requiring hospital treatment. Other afflictions suffered by the LRDG were mild conjunctivitis, as much due to wind as glare, and Lawson was surprised to discover that 'athlete's foot, heat exhaustion and sun stroke were rare … in spite of the fact that some men wore no caps and others balaclavas, the sun did not appear to affect them under normal working conditions'.[14] As for the soldiers' mental well-being, or 'morale', as Lawson termed it, he made the following personal observations:

> The unit was made up of picked men and officers, the majority of whom had a definite individual responsibility either in regard to their patrol, their truck, their gun or their speciality … For the most part the unit was away from other troops and away, except on leave, from the towns and their softening influence. The men were doing work of which they were proud and which was novel. Their badge and shoulder tabs gave them a distinction. These points contributed to form a loyal and contented unit, proud of itself and with the spirit of an expedition. This was helped by the successful thoroughness with which the senior officers organised the work and rest periods. Arising from this, the sick rate was genuine and there was little neurosis and no malingering.[15]

Siwa at the Time of the Malaria Outbreak

Some photographs of Siwa Oasis in 1942. An outbreak of malaria struck down many men from the LRDG and the unit was pleased to withdraw following the Afrika Korps' offensive in June that year. (Courtesy of the SAS Regimental Archive)

Paddy Allen wearing a cap comforter, the most popular form of headgear among the LRDG. (Courtesy of the SAS Regimental Archive)

The LRDG's new base at Fayoum also had other advantages beside being more salubrious, explained Bill Kennedy Shaw, providing them with a 'back door to the country behind Axis lines'. The back door was through the Qattara Depression, a remarkable natural feature 150 miles long, half as broad, and 450 feet below the Mediterranean at its deepest point. It was a pin-prick on the earth's surface, but a crueller, more desolate spot would be hard to imagine, particularly at the height of the North African summer. 'In the basin the heat is stifling,' recorded Kennedy Shaw. 'No hill gives shade, no tree breaks the monotony of the salt marshes. Drive your truck two yards from the beaten track and it will be sunk to its axles in the quicksands.'[16]

From the start of July LRDG patrols began using the Qattara Depression as the back door into the enemy's territory, undertaking the orders of Auchinleck, who told them 'to do everything possible to upset the enemy's communications behind the Alamein line and to destroy aircraft on his forward landing grounds'.[17] These were the last instructions given to the LRDG by 'The Auk'; he was soon replaced as commander-in-chief at the instigation of Winston Churchill by Lieutenant General Sir Harold Alexander, with Lieutenant General Bernard Montgomery assuming command of the Eighth Army.*

---

* Lieutenant General William Gott was the initially the choice as Eighth Army commander but en route to Cairo to take up his appointment in early August his plane was shot down.

One of the first LRDG patrols to follow Auchinleck's instructions was Robin Gurdon's G2 Patrol. Since joining the unit the previous February, the 38-year-old lieutenant had proved himself an officer of initiative and endurance, forging an excellent working relationship with David Stirling, CO of the SAS, and like Gurdon a member of the British aristocracy. On 3 July Gurdon led his patrol west with the aim of attacking landing grounds west of the El Alamein line; they were accompanied by Stirling and some of his SAS raiders. On 6 July they arrived at Qaret Tartura on the north-western edge of the Qattara Depression, where they were greeted by Alastair Timpson's G1 Patrol and also Y2 Patrol under the command of Tony Hunter.

From the remote base of Qaret Tartura, Stirling planned to attack 'the enemy's landing grounds from Ed Daba to Sidi Barrani [and] the road from Ed Daba to the Halfaya Pass' as the Eighth Army counter-attacked.[18] Timpson was impressed by Stirling, a man he described as having 'extraordinarily little fear, largely because he was so pre-occupied with how to execute an operation he was engaged in'. In addition, the SAS commander 'liked to deal with people who said "yes" or "no", preferably not "no". Those who wanted to take a lot of time in coming to a decision angered him'.[19]

Timpson was delighted to see Gurdon, but the pair had little time for a chat; at midday the three LRDG patrols headed off to the six targets selected by the SAS. Stirling would attack the airfields at Bagush, while Lieutenant Bill Fraser and Lieutenant Augustin Jordan would lead British and French parties to airfields at Fuka, east of Bagush, and a fifth unit would lay waste to Sidi Barrani. Finally, Earl George Jellicoe would jointly command an Anglo-French raid on the coast road from Fuka to Galal.

The results were mixed. At Sidi Barrani it was discovered that the airfields were used only during the day, to bring in supplies on transport planes; Jellicoe captured 'a few stray prisoners' but encountered no vehicles on the road from Fuka to Galal; the attacks on the landing grounds at Fuka resulted in the destruction of ten aircraft, while Stirling and Paddy Mayne scored a first for the SAS by approaching Bagush airfield not on foot, but in a jeep and Stirling's 'Blitz Buggy' (a stripped down German staff car). Stirling had improvised after discovering that the primers on many of their bombs were damp, so, unwilling to leave without attacking the target, he led his men onto the airfield where they machine gunned around 14 aircraft. The success of the attack persuaded Stirling that the SAS could become self-sufficient and no longer required the support of the LRDG. ★ [20]

★ In the view of David Lloyd Owen, later the CO of the LRDG, this was an imprudent decision. 'From the moment [Stirling] began to get his own transport, and became independent of the LRDG, he began to lose his effectiveness because he necessarily had to concern himself with the mechanics of administration,' he

Following the attacks, the raiders moved their base 25 miles west from Qaret Tartura to Bir el Quseir because of a fear they'd been spotted by Italian aircraft. Then on the afternoon of 11 July Gurdon led G Patrol towards the airfields between Fuka and Daba, their four trucks containing a party of SAS men led by a French officer called François Martin. The first 24 hours of their journey were uneventful, and in the late afternoon of 12 July they passed through some hills and out into the plain beyond. Dusk was approaching and Gurdon gave instructions for the trucks to disperse and camouflage for the evening. Suddenly from the west three aircraft were spotted. They were soon identified as Italian Macchi fighters. Unfazed, Gurdon clambered atop one of the trucks and gave a friendly wave of his arms, hoping the pilots would think them on their side. The aircraft made a pass, then rose into the air, circled, and came in again, this time firing as they swooped.

––––––––––––

The next day a solitary LRDG truck arrived at its base at Bir el Quseir. Most of the SAS soldiers had returned to Cairo with David Stirling to acquire jeeps and further supplies that could operate independently of the LRDG. A few remained, however, at the remote desert hideaway, sweating silently in one of the many caves sunk into the rocks. Captain Malcolm Pleydell roused himself when he heard three long blasts on a whistle, the signal of an approaching vehicle. 'We grouped round it as Corporal Preston, the navigator of Robin Gurdon's patrol, lowered himself down wearily from his seat next to the driver,' he wrote subsequently. 'His leg was bandaged; a dirty old bandage through which the blood had soaked and dried in irregular dark patches. He looked as if he was exhausted, and his eyes were reddened with fatigue. When he spoke, it was almost with a tired resignation in the very words.'[21]

The first thing Preston said was that 'Mr Gurdon is badly wounded'. He required medical attention, urgently. So did another member of the patrol, Murray, who'd been shot through the elbow. Pleydell grabbed his medical bag and within minutes he was in a truck with Preston explaining the sequence of events of the previous day.

The aircraft had failed to inflict any damage in the first attack, and as they circled for a second strike, Gurdon ordered his men to seek cover. As his truck began to move off, it was targeted in front by one of the Italians. Gurdon was hit twice by cannon fire, in the stomach and the lungs, and Murray was caught in his elbow. The pair were dragged clear of the burning truck before it exploded, the bulk of their medical supplies going up in flames. There was a small amount of

wrote. 'David Stirling was a magnificent fighting leader, but the tedious business of worrying where the food, the ammunition, the communications, the fuel and water were to come from was something with which he did not want to concern himself. Up until then the LRDG had done all that for him.'

Four members of the Rhodesian LRDG patrol with the original caption reading: Dod, Joe, Skinner and Mac. (Courtesy of the SAS Regimental Archive)

morphia, but it was clear that Gurdon's wounds were grave. Pleydell had known Gurdon for years, and could scarcely comprehend that he was, after all mortal. 'That sort of thing would not happen to him,' he reflected. 'He was too proud, too lordly, to die ungraciously like this in the wilderness.'[20]

But any faint hope Pleydell had that his friend's wounds were not as serious as Corporal Preston described vanished when they reached 'a small saucer-like depression in which were scattered elevations and rocky cliffs'. It was there the rest of G2 had sheltered during the 45-minute attack, and it was here that Gurdon died. Pleydell realized at once from the bearing of the men who came to greet their truck. 'When I inquired, they just nodded and pointed to two small stony hills to the south, saying that that was where they had buried him.'

Gurdon's batman began explaining his officer's end, but he broke down and wept. Pleydell put an arm round the soldier's shoulder and then he, too, cried for his dead friend. The rest of the soldiers moved discreetly away. Eventually a French soldier approached and offered his hip flask. Pleydell took a swig. It was water laced with rum. 'I wiped my eyes on a dirty rag of a handkerchief, and blew my nose vigorously,' said Pleydell.[23] Then he set about tending Murray's shattered elbow.

The death of Gurdon, and the acquisition by Stirling of 20 jeeps mounted with Vickers and Browning machine guns, signalled the end of the LRDG providing the SAS with a 'Taxi Service'.

In the first six months of 1942 the SAS, thanks in large measure to the LRDG, had destroyed 143 enemy aircraft. As David Stirling noted: 'By the end of June L Detachment had raided all the more important German and Italian aerodromes within 300 miles of the forward area at least once or twice. Methods of defence were beginning to improve and although the advantage still lay with L Detachment, the time had come to alter our own methods.'[24]

Indirect pressure may also have been brought to bear on Stirling to become self-sufficient by Guy Prendergast, CO of the LRDG, who was running out of patience with the SAS. According to Alastair Timpson, Prendergast was increasingly exasperated by what he considered Stirling's rather cavalier approach to logistics. 'One cannot blame Prendergast for being a little sour about the episodes when he had to cope with what went wrong in the administration of Stirling's glamorous sorties,' said Timpson.[25] Timpson's view was shared by Lieutenant Colonel John Hackett, a staff

LEAVE AT CAIRO

TOP LEFT
The reward for weeks operating behind enemy lines deep in the Libyan Desert was a few days' leave in Cairo. (Courtesy of the SAS Regimental Archive)

TOP RIGHT
A member of S Patrol on leave in January 1942 at the Rhodesian Club, with Cairo in the background. (Courtesy of the SAS Regimental Archive)

BOTTOM LEFT
Some of S Patrol relax in the Rhodesian Club in Cairo. (Courtesy of the SAS Regimental Archive)

BOTTOM RIGHT
Ginger Low, Dopey Torr and Pluto Endersby in the Rhodesian Club, January 1942. (Courtesy of the SAS Regimental Archive)

officer supervising light raiding forces in North Africa in 1942 (who would later command the 4th Parachute Brigade at Arnhem. After the war he recalled:

> One of the chief problems was to keep these little armies out of each other's way … There was the LRDG practising its intricately careful, cautious, skilful reconnaissance … but the SAS would come out to blow up some aeroplanes and they were very careless about it. Lovely men, but very careless and they would leave a lot of stuff around, and they would stir the thing up no end and out would come the Axis forces to see what had stirred it up, and they would find the LRDG.[26]

Road watching for the LRDG continued throughout July into August, but at the start of that month Timpson's G1 Patrol was granted ten days' leave. Timpson, like many Guards officers, was frightfully well-connected and one evening found himself dining at the British Embassy in Cairo. On his right was Lady Jacqueline Lampson, vivacious wife of the ambassador, Sir Miles, and on her right was a brigadier in military intelligence. At an opportune moment the brigadier – rather impertinently, in Timpson's view – leaned across Lady Lampson and requested his presence at his office the following day. When he arrived at the brigadier's office, Timpson was told that, with the way the war in North Africa was going, military intelligence thought it might be a boost if an LRDG officer broadcast a dashing account of the unit's exploits on the BBC to help boost morale. Timpson didn't like the idea. It was anathema to what the LRDG, and indeed all special forces, hoped to achieve, 'which was trying to be as clandestine as possible'.

Timpson discussed the matter with Prendergast and Jake Easonsmith, who appreciated the reasoning of military intelligence but agreed that security must not in any way be compromised. The upshot was that Timpson 'decided to do something as helpful as I could without saying anything which we presumed they must know or guess, and even [giving] some misleading remarks'.[27]

Timpson was taken in hand by the distinguished war correspondent Richard Dimbleby, who was working for the BBC in North Africa. 'It was of the greatest importance that London should have accurate information as quickly as possible,' he wrote of the summer of 1942. 'The need for frequent despatches of a reasonably authoritative nature tied me to battle headquarters for long periods.'[28] The pair lunched together, and in the afternoon Dimbleby coached Timpson in a broadcasting crash-course. The talk, which had been written by a member of military intelligence, ran for six minutes and Timpson delivered it, so said Dimbleby, in an 'excellent' style. It began:

Far from being all what the adventurous-minded would call fun and having a good party, being completely on one's own with one's patrol, often hundreds of miles behind the enemy's forward positions, not knowing when one may run into his forces, we must be constantly on the lookout. For the reconnaissance work, when it is essential to avoid detection, we have to be particularly vigilant, often creeping past enemy occupied posts at night. But when on a raiding party detection does not matter so much, we can shoot up anything we meet on our way to our objective, and besides, if we see some enemy tracks we can generally pass them quite close without them suspecting that we are anything but their own people.[29]

The rest of the address was in a similar vein, what Timpson described as 'incredibly dull'. He mentioned no names, either of soldiers or places, and his account of the firefight in Wadi Cahela that cost George Matthews his life was told in dry, colourless prose. 'Unfortunately the enemy somehow discovered our hideout at around midday, our sentry did not spot them until they came over the brow of the *wadi* side about 200 yds away,' Timpson told his audience.

They opened fire on us at once. They were Italian troops, about 30 or 40 of them. We were a good deal less. It took us some time to get the automated guns … because they were covered in bushes and nets. And to fire from the tops of the trucks meant being very exposed to the enemy fire. The first man to get to his guns, a Coldstream Guardsman, and one of my best men, got a bullet through his head, but we got most of the guns firing soon. Then followed a quarter of an hour of exchange of fire, with the enemy's fire slackening.[30]

CHAPTER 11

COURAGE IN THE FACE OF CALAMITY

T he Allies and the Afrika Korps had both been busy augmenting their armies in the late summer of 1942. The former had been reinforced by the arrival of 44th and 51st divisions, plus two armoured divisions, while Rommel had finally winkled some infantry and artillery reinforcements from Germany.

General Montgomery arrived in Egypt bursting with 'binge', his word for fighting spirit. He was confident he had the measure of Rommel, the 'Desert Fox', and had already begun drafting plans for a big offensive in the autumn. But in the meantime Montgomery wanted to disrupt the enemy's supplies arriving in the ports of Tobruk and Benghazi, despite the fact they were still woefully inadequate for Rommel (in August 42,000 tons of supplies were shipped across the Mediterranean to Axis forces in North Africa, 32 per cent of what the Afrika Korps required).

What Montgomery had in mind were simultaneous attacks against Tobruk and Benghazi, and an airfield at Barce (now called El Marj), 40 miles north-east of Benghazi. A fourth assault would be launched against the Italian garrison at Jalo, a strategically important base for whoever was in possession. The first the LRDG knew about the attacks was when Prendergast and his officers were summoned to the office of John Hackett at GHQ.

OPPOSITE
Captioned 'Patrols Meeting at Bir Etla', this photo is believed to have been taken in late 1941. (Courtesy of the SAS Regimental Archive)

When they departed there was little enthusiasm for what they had just heard. The raids would be launched on the night of 13 September, except for Jalo, which would occur four days later. The attack on Barce airfield would be the only purely LRDG affair, led by Jake Easonsmith. Stirling would lead a 200-strong party to Benghazi, the SAS supported by the two Rhodesian patrols of the LRDG. A third raid, against Tobruk, was the most daring. It involved naval co-operation and the use of a small unit of Palestine Jews recruited from Middle East Commando into the Special Interrogation Group (SIG), alongside the LRDG, Commandos, gunners and engineers. They would attack from the desert, neutralizing the coastal guns, allowing two Royal Navy destroyers to land soldiers from the Northumberland Fusiliers and Argyll and Sutherland Highlanders in the harbour. Once these objectives had been gained, Y2 Patrol under the command of Captain Tony Hunter would guide the Sudan Defence Force (SDF, designated Z Force) to Jalo, where the garrison would be captured so that the SAS could use it as a base from which to launch a series of hit-and-run raids on the enemy's line of communication once Montgomery launched his major offensive (El Alamein) in October.

The whole plan was magnificent in its ambition, impressive in its audacity and doomed to fail from the outset. Such a large operation, involving thousands of troops, ran counter to every principle that had guided the LRDG and the SAS from their formation. Their success of the previous two years had been built on secrecy, speed and surprise. What the Eighth Army proposed was amassing in Kufra what amounted to a small army – including two tanks for the attack on Benghazi – and sending it out into the desert over hundreds of miles. Not only were the chances of detection from the air considerable, but assembling the force without arousing the suspicion of the scores of German spies operating in British-held territory was highly unlikely.

Lloyd Owen was as 'horrified [by] how unwieldy the whole thing was', as he was at the indiscretion of some of the raid's participants. 'It was very clear to me when I arrived [in Kufra] from Fayoum at the end of August that far too many of those who were to take part in these raids were talking too much,' he wrote. 'I had heard rumours; and I heard these through gossip at parties and in the bars of Cairo. I was very suspicious that security had been blown.'[1]

Of the four raids, only the attack by T1 and G1 patrols on Barce met with success. The SAS were ambushed on the approach to Benghazi and forced to withdraw in the face of heavy enemy fire towards the shelter of a faraway escarpment. Dawn broke soon after and those vehicles still out in the open were picked off by enemy aircraft. 'It was a sharp lesson which confirmed my previous views on the error of attacking strategical targets on a tactical scale,' reflected Stirling.[2]

The attack on Jalo by the Sudan Defence Force (SDF) augmented by 18 men of Y2 Patrol was also a fiasco, and confirmation that the Axis had learned of the attack. The Italians had been reinforced by a company of Afrika Korps, and all hell broke loose as the attackers approached the fort. Most of the SDF fled in the face of the withering fire, and the next morning Lofty Carr, one of the few men to stand and fight, was captured as he tried to escape. The loss of arguably the LRDG's best navigator was a heavy blow. 'The enemy obviously knew of the operation and were waiting for it,' wrote Captain Tony Hunter in his report on the raid.

Unlike the operations against Benghazi and Jalo, the raiders tasked with attacking Tobruk reached their target without incident, having been escorted from Kufra by David Lloyd Owen's Y1 Patrol. The LRDG wouldn't be participating in the assault: they were to wait at a pre-arranged RV for the raiders (known as B Force), who made the final approach to Tobruk in four trucks daubed with the insignia of the Afrika Korps. The German soldiers on board the trucks were actually German Jews belonging to the Special Interrogation Group and the British prisoners they were supposedly guarding were actually British Commandos, their weapons concealed in the vehicles.

The raid on Barce took a heavy toll on the LRDG and here Captain Nick Wilder and troopers Dobson, Burke and Parker of T Patrol await evacuation by air to a Cairo hospital. (Author's Collection)

A wounded LRDG soldier enjoys a cup of tea at Kufra as he waits to be flown to a Cairo hospital following the failed raids in September 1942. (Author's Collection)

John Haselden, MC and Bar, worked closely with the LRDG in his role as the Western Desert Liaison Officer at 8th Army HQ. He was killed leading a gallant charge against the enemy during the Tobruk raid in September 1942. (Courtesy of the SAS Regimental Archive)

Having tricked their way into Tobruk, the Commandos set out to eliminate the gun positions to the east of the port, while Lieutenant Colonel John Haselden, in overall charge of the raid, established his command post in a small house close to the harbour. But soon the operation began to go wrong. The commando charged with signalling in the Royal Navy motor boats got lost. As the amphibious force circled waiting for the light from the shore, they were spotted by the enemy. So too were the destroyers transporting the Northumberland Fusiliers and Argyll and Sutherland Highlanders, both of which were eventually sunk. With the element of surprise gone, the Commandos and SIG were trapped inside Tobruk. The raiders fought valiantly, none more so than Haselden, who was killed leading a charge against the Germans. In all just four men – three Commandos and a 19-year-old member of the SIG – managed to slip out of Tobruk. Unable to reach the LRDG rendezvous, the quartet set off on foot along the coast in an easterly direction. Forty days and 400 miles later they reached Allied lines, having survived on bully beef, goat meat and a few bottles of water.

At the LRDG rendezvous on the eastern perimeter of Tobruk, Jim Patch recalled: 'We installed ourselves near the road in a bit of a depression to keep out of sight. There were searchlights scouring the land for anything they could pick up but we were too low for them to pick us up.'[3] By first light it was clear the raid had failed, so Lloyd Owen and his patrol reluctantly drove away from Tobruk.

———————

Jake Easonsmith led his force out of Fayoum on 1 September. There were 47 men in total, travelling in 12 trucks and five jeeps, including Captain Nick Wilder, a New Zealand sheep farmer before the war, who was in charge of T1 Patrol, and Captain Alastair Simpson, in command of G1 Patrol. Between Fayoum and Barce lay 1,155 miles of desert, which entailed traversing the Great Sand Sea between Ain Dalla and Big Cairn. No one was relishing the prospect of tackling its monstrous dunes. The convoy was accompanied by two 10-ton lorries carrying petrol for the first 250 miles as far as Ain Dalla; there they were refuelled and took on fresh supplies of water. It was after Ain Dalla that the going got tough, their route guarded by row after row of dunes. 'They came out of the north in long, white barriers, towering into razorbacks 300 feet high at times and mostly sharp at their crests, and so stretching away endlessly south,' recalled Timpson.[4] There was on average a mile between the crest of one range and that of the next. The deeper they penetrated into the Sand Sea, the harder it became to surmount the waves of sand. They were bigger, steeper and softer. Timpson described it as 'a world of nothing but sand'. The convoy was approaching the dunes from the east, the steep side, which required vehicles to accelerate towards the crest, slow, and then with wheels aligned, gently

If a vehicle took a sand dune too fast it could well topple over, as was the case with Captain Alastair Timpson's jeep. (Courtesy of the SAS Regimental Archive)

topple over the tip and surf down the gentle undulation of the western side to the trough below the next formation.

Six days out from Fayoum, Timpson crested a dune too quickly. The jeep flipped over, fracturing Timpson's skull and breaking the spine of Thomas Wann alongside him. Easonsmith organized an aerial evacuation while Captain Richard Lawson, the medical officer, stabilized Wann, a big man who on the troopship from Britain to Cairo had won the Scots Guards heavyweight boxing championship.

'Wann and I were carried on the backs of two of our trucks with awnings spread over us until we reached the gravel country,' wrote Timpson. 'After two days a Hudson aircraft arrived from Kufra ... and flew us back to Cairo.' [5] ★

The rest of the patrol continued towards Barce, reaching the foothills of the Jebel Akhdar without further mishap. On 13 September they reached Benia, approximately 15 miles south of Barce, and concealed themselves within some of the trees in the green, wooded countryside. Three guides – including two Senussi – were sent forward to reconnoitre the target and obtain what information they could from their brethren in Barce. At nightfall Easonsmith led his men north. 'At nine o'clock we moved northward through the warm darkness,' recalled Corporal Arthur Biddle, a British signaller attached to Wilder's Kiwi Patrol. 'Everyone detailed for the road had been primed in his particular task, and we drove hard for Barce confident of catching the Italians on the hop.' [6]

They drove up a deep winding *wadi* when suddenly a challenge rang out and a figure stepped in front of the lead truck. Easonsmith switched on the headlights, blinding the man temporarily and allowing his noiseless capture. He was a native soldier, only too willing to tell the LRDG that an Italian officer was nice and warm in the guardhouse 200 yards away. The native soldier called out to the Italian. He appeared a few moments later, striding towards the trucks, whereupon he was shot dead.

By 2300 hours, the convoy had rendezvoused with the guides and reached the road running eastward from Barce to Maraua. Everything was on schedule and going according to plan. They turned westward, cutting the telephone wire as they went, and motored along the road that led into Barce. Up ahead, two light tanks were seen. Easonsmith in the lead jeep held his nerve, banking on the Italian tanks mistaking them for their own vehicles. It was a gamble. Like everyone else, Easonsmith suspected details of the raids had been compromised. The tanks were

---

★ Wann spent the rest of his life in a wheelchair. He died in 1987 and Timpson – who returned to the Scots Guards at the start of 1943 – wrote his obituary. He finished with an anecdote about one of his many visits to Wann in his native Edinburgh. 'I always feel dreadful about my responsibility for what happened to you,' he told Wann. 'You should not worry, sir, I never regret having gone with you to the LRDG.'

An LRDG patrol examine the wreckage of an aircraft south-west of Sirte in September 1941. (Courtesy of the SAS Regimental Archive)

now only a matter of yards away. Still Easonsmith kept his composure. They drew level with the enemy armour, and then Easonsmith gave the order to fire. The gunners in his jeep opened up with their Vickers and Browning, as did those on the other vehicles, subjecting the crews of the two tanks to such a firestorm that they were able to race off into the darkness without receiving any return fire.

When they reached a crossroads on the outskirts of Barce, Easonsmith despatched the various patrols to their targets. The Guards Patrol took the road to the main army barracks and workshops, Wilder and his New Zealanders headed towards the airfield, and Easonsmith and his driver, Gutteridge, went off in his jeep to 'shoot up anything they could find'.

Wilder led his four trucks towards the airfield, but found their route blocked by a dozen Italians behind a barrier. 'We wiped them out without leaving our seats,' Wilder told Eric Bigio, the war correspondent for the *Daily Express*, in an article that appeared nine months later.[7] 'But it was only the beginning of the battle. We had to shoot our way onto the 'drome. Once inside, we found the main track of the landing ground blocked by a huge petrol tanker-trailer. We set that alight with our machine-guns and it made such a big blaze that the whole surroundings lit up: that helped us find our bearings.'

The truck containing Arthur Biddle had been detailed to remain at the airfield's perimeter fence and, as Wilder drove onto the strip, he opened up with the Vickers. 'The target was a number of Italians who had suddenly appeared and made a dash for cover, firing wildly as they went,' he recounted.[8] He continued to blaze away whenever he saw an Italian, amusing himself in the interim by firing the occasional burst at the buildings on the edge of the airfield, which included a pilots' mess, barracks and workshops. Biddle had to be careful not to hit Wilder, whose vehicle was now circling a large red-brick building used as a mess, its gunners raking the walls and windows. Wilder slowed and managed to throw a couple of hand grenades, and by the time they had completed two laps of the building it was well ablaze.

The other trucks had been laying waste to some petrol dumps while Wilder attacked the building, but once reassembled the New Zealand officer led his men through a hedge and onto the airstrip. 'There were 30-odd German and Italian fighters and we set to work to destroy them methodically,' Wilder explained. 'We went round the 'drome in our vehicles in single file, each one of us pouring a hail of machine-gun bullets.'[9] Any aircraft that wasn't sent up in flames from the stream of incendiary bullets was left to the truck bringing up the rear. 'Its occupants had to place a bomb in the fuselage, pull the pin and then fling themselves to the ground and wait for the explosion ten seconds later. Fourteen planes were destroyed in this way. Six others were blazing beautifully and a dozen more were well alight by the time we had gone right around the field. I wish you could have seen the scene.'[10]

Arthur Biddle had a grandstand view of the attack from his position at the perimeter fence. 'One after another the machines caught fire,' he recalled. 'And when a petrol lorry flared up the whole town was illuminated.'[11]

Wilder had been surprised initially at the light resistance encountered. It may have been because the Italians believed there was an airborne assault in progress, because he saw a lot of tracer being fired into the air. Gradually, however, the Italians understood the nature of the raid and subjected the LRDG to machine gun and mortar attack. But it was now an hour since Wilder had driven through the perimeter fence, and 20 aircraft had been destroyed and four more were badly damaged. It was job done, and time to get the hell out of Barce.

On watching Wilder and the Guards Patrol set off to their targets, Jake Easonsmith drove towards the town centre to cause as much diversionary havoc as he could in the space of an hour. He soon spotted some small detached bungalows that he suspected were officers' quarters, and lobbed a grenade onto the flat roof of the one bungalow showing a light. Driving on, his next victims were two light tanks, both hosed in machine gun fire from the twin Vickers. Once in the centre of town, Easonsmith told his driver to pull off into an alley. Scrambling out, Easonsmith went off exploring, eventually finding himself 'in what seemed in the dark to be some sort of market place, a building with arcades and pillars'. Then he literally bumped into a patrol of Italian soldiers. Easonsmith later described to Bill Kennedy

Shaw how 'for a time [I] chased them around the columns, bowling Mills bombs [hand grenades] among their legs'.[12] The Italians eliminated, Easonsmith returned to the jeep and drove off on a new hunt, one which ended in the destruction of a dozen military vehicles in a motor transport park.

As for the Guards Patrol, led by Sergeant Jack Dennis following Timpson's mishap, they first cut the telephone wires to Benghazi and Tobruk and then headed to the large barracks two miles east of the town. En route to their target they passed a military hospital, and the two sentries on duty outside issued a challenge. 'I placed a four second grenade between them and continued driving up the road,' Dennis wrote in his report, adding that 'both sentries were seen to be blown down by the blast.'[13] A similar challenge at the entrance to the barracks met with a similar response, and grenades were also hurled at a group of Italians on the steps that led to the main building. 'By this time the trucks were covering two sides of the barracks and were emptying their guns into the buildings,' wrote Dennis. 'When presumably an ack-ack sentry opened up with small arms fire on to the trucks from a gun post situated on the top of a brick-built tower, he was quickly silenced as all our guns immediately turned on him.'[14]

Dennis led a party on foot to attack the barracks, but they were beaten back by accurate small arms fire from Italians now in slit trenches. They threw some more grenades at the building before returning to the trucks and subjecting the defenders to several thumping bursts of fire from the Vickers and Browning. Suddenly someone shouted a warning. 'Tanks!' On seeing the approach of two light tanks

A dead animal discovered in the Haruj hills. (Courtesy of the SAS Regimental Archive)

Skinning a gazelle.
(Courtesy of the SAS
Regimental Archive)

(probably the two that the LRDG had encountered on the outskirts of Barce), Dennis ordered G Patrol to withdraw.

Wilder's T1 Patrol was also having problems with tanks. Three of them blocked their escape route from the airfield. 'There was nothing to do but rush them,' he reflected. 'So we charged straight into them with guns blazing. I was driving the leading truck and ran down one of the tanks with it. The truck was smashed to pieces, the wheels flung off and the engine knocked back – but the tank was knocked over on its side.'[15] Wilder suffered some minor injuries in the collision, but everyone else in the truck was unhurt. But it was utter pandemonium on the road. A couple of the tank crew had already scrambled to safety, and instead of fleeing they advanced on the LRDG, trading blows with Wilder and his men. 'For three minutes there was a glorious all-in scrap,' said Wilder.

Sergeant H.R.T. Holland was beaten to the ground, and another soldier, Lance Corporal Alan Nutt, a farmer from Motukarara, vanished after leaving his vehicle to aid Wilder and his men (both were captured, but Nutt escaped the following year). Wilder leapt into a jeep driven by Trooper Burke and opened fire with the Vickers, sending a torrent of tracer into one of the two remaining tanks. Burke, 'dazzled' by the tracer, drove the jeep into the kerb and the vehicle overturned, trapping himself, Wilder and Parker. Meanwhile two of the LRDG had climbed onto the stricken tank and dropped hand grenades through the slits, and the valiant pair then immobilized a second tank with a grenade under its tracks.

Wilder and the other men were pulled from under the jeep, loaded onto a truck, and the raiders then careered into the night. But their ordeal was not yet over. The rear truck, driven by Merlyn Craw, was intercepted by three armoured cars that had arrived on the scene. Turning into a narrow side street, Craw's vehicle came under fire and he crashed into a concrete air-raid shelter. Within seconds Italians were upon them, and Craw and his three comrades on the truck were all captured.

'We drove straight down the main road the way we had come,' said Wilder, adding that Italians were lined up on both sides of the route, firing at will as the convoy passed. 'Some of them can't have been more than 30 yards from the track,' explained Wilder. 'It was a sort of ambush and inevitably some of our men were wounded. But all got through, even the truck which burst a tyre halfway through the *wadi*. I will never forget that. The sergeant in charge of the truck calmly got out and we changed the wheel there in the middle of the ambush with bullets flying all around us.'[16] The sergeant who changed the wheel in the middle of an ambush was Jack Dennis, and once done the convoy was able to turn off without further damage to the vehicles. Five miles on, it was deemed safe enough to find cover and let the fitters repair all the damage.

Simpson of S1 Patrol was wounded in the shoulder during an attack on an Italian roadhouse at Tmed Hassan on 8 November 1941. (Courtesy of the SAS Regimental Archive)

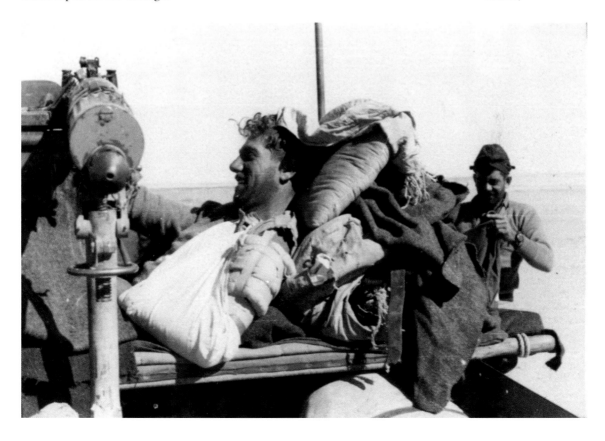

KUFRA, 1942

TOP LEFT
Kufra offered plenty of shade from the sun, but also attracted the flight of German Heinkels who attacked the oasis following the failed raids at Tobruk, Jalo and Benghazi in September 1942. (Courtesy of the SAS Regimental Archive)

TOP RIGHT
Jacko Jackson and Pluto Endersby, one of the unit's signallers, at Kufra in 1942. (Courtesy of the SAS Regimental Archive)

ABOVE
The living quarters of the LRDG at Kufra. (Courtesy of the SAS Regimental Archive)

In all, G Patrol had lost four men and a truck, and T1 Patrol was down two trucks, a jeep and six men. The following day they were located by the Italians, attacked from the ground and from the air, resulting in the loss of all vehicles except one truck and a jeep. More men were also wounded. The situation was grim. Easonsmith detailed the medical officer, Richard Lawson, to load the six most seriously wounded men into the truck and two jeeps, and head south to a RV point with David Lloyd Owen's Y1 Patrol. The rest of the men organized themselves into two parties. Easonsmith led 14 men some 80 miles, the men taking it in turns to ride in the other jeep, which also carried water and rations, before they were met by another LRDG patrol. The second group consisted of nine guardsmen and Frank Jopling, the New Zealander who had been in the unit since day one. Jopling was carrying a nasty flesh wound to his leg, which soon turned gangrenous. Unable to keep up with the rest of the party, Jopling and another ailing soldier urged the others to press on. They reached safety, but Jopling and his comrade, despite covering an extraordinary 150 miles in total, failed to locate any British units and were picked up a week after the raid by the Italians. 'The whole saga of the raid that Jake led on Barce is one that is resplendent in adventure, in courage, in fortitude and leadership,' wrote Lloyd Owen, who was the first friendly face Lawson saw when he reached the RV on 16 September.

Nonetheless, overall the four raids on Tobruk, Benghazi, Jalo and Barce had come at a heavy price: a dozen men wounded, ten captured and the loss of many vehicles. At least there had been no deaths, and Lloyd Owen considered that the unit was 'bloodied but unbowed'. But the Axis retribution was not finished. On 25 September, not long after the LRDG had arrived at Kufra for a well-deserved rest, the peace was shattered by a series of sharp whistles. Aircraft! Suddenly a flight of eight Heinkel bombers swooped over Kufra. 'I was standing looking up into the small area of sky that I could see through the trees when suddenly I saw a great shiny silvery Heinkel come bearing down on us,' wrote Lloyd Owen. 'Its four cannons were spitting flame and lead as it roared towards us.'[17]

The next thing Lloyd Owen remembered was being dragged under cover by two of his men. He was in dreadful pain, shot in the back and left arm, the most serious casualty of the sudden air strike. It was a suitably dispiriting end to what had been for the LRDG an ill-conceived if gallantly executed operation. 'The British suffered considerable losses in killed and prisoners,' noted Rommel, who personally flew to Tobruk to congratulate his men on repelling the raiders. He was particularly pleased to discover the SAS and LRDG were involved in the raids, soldiers who have 'caused considerable havoc and seriously disquieted the Italians'.[18]

CHAPTER 12

THE EYES OF THE ALAMEIN OFFENSIVE

The failure of the SAS raid on Benghazi didn't detract from what they had achieved in the year since their formation. Far from it. Not long after his appointment as commander-in-chief of Middle East Command, General Harold Alexander received a memo from General McCreery, his chief of staff. It was about a small unit operating in the desert that had enjoyed 'conspicuous success in the past'. He continued:

> The personality of the present commander, L Detachment S.A.S. Brigade, is such that he could be given command of the whole force with appropriate rank. In view of this I make the following suggestion. That L Detachment S.A.S. Brigade, 1 S.S. [Special Service] Regiment, Special Boat Section should all be amalgamated under L Detachment S.A.S. Brigade and commanded by Major D Stirling with the rank of lieutenant colonel.[1]

Alexander accepted the recommendation and on 28 September 1942 GHQ, Middle East Forces, issued an order promoting the 26-year-old David Stirling and authorizing him to expand his unit into a regiment.

While Stirling embarked on a recruitment campaign to fill what he envisaged would be a regiment of five squadrons of 29 officers and 572 other ranks, the Long Range Desert Group was also on the hunt for new blood. As well as the men

OPPOSITE
A bust of Mussolini makes an ideal footrest for this LRDG soldier as the Allies begin liberating western Libya from Italian rule. (Courtesy of the SAS Regimental Archive)

captured during the raids on Barce and Jalo, David Lloyd Owen, Nick Wilder and Alastair Timpson were recovering from their wounds in Egyptian hospitals. On a more positive note for Lieutenant Colonel Prendergast, now that the SAS was able to stand on its own two feet, no longer requiring the LRDG to act as its 'aunt', the unit was able to revert to Bagnold's original idea: a small reconnaissance force exploiting its mastery of the desert. To clarify the roles of the LRDG and SAS during the launch of the impending offensive by the Eighth Army, Lieutenant Colonel John Hackett, in charge of supervising light raiding forces in North Africa, called Stirling and Prendergast into his office and 'drew a line down the map like a medieval pope separating out the Italians from the Portuguese in the Atlantic. And I said, "West of this line LRDG only, east of this [line] SAS only", and that kept them more or less out of each other's hair.'[2] The line designated by Hackett was the 20th meridian of longitude east, a line that ran north to south through Jedabia. For the LRDG, that meant a move from their base at Fayoum back to Kufra.

For the next two months the LRDG, comprising 25 officers and 278 other ranks, was the eyes and ears for the Eighth Army as the great battle of El Alamein that had begun on 23 October gathered an inexorable momentum.

Yeomanry Patrol, now under the command of Captain Ken Spicer, left Kufra on the same day as the offensive began, and headed north, 700 miles west of El Alamein. Spicer's orders were to conduct a census of the vehicles using the Benghazi–Tripoli road, just east of Marble Arch. From 1900 hours on 30 October until relieved by the New Zealand R2 Patrol at 1900 hours on 8 November, the Yeomanry Patrol watched the road, recording every vehicle that passed in either direction.

Sunset in the Haruj, a range of hills in Libya reconnoitred by the LRDG in October 1942. (Courtesy of the SAS Regimental Archive)

LRDG ROAD WATCH

Taken in central Libya in 1942, this series photographs an LRDG patrol on its way to a road watch. (Courtesy of the SAS Regimental Archive)

It was during their reconnaissance in October 1942 that S2 Patrol discovered a new route for the advancing Allied army. (Courtesy of the SAS Regimental Archive)

The LRDG didn't just note the weight of traffic on the road, they broke their surveillance down into motor cycles, staff cars, 15cwt trucks, 30cwt trucks, oil tankers. They even described – if they could see it through their binoculars – what the trucks were carrying: barrels, rations, barbed wire, tents and poles. On one occasion, there was an 'Italian girl inside'. In the ten days of the Y1 Patrol road watch, the average number of vehicles in both directions was just under 100. Yet within three days of the New Zealanders relieving their British colleagues, they were reporting to Kufra that enemy transport was streaming westward at a rate of 3,500 vehicles a day.

By the second half of November the LRDG was ordered to a new observation area, 40 miles west of Marble Arch, where they remained for the next eight days. The huge numbers of enemy troops heading west made the task of the LRDG all the more dangerous; the Afrika Korps were retreating, but they were doing so in a disciplined and orderly manner.

The survivors of Nick Wilder's T1 Patrol had spent much of October resting and refitting in Cairo. On the penultimate day of the month they left the Egyptian capital for Kufra, arriving a week later to find the place hadn't changed much. It had been 18 months since Lance Corporal Jack Davis had last been at the oasis. A 28-year-old from Stratford, a town in New Zealand's North Island, Davis was one of the original members of the LRDG, what he referred to as 'the pioneer days of the L.R.P.'.[3] When T1 Patrol – commanded by Captain Ron Tinker in the absence of Wilder – started out on a road watch west of Nofilia, Davis noted that 'our old spot is now a German camp so a new one had to be found'. They found a new camp to the north-east of the oasis of Zella, but on the first day of their road watch, 25 November, Ron Tinker's truck drove over a mine in a *wadi*. Fortunately only one trooper was wounded – a broken ankle – but it meant the patrol had to return to Kufra, as it wasn't possible to evacuate the casualty by air because of the proximity of the enemy.

To Davis's delight the patrol was welcomed on its return by Nick Wilder, fully recovered from the wounds received at Barce. He led T1 Patrol on their next assignment, a road watch on the Hon branch of the Tripoli road. They rendezvoused with Captain Tony Hunter's Y2 Patrol, got caught in a fierce desert storm that turned the *wadis* into rivers of raging water, and blazed a trail west in country that had hitherto been out of the LRDG's reach. 'Passed through unexplored country,' wrote Davis in his journal, 'thus finding many prominent features – *wadis* and basins – not marked on our maps.'[4]

The two patrols continued west, mining roads as they went. Wilder, never one to pass up the opportunity to attack the enemy, waylaid an Italian truck, killing one soldier and capturing two others. On 23 December Y2 Patrol was recalled to Kufra, and they took the pair of Italians with them, leaving T1 Patrol to celebrate Christmas alone. It was, recorded Davis, 'an unforgettable one – a double issue of rum gave us the stimulus to sing all the popular melodies and parodies, and we had a merry time'.[5]

Come Christmas Day, the patrol was ready to give the enemy their own unforgettable experience, as Davis described in his journal:

Although a road watch could be excruciatingly tedious, the information provided by the LRDG was of immense value, particularly in the weeks after the El Alamein offensive. (Courtesy of the SAS Regimental Archive)

Winter in the desert brought bitter temperatures and required the LRDG, like Bill Lothian, seen here, to wear their greatcoats. (Courtesy of the SAS Regimental Archive)

[At] 0950 hours, two trucks and trailers approached. They were ammunition trucks – a good haul. Once again a few surprise shots. They do not stop, so they 'get it!!'. Three were killed and three were wounded. They were on their way to Tripoli for supplies of ammo. We made a good job of destroying the trucks, and they were blazing merrily when we left. We moved off the road for a few miles and attended to the enemy wounded.[6]

T1 Patrol arrived at Zella, now being used as an LRDG base, on 28 December, and a sackful of mail from New Zealand was given to them, a welcome late Christmas present. Zella was an oasis in the Fezzan region of south-west Libya, described in the journal of Richard Lawson, the medical officer, as lying 'in very broken country and oases lie between the tongues of limestone'.[7]

With T Patrol safely returned, the LRDG threw a belated Christmas party at Zella on 1 January. Menus were published with the LRDG scorpion insignia at the top and at the foot the message: 'Enjoy yourself Boys'. Sandwiched between was the menu:

Potage pomme d'amour
Croquettes d'homade à Keeler
Venison *au E.T.A roti*
Plum pudding
Coffee, cigars, port and cherry brandy

The New Year brought a new role for the unit, one that adapted to the fluidity of the Allies' advance. Tony Brown and his patrol had guided the New Zealand Division and the 4th Armoured Brigade round Rommel's defensive line at El Agheila in late December, the Kiwis outwitting the Desert Fox so that he was compelled to withdraw to the Mareth Line, approximately 170 miles west of Tripoli. Bernard Montgomery informed Lieutenant Colonel Prendergast that the Eighth Army would launch a 'holding frontal attack on the Mareth position, while his main effort would be swung round to the south to outflank it'. The task of reconnoitring the country over which this 'left hook' into Tunisia would be

An LRDG patrol prepares to begin a road watch near El Agheila in October 1942. (Courtesy of the SAS Regimental Archive)

delivered fell to Wilder's T1 Patrol. They left Zella on 3 January in a terrific sandstorm and two days later rendezvoused with Tony Hunter's Y2 Patrol. 'We travelled together, refuelled and spent the rest of the day cleaning our guns in preparation for crossing the Hon-Dun'Gem Road,' wrote Davis.

On 8 January the LRDG unexpectedly encountered a unit of SAS. They were surprised to meet the SAS so far west, but this was a party commanded by David Stirling, who, with his customary audacity, had secured permission from MEHQ for one final scheme before the end of the war in North Africa. He was intent on attacking the Germans as they retreated into Tunisia while also reconnoitring the Mareth Line to see if the Afrika Korps were preparing for a final stand. That was the role of the LRDG, but Stirling's overriding objective was to seize the glory of being the first unit from the Eighth Army to link up with the First Army, which was advancing east from Algiers.★

9 January was Davis's 29th birthday and his present came in the form of two German Heinkel bombers, which passed overhead without noticing them. A similar thing happened the next day and Davis attributed it to either poor eyesight on the part of the pilots, or more likely the fact that they assumed the vehicles below were theirs, as no Allied units were believed to be so far west.

★ Stirling paid a high price for his hubris when, a couple of weeks later, his patrol was captured by the Germans, just beyond the Gabes Gap, a geographical bottleneck between the Tunisian salt-flats and the Mediterranean Sea. Stirling spent the remainder of the war a prisoner and Paddy Mayne assumed command of the SAS.

Getting stuck on a dune was an occupational hazard for the LRDG. (Courtesy of the SAS Regimental Archive)

The LRDG exchange pleasantries at Bezema with some natives, the majority of whom favoured the Allies because of Italian barbarity during colonization. (Courtesy of the SAS Regimental Archive)

The next few days were tough going. The country was very rough and the vehicles were taking a hammering. A couple of springs had to be repaired and the petrol consumption was greater than Wilder had envisaged. On 15 January the terrain was so bad the patrol had to continue the reconnaissance on foot in three parties. 'All parties found the mountains impassable,' wrote Davis on 16 January. 'They discovered signs of recent gun pits, and small blockhouses were seen all along the escarpment. At that time they were not manned.'[8] They returned to their vehicles the following day and on 19 January finally encountered a 'clear gap through the escarpment, passable for MT [Motor Transport]', which was 25 miles

south-west of Foum Tatahouine. Wilder radioed HQ with the news and, with their mission accomplished, they turned south for the long journey back to base. On their return they saw overhead dozens of American Flying Fortresses on their way to bomb the retreating Germans. Wilder's T1 Patrol encountered T2 Patrol on 24 January, the latter heading in the opposite direction on the route pioneered by their comrades. Also travelling north was Indian (3) Patrol of the LRDG, one of four Indian patrols that had been raised a few weeks earlier with British officers commanding Indian soldiers.

Gordon Rezin was killed in February 1943 in Tunisia when his LRDG patrol was mistaken for Germans by a unit of Free French. (Courtesy of the SAS Regimental Archive)

The gap discovered by T1 Patrol was named after its officer, Wilder, and proved of great value when Montgomery launched his attack on the Mareth Line. By this time Nick Wilder had been recalled to the New Zealand Divisional Cavalry, much to the regret of Jack Davis. 'Nick is a grand chap and a great soldier,' he wrote on 29 January on learning of Wilder's recall. For the next few weeks the men of T1 Patrol amused themselves at their new base at Hon. There were lectures, rugby matches and reunions with former comrades from the New Zealand Expeditionary Force who passed through en route to Tunisia.

On 20 March the Eighth Army launched a frontal attack on the Mareth Line. It was checked initially, but not for long. The New Zealand Division, guided by Ron Tinker's T2 Patrol on the route pioneered by Nick Wilder, delivered a 'left hook' to the Afrika Korps, capturing El Hamma, 18 miles west of Gabes, on 28 March. The Mareth Line had been breached and defeat was now inevitable for Rommel. Their services no longer required, the Long Range Desert Group began to withdraw east, heading all the way back across Libya to Alexandria. Bernard Montgomery took a moment to convey his thanks to the unit's commander in a letter dated 2 April:

Scott and Moyes in front of a lake in the Haruj region. (Courtesy of the SAS Regimental Archive)

My dear Prendergast

... I would like you to know how much I appreciate the excellent work done by your patrols and by the SAS in reconnoitring the country up to the Gabes Gap. Without your careful and reliable reports the launching of the 'left hook' by the NZ Division would have been a leap in the dark; with the information they produced, the operation could be planned with some certainty and as you know, went off without a hitch.

Please give my thanks to all concerned and best wishes from Eighth Army for the new tasks you are undertaking.

B. L. Montgomery[9]

Salt lakes, like this one in Kufra, were a favourite bathing spot because one could float in the water and read a book. (Courtesy of the SAS Regimental Archive)

Once in Alexandria, the men of the LRDG went into camp on the beach, swimming, sunbathing, and sleeping. 'Letters add to our pleasure at this summer resort,' wrote Jack Davis. To use the words of the colonel [Prendergast], 'people in peacetime pay lots of money to experience what we are enjoying'.[10]

CHAPTER 13

ADVENTURES IN THE AEGEAN

The weeks in Alexandria were blissful for the Long Range Desert Group. 'Unfamiliar laziness', as Ron Hill of Y Patrol called it. 'Then came the order,' he recalled, 'that as we were now back under Army Command all beards were to be shaved off by 0800 hours or some such.' Most of the LRDG were given leave of varying duration, and when they were all back in Alexandria they learned what the future held. It had been a subject of intense speculation for the men in the preceding weeks, and while many theories were expounded, what they all could say with any certainty was that 'no longer would we be able to rely on the wide open spaces of the desert wildernesses in which to hide'.[1]

Eventually Hill and his comrades were informed by Lieutenant Colonel Prendergast that they were off to the British Army Ski School in the Lebanon. The first squadron to arrive at the school was B, on 20 May, followed on 21 June by A Squadron. The school had been the Cedars hotel in peacetime, boasting among its amenities a ski resort at an altitude of 6,000 feet a few miles above the village of Becharré and named after the small grove of the original cedars of Lebanon nearby. Originally the idea of the Australian Imperial Forces, the ski school opened for business in December 1941 and such was its success it soon expanded to house the Mountaineering Wing of the Middle East Mountain Warfare School based close to Tripoli.

OPPOSITE
Ron Low fills up
the petrol tank of
his vehicle prior to
another day's patrolling.
(Courtesy of the SAS
Regimental Archive)

The LRDG medical officer, Captain Richard 'Doc' Lawson, awarded a Military Cross for his devotion to duty on the Barce raid, wrote in his journal that the hotel and grounds 'were dirty after a winter of snow and because of large oil stoves at the end of the building from which the wind came'. Lawson had explicit instructions from Prendergast, which were to 'find out the best way to change completely motorised patrols into small groups of mountaineers carrying everything they needed from start to the finish of their objective'.[2]

There was only one practical way to achieve such an aim: weed out the weak. 'Training began with three hour walks without packs and later with empty packs working up to 40lbs and 2 day trips by the end of the month,' recalled Lawson. Some men dropped out, most didn't, and they were soon embarking on 100 mile marches with 80lb packs. 'The training was tough and tested us to our limits,' recalled Ron Hill.[3]

The men experimented with clothes, equipment and weapons, and took stock of the very latest in communications technology, the Eureka radio directional hand set, which as Hill discovered 'enabled us to call in aircraft without the need to lay out markers'. Lawson monitored the men's physical condition and concluded: 'The ration was not wholly satisfactory and more sugar was added. The dehydrated meat was too fat for the hot weather.' There was also one case of heat stroke as the intensity of the training increased, and Lawson noted that 'difficulty was experienced in replacing the water lost by sweating'.[4]

Lieutenant Colonel Prendergast required soldiers who 'had ideas and sympathies in common', who were friends as well as comrades, as so much of their time would be shared in close proximity to one another. With several old hands returned to their former unit during the mountain training, the LRDG once more had to recruit. Prendergast drafted a list of requirements in any potential member of his unit:

Tact, initiative, and a keen understanding of his fellow men.

Intelligence above the average, and a sound military background.

Courage and endurance.

Perfect physical condition.

A readiness to undertake any task that might be required of him.

Some technical or language qualification.

Youthfulness. Few men over the age of thirty [will be] accepted.

That was the other ranks. For officers, Prendergast expected all of the above as well as a 'knowledge of men'. 'For days on end he [the potential officer] would have to live with his men, endure their hardships, share their disappointments, and rejoice in their success,' stated Prendergast. 'Not only did he need to know more about their job than they knew themselves, but he also had to be more expert than they in handling weapons and equipment.'[5] The final characteristic sought by Prendergast applied to both officers and men, and was arguably the most important trait in any potential LRDG recruit: 'A man who had the reputation of being "tough" was by no means a first choice,' said Prendergast. 'Too often the "tough" man is the man who lacks intelligence, initiative and discipline; often enough he lacks courage as well.'[6]

'A man who had the reputation of being "tough" was by no means a first choice. Too often the "tough" man is the man who lacks intelligence, initiative and discipline; often enough he lacks courage as well.'

Guy Prendergast

The final part of the training was also for most of the LRDG the worst – parachute training. They'd heard tales in the desert from the SAS about the terrors of jumping out of an aircraft, an activity that had cost two SAS men their lives in the early days of training when their parachutes failed to open. In August 1943 rumours began to circulate within the LRDG that they were to be sent to the British Army parachute school at Ramat David in Palestine. Then one morning their worst fears were confirmed. 'The CO got us altogether and explained the reasons,' related Hill. 'It was a way to get behind the enemy lines in the new conditions of fighting on mainland Europe.'[7] Nonetheless, continued Prendergast, he appreciated that when the men had volunteered for the LRDG they had not been expected to jump out of aeroplanes. If any man didn't wish to go to the parachute school, he would 'not be discriminated against or thought any the worse of'. Hill recalled that only six men declined the opportunity to learn to parachute. Hill's great pal, Jim Patch, was one of the many volunteers, although he had a nervous moment at the medical examination when they were tested for colour blindness. 'We were all lined up in front of [Doc] Lawson,' remembered Patch. 'The only means he had to test us was the coloured cover of a magazine. He would point to different colours and we had to say which they were. I was colour blind as could be.'[8] Lawson passed Patch, although he offered a word of advice as he did so: namely that when he had to leap out of the aircraft he should 'just follow the man out in front' rather than waiting for the green light to flash. They headed to Ramat David in small groups, but Hill and Patch never got the chance to earn their 'wings'. Instead, as they began to learn the rudimentaries of parachuting a message arrived from Lieutenant Colonel Prendergast ordering all LRDG personnel to Haifa.

TOP
Men of S1 and S2 patrols undergo parachute training at the British Army school at Ramat David, Palestine, in December 1943. (Courtesy of the SAS Regimental Archive)

ABOVE
Dick Edwards awaits his turn to jump. (Courtesy of the SAS Regimental Archive)

RIGHT
The training began with a gentle introduction using the scaffold. (Courtesy of the SAS Regimental Archive)

Initial rumours suggested they were bound for Rhodes, an island that since the previous May had been targeted for invasion. By the start of September, however, the British chiefs of staff recognized that they didn't possess the resources to overpower the 7,000-strong German division on Rhodes. After the successful conquest of Sicily, the Allies were about to invade the Italian mainland, so rather than attack Rhodes it was decided to invade the smaller islands of the Aegean.

In the context of the war as a whole, the Aegean appeared at first glance an insignificant backwater, but it contained three groups of islands that were of strategic importance: to the north the Sporades, the Cyclades in the west and in the east the Dodecanese. It was the latter that were considered key to the Aegean with Rhodes, Kos [also spelled 'Cos'] and Leros among the most important islands. Rhodes was too well defended to attack, but Kos and Leros weren't.

The lead elements of the LRDG began departing the Middle East in the second week of September, sailing from Haifa aboard a Greek sloop. David Lloyd Owen held deep reservations at the haste at which they were being despatched. 'The lack of reliable information was disgraceful,' he recalled, though he and the men welcomed the prospect of putting into practice all they had learned in the Lebanon.

In the evening of 13 September, Lloyd Owen and some 100 men arrived at the port of Castelrosso, the principal settlement in Castelorizzo, the most easterly of the

Few men enjoyed parachute training but the soldiers of R2 put on a brave face for the camera. (Courtesy of the SAS Regimental Archive)

LEFT
These photos of
new LRDG recruits
learning to parachute
in 1943 were taken by
Wally Smart. (Courtesy
of Jack Valenti)

RIGHT
Broken bones were a
common occurrence
during parachute
training as the men
jumped from moving
trolleys. (Courtesy of
Jack Valenti)

Dodecanese islands, lying just off the Vathi Peninsula on the Turkish mainland. 'We were received rapturously by the inhabitants and we spent a night there,' recalled Jim Patch.[9] Their stay was brief, however, and the following day Lloyd Owen was instructed by Cairo to take his men north to Leros, approximately 170 miles north-west.

On the same day, S Squadron of the Special Boat Squadron [SBS] arrived on Kos with another section, led by their commanding officer, Major George Jellicoe, travelling on to Leros. By the end of September, the British controlled all of the Dodecanese islands except for Rhodes, a state of affairs that was discussed by Adolf Hitler and his senior officers. There was a body of opinion among some, notably Grand Admiral Donitz, that the best course of action was to leave the Aegean to the British and instead concentrate their forces in defending the Balkan Peninsula. Hitler disagreed. 'Abandonment of the islands would create the most unfavourable impression [among our Allies],' declared the German leader. 'To avoid such a blow to our prestige we may even have to accept the loss of our troops and material. The supply of the islands must be assured by the Air Force.'[10]

By the start of October, the LRDG were doing what they did best; travelling far and wide on reconnaissance patrols, only this time on water not sand. They patrolled the shipping lanes around islands such as Pserimos, Calinos, Kithnos and Syros. One of the most successful recces was the New Zealand T1 Patrol skippered by Captain Charles Saxton. On the afternoon of 6 October they reported 'a convoy of 6 LC [Landing Craft], one tanker and one minesweeper', intelligence that resulted the next morning in the destruction of the convoy by the RAF in the waters close to the island of Stampalia, west of Rhodes.

In the same week, Prime Minister Churchill was doing his utmost to persuade President Franklin Roosevelt to collaborate with Britain in the Aegean. 'I have never wished to send an army into the Balkans,' emphasized Churchill in a cable sent on 7 October to the White House. 'But only by agents, supplies and commandos to stimulate the intense guerrilla movement prevailing there.'[11]

But Roosevelt was deaf to Churchill's entreaties, Congress believing the prime minister was intent on embroiling himself in a Balkan campaign every bit as ill-conceived as his disastrous Gallipoli adventure in 1915 when the attempted Allied invasion of western Turkey came to grief in the Dardanelles Straits. The Americans told Churchill their focus in the coming months was on maintaining pressure on Italy ahead of the planned invasion of France in 1944. 'It is my opinion that no division of forces or equipment should prejudice "Overlord" [the codename for the invasion of France] as planned,' Roosevelt wired Churchill in response to the PM's cable. 'The American Chiefs of Staff agree.' The British were on their own in the Dodecanese.[12]

In mid-October it was reported that a 3,000-strong force of Germans had come ashore on the island of Kalymnos, which lay to the north of Kos and the south of Leros. A small reconnaissance party from a Rhodesian patrol of the LRDG was ordered to land on Kalymnos and investigate. Setting out from Leros, Lieutenant Stan Eastwood and his four men were dropped close to Linaria Bay with enough rations for five days; the Royal Navy commander in charge of the motor launch arranged to return in 48 hours. But when the launch returned on the night of 20/21 October, there was no one waiting for them; they came back the following

Wally Smart, sitting on the wheel of the WACO, and his pal William Dougan, joined the LRDG from the Royal Electrical and Mechanical Engineers and served in the Aegean and Adriatic. (Courtesy of Jack Valenti)

night, and this time Corporal Tant went ashore in an attempt to make contact with Eastwood. He never reappeared. The launch made one final attempt to contact the LRDG men on the next evening, 22/23 October, but when the commander neared the shore in his dinghy, signalling with his torch as he heaved to, 'low whistles on shore were obviously made by the enemy'. The Royal Navy commander rowed back to the motor launch, and on arriving at Leros reported that in his estimation Eastwood and his party had been captured.

––––––––––––

When Eastwood and his four men – corporals Harry Whitehead and Alf Curle, private Neddy Edwards and private Reed – landed on Kalymnos, they did so unobserved. They made their base in a cave on top of a mountain, and the next morning began their reconnaissance, while also establishing contact with a civilian informer. Assured that the Germans didn't patrol at night, Eastwood led three of his men (Edwards remained in the cave) along a mule track towards the village of Linaria on the evening of 19 October. 'Suddenly we saw a patrol with mules less than twenty yards in front of us,' recalled Corporal Curle. '[We] took cover behind large rocks next to the track, hoping we had not been seen.'[13]

It appeared they hadn't. Curle said that the enemy passed by and 'gave absolutely no sign of any knowledge of our whereabouts'. Just as the LRDG thought they had got away with it, the Germans went into action, wheeling round with their weapons pointed at the men crouched behind the rocks. One of the Germans pulled a grenade from his belt. Eastwood emerged, his hands in the air. At the same moment, Whitehead broke cover and tore down the hill towards the sea. Curle and Reed stood up with the intention of blocking the Germans' view. A couple of shots were fired after Whitehead, but the Germans didn't give chase. Instead they disarmed the three LRDG men and escorted them down the mule track, their hands on their heads and under strict instructions to remain silent. They spent the rest of the night at the German HQ in Calino, and the next day their interrogation commenced. It was civilized and the trio declined the Germans' invitation to speak. 'Enemy friendly but watchful,' reported Curle. 'Consider the British are gentlemen in fighting and [we] were treated accordingly. Received some food as Germans [have] more than sufficient quantities.'[14]

In the early morning of 23 October, Eastwood, Curle and Reed were joined in captivity by Edwards and Tant. The latter had been captured by a German patrol as he searched for his comrades. So, too, was Edwards, an indication that the Germans on Kalymnos were experienced troops and not soldiers deemed unfit for combat on the Eastern Front. The five LRDG soldiers were transferred to Kos, now in the hands of the Germans, where they were lined up on the quayside. General Friedrich-

Wilhelm Müller appeared, the officer in charge of German forces in the Dodecanese. Known as the 'Butcher of Crete', Müller had a reputation for brutality in responding to any sign of resistance among the local population. He moved down the line of the prisoners, recalled Curle, 'and after looking at us for about five minutes walked inside. He did not say anything.'[15]

If Müller had intended to intimidate his prisoners into meek obedience, he failed. Within a few days, all had escaped. It was on 27 October that Corporal Curle detected a possible route to freedom. Imprisoned with other Allied soldiers in the village of Antimachia, 15 miles from Kos harbour, they were taken each day to an ablutions block. 'On returning [I] noticed a possible chance of escape,' remembered Curle. They were marched in single file with one guard ahead and one behind. 'The rear guard was blind for a few seconds and a good hideout was only a few yards away.'[16]

Curle discussed the matter with Eastwood and the others, and they all agreed it was worth a go. Eastwood, Edwards and Reed were the first to try, slipping away unobserved from the disinterested guards. Tant was next to go, and Curle made his bid on the morning of 29 October. It was surprisingly easy to get away unseen, and having spent the day in hiding, Curle emerged at dusk and headed into the mountains. The few civilians he met were only too happy to provide directions and share what little food they had. On 30 October he was reunited with Tant and the pair were soon put in contact with a Greek intelligence officer living rough in the mountains. He organized their evacuation off Kalymnos and Curle and Tant were soon back in Leros, as were Eastwood, Edwards and Reid, also on account of the intelligence officer.

There they were reunited with Corporal Whitehead, who had quite a tale to tell. Having fled downhill, he avoided the bullets from the German patrol and dived into the sea in the belief they were in hot pursuit. He swam quite a distance away from the shore, 'hoping to mislead the enemy', and then changed direction, swimming parallel to the coast, eventually landing about 500 yards from his taking-off point. He made his way carefully back up the hillside, but Edwards wasn't in the cave. The mountains were now thick with Germans, so Whitehead sought sanctuary from an old shepherd, 'who fed me and gave me clothes and a place to sleep'. At great risk to himself, the shepherd sheltered Whitehead for four days before the soldier made contact with members of the local resistance. He was eventually picked up on the night of 5 November and returned to Leros, furnishing the Allies with a detailed report on the strength, location and morale of the Germans. Whitehead ended his report with a word about the locals: 'During my stay on the island everyone did all they could to help me, despite the fact that the day following our route the Germans published a proclamation stating anyone harbouring British troops or agents would pay the ultimate penalty of death.'[17]

CHAPTER 14

THE BATTLE FOR LEROS

With Kalymnos and Kos in the hands of the Germans and the Americans adamant that they weren't going to become involved in the Aegean, Britain by the start of November had abandoned any pretence that its strategy in the region was anything but defensive; instead of trying to seize the islands from the Germans, the focus switched to reinforcing the existing garrison on Leros.

The SBS arrived on the island in the first week of October, disembarking at the deep-water port of Lakki (known to the Italians as Porto Lago) on the south-west coast of the island. Their commanding officer, David Sutherland, wrote: 'Leros is eight miles long and four wide with two narrow mile-long beaches in the middle … There are three barren, hilly features, each about 1,000 feet high. In the south-west corner is the all-weather harbour Porto Lago Bay.'[1] The joke among the SBS, as told to them by the LRDG, was that Leros resembled in shape 'a large cowpat trodden on by two feet!' But this particular 'cowpat' wasn't soft and flat; its surface was rocky and mountainous, wholly unsuitable for an airfield. What Leros did have, however, was a chain of formidable coastal batteries overlooking the island's six bays. By November Leros had been divided into three defensive zones – north, south and central – with the 4th Royal East Kent (The Buffs), 2nd Royal Irish Fusiliers and 1st King's Own Royal Regiment responsible for the sectors.

This force was strengthened by sappers, Ordnance Corps and the SBS and LRDG, as well as the existing Italian garrison. In overall command of the island's defence was Brigadier Robert Tilney, whose fortress HQ 'consisted of a single twisting tunnel blasted right through the peak of Meraviglia', in the centre of Leros. Alongside him in his command post was Guy Prendergast, recently appointed second-in-command of 'Raiding Forces', the co-ordinating headquarters of all the disparate special forces units operating in the Aegean. Now, the LRDG, the SBS, the Levant Schooner Flotilla and the Greek Sacred Squadron – two other special forces units, the former comprising Royal Navy personnel who ferried the raiders to targets in Greek fishing boats, and the latter similar in modus operandi to the SBS – were under the command of Colonel Douglas Turnbull, with Prendergast his second-in-command. It was not an appointment welcomed by the LRDG (although the appointment of Jake Easonsmith as the new CO met with approval nonetheless), who considered that Prendergast's experience and expertise would be better used commanding the LRDG, a position from where he could liaise closely with Raiding Forces HQ.

Tilney and his HQ staff were well protected from the daily air raids on the island, but not so the men under his command. Since October they had been dive bombed by Stukas with a regularity that was fraying the nerves of everyone cowering in the fox-holes and slit trenches. The men dug in around the gun batteries came in for particular attention from the Stukas. One such 6-inch battery was reinforced by Captain John Olivey and his S1 Patrol of southern Africans. They were positioned on Point 320, which in Olivey's words was 'an almost sheer rock mound rising 1,000ft above the sea [also known as Mt Clidi]. It commanded a complete view to the north with the exception of the N.W. corner.'[2] To the north, approximately two miles away, were two large bays and dotted beyond them was

The aftermath of the bitter battle for Leros. Despite the wreckage of these vessels, the LRDG managed to evacuate the majority of its men in the days after the island fell. (Getty)

a smattering of small islands. To the east, the coast swung round past a sandy beach on the southern end and disappeared from sight behind Mt Vedetta. One of the men with Olivey was signalman John Kevan, who one morning was making his way back to the battery from answering a call of nature further down the mountain. As the Stukas swooped with a terrifying shriek, Kevan 'flattened myself against the almost perpendicular rock about twenty feet below the guns, taking what cover I could under a slight overhang of rock'.[3] The whole mountain seemed to shake and roar as the bombs fell. Kevan covered his head with his hands as lumps of rock bounced off his body and his ears rang with the thunderous noise. When he emerged from the rock he discovered the battery had taken a direct

Lt John Olivey, seen here plotting the course for the day's travel, was a brilliant special forces soldier who served in the LRDG right up until the last days of the war. (Courtesy of the SAS Regimental Archive)

hit. There were no casualties, but the gun had had its barrel blown off. Olivey gave a rueful shake of his head as he and Kevan stood among the devastation. 'While he and I were discussing the damage, he said "have faith", and produced a bottle of whisky from behind his back,' recalled Kevan. 'How I blessed him!'[4]

Secure in his underground HQ, Brigadier Tilney continued to strike a defiant note despite the increasing intensity of the aerial attacks on Leros. 'No enemy shall set foot in this island unless to be a prisoner of war,'[5] he assured the men under his command. Tilney was confident the Germans would not be able to establish a beachhead, though some of his officers believed that this confidence was misplaced because he had deployed his forces along too wide a front.

As for the LRDG and SBS, Tilney held them in reserve, in effect a rapid reaction force, in the unlikely event that the Germans did land in sufficient force. On the gun battery at Point 320 on Mt Clidi, S1 Patrol had started to become accustomed to the air raids. Signalman Gordon Broderick, a 22-year-old from Hartley (now Chegutu) in Rhodesia, said 'they learned to judge where the bombs were headed' and a certain nonchalance took hold. Nonetheless, they remained alert for an invasion, and one night Broderick, on guard duty, observed some 'silver shapes' in the water below. He roused John Olivey, who rushed to investigate, only to point out that the 'silver shapes' were in fact cloud shadows. 'I had to counter the derision next day by stating that at least it proved that those on Clidi were awake at that early hour,' reflected the young Rhodesian.[6]

In the early hours of 12 November, Broderick was once more manning the observation post. There were no silver shapes visible in the darkness, but when the first grey strands of dawn started to lighten the night sky, Broderick gasped in amazement. 'A fleet of barges and other craft could be seen heading into a dead field of view beyond Mount Vedetta,'[7] he recalled. He gave Olivey an 'urgent call', and the officer appeared. This time there was no scorn.

As Olivey observed the first wave of the German invasion fleet – 800 troops in total – approach the north-east of Leros, he knew exactly where they were headed. 'The enemy's objectives were obvious, the cove below us,' he wrote, 'and the dead ground behind the hill to our N.E.'[8]

As the Italian battery crew manned their guns, Olivey ordered his men to open fire on the invasion fleet. Broderick and Harold Todman, best friends who had volunteered at the same time for the LRDG, clambered into a machine gun pit below the gun that had been destroyed in the previous Stuka attack. They were joined by the Italian artillery officer, who directed his crews' fire via a short-wave radio. 'Seeing some Germans setting up an 88mm mortar, I asked the artillery officer to take it out,' recalled Broderick. 'But he replied that he should not protect himself and proceeded to fire at a barge slipping through towards Partheni Bay.'[9]

The Italian crew disabled the barge but Broderick's Bren gun proved ineffective against the mortars. More and more Germans were now coming ashore, and the mortar crews were starting to range in on the defenders above them on Mount Clidi. One battery received a direct hit, disabling the gun and sending the Italian artillerymen running. Then a mortar bomb landed on the lip of the gun pit containing Broderick and Todman. Shrapnel lacerated Broderick's shoulder but, after having the

An Italian anti-aircraft battery on Leros, similar to the one defended by John Olivey and his LRDG patrol when the Germans invaded the island in November. (Getty)

wounds dressed by a medic, he and Todman moved the Bren gun to a different position and continued to fire at the Germans advancing slowly up the mountainside.

During a break in the firing, Broderick heard a noise. A hum. It grew louder and then he spotted a 'thin black line close to sea level, which approached rapidly from the south-west'. Olivey had also seen the strange apparition on the horizon. Then it dawned on him. Aircraft.

Inside the fleet of Junkers 52 transport planes was a battalion of paratroopers from the elite Brandenburg Division, the closest German equivalent to the SBS. Olivey watched as the 40 aircraft approached in perfect formation at a height of 300 feet above the island's narrow waist between Alinda and Gurna bays. 'Everything was silent, every man on his gun, every gun pointing in their direction,' recalled Olivey.[10]

Broderick, like most of S1 Patrol, readied themselves for the bombs to start falling. Then Olivey realized the aircraft weren't bombers. 'Paratroops!' he screamed, and ordered his men to open fire. 'Every gun and firearm available to the British opened up from both sides of the central valley,' said Broderick. 'It was a wonder to see those planes run this gauntlet. Those of us on Mount Clidi looked straight into the flight decks of the Ju 52s and we added our contribution to the firepower.'[11]

Olivey and his men had nothing but respect for the courage of the men hurling themselves into the air from the transport planes. But they still tried to kill as many as possible. Of the 470 paratroopers who emplaned for Leros, 200 were killed on the drop, either shot as they floated to earth or drowned in the Aegean. Another 100 sustained injuries as they landed on the rocky slopes of Leros. Nonetheless, nearly 200 airborne troops landed in the middle of the island, with orders to dig in and effectively sever Leros in two.

The bulk of the Germans landed close to the position occupied by Major Alan Redfern and his LRDG force. 'They dropped right across the narrowest part [of Leros] on the west of island, quite within easy range of our weaponry and it was impossible to miss firing into the clouds of paratroops coming down,' recalled Ron Cryer, a Bren gunner.[12]

Meanwhile, on Mount Clidi the German infantry were making good progress towards the summit, their progress no longer impeded by the Italian battery. A company of British infantry arrived to bolster the LRDG and together they dug new defensive positions in between holding off the advancing enemy. 'Jerry was already at the perimeter trench,' remembered Broderick. 'A British officer ordered his men to fix bayonets but he was shot and the order was not carried out.'[13]

One of the Rhodesians fighting alongside Broderick was Don Coventry. He recalled that 'as it got dark we were engaged in hand to hand fighting'.[14] The British beat off the Germans, although as the enemy withdrew back down the mountain,

Olivey realized they were dangerously low on ammunition. He contacted HQ and received permission to fall back. 'We withdrew to a position on a ridge some 400 metres distant,' said Coventry, the orders of the LRDG being to prevent the Germans from pushing north from the ridge. The next day, 13 November, was relatively quiet for S1 Patrol, but at 0200 hours on 14 November the British launched a counter-attack against the Germans dug in on the mountainside. The attack failed, and Harold Todman was mortally wounded. The British withdrew once more. There was an air of weary resignation, and a feeling that the battle was slipping away. But similar sentiments were felt by the Germans. On 15 November the Wehrmacht war diary was pessimistic as to the chances of success, noting: 'The fighting is confused and information scarce, and changes in control by the enemy results in a confused crisis.'[15]

Ultimately it was German air superiority that wore down the British resistance, or at least the confidence of Brigadier Tilney. With him in his command HQ inside the Meraviglia rock was Colonel Prendergast and Major Jake Easonsmith, now in charge of the LRDG, both of whom had been sent by Tilney to scout Leros town in previous days. On the night of 15/16 November, Easonsmith was despatched once more to ascertain if German troops were in the town. He never returned. Word reached Prendergast that he had been shot dead as he approached Leros town. Prendergast assumed command of the LRDG. 'I made a personal reconnaissance up to the top of the Meraviglia feature to see for myself was what happening above our heads,' he wrote subsequently. 'I found the top of the feature to be a very uncomfortable spot.'[16] The air was thick with enemy aircraft, Prendergast counting several Stukas circling overhead searching 'for a suitable target to attack', while Junkers 88 were also dropping anti-personnel bombs on the feature.

Worse, there were soldiers coming towards Prendergast. German soldiers. 'We exchanged a few shots and then I went down to the main HQ and told the Brig[adier] that in my opinion it was essential immediately to stage a counter attack on those troops to push them off the Meraviglia feature,' wrote Prendergast. Tilney absorbed the advice and said 'he would see what could be done about collecting the necessary troops for the counter attack.'[17]

Tilney's bullishness of the previous month had vanished. He was now diffident and indecisive. At 0800 hours on 16 November Tilney informed Prendergast 'that he was unable to stage this counter attack and was proposing immediately to evacuate his HQ from the Meraviglia cave'. Prendergast was ordered to do the same, even though he wondered how on earth Tilney intended to control British resistance if all the wireless sets, as was the instruction, were left behind.

'I told the LRDG HQ personnel to destroy all wireless sets and make their way to a certain house in Porto Largo which we all knew as it had been the HQ of Brig.

Turnbull when we first reached the island,' recollected Prendergast.[18] On his way to Porto Largo Prendergast changed his mind. It was madness to evacuate the cave without any wireless sets. He returned to the HQ and was relieved to find the men still there had yet to destroy the radios. Contacting Tilney, Prendergast informed him of what he'd done and was told by the brigadier 'to remain in the main HQ and run the battle to the best of my ability until he should return'.

Tilney showed up a short while later with a few of his staff. None inspired much confidence. Many of the hours that followed were confusing. At 1600 hours Tilney instructed Prendergast to go to Porto Largo and round up as many men as he could. The time had come for a final stand. 'After I had been on my journey for about 20 minutes I looked back at the Meraviglia feature and saw a large number of Germans on the top,' said Prendergast, 'and what appeared to be the whole of the HQ staff lined up outside. I continued to Porto Largo to look for my LRDG personnel.'[19] Not long after Major George Jellicoe, commanding officer of the SBS, arrived at Meraviglia in a jeep having been unable to raise HQ on the wireless. He was furious to discover Tilney discussing surrender terms in the presence of several other senior British and German officers.

Concealing his disgust, Jellicoe listened to proceedings and then made for the exit. The Germans blocked his path. 'Where did he think he was going?' they demanded. With his customary charm, Jellicoe explained that if the Germans wished his unit to surrender they must hear the news from their commanding officer in person. The Germans stepped aside and Jellicoe raced back to the squadron. His men greeted the surrender, what Jellicoe dubbed 'the Anglo-German Peace Conference', with a mix of 'surprise and horror'. Neither they nor their CO had the slightest wish to spend the rest of the war a prisoner.[20]

Guy Prendergast deployed a similar trick in Porto Largo when 'the brig drove up in a jeep with Capt. Baker RN [Royal Navy] and two German officers and told me that he had to capitulate'. Prendergast nodded and said he would bring his LRDG men in. He had no such intention. Anticipating a surrender, Jellicoe and Lieutenant Commander Frank Ramsayer [RN] had 'selected a number of places around the island from which the navy had been briefed to take off escapers'. One of the first LRDG men encountered by Prendergast was Captain Dick Croucher, an experienced desert veteran and brilliant navigator. He informed Prendergast that a party of LRDG, led by Richard Lawson, the medical officer, was assembled and ready to head to one of the escape points.

The artistic flair of Bill Morrison of the LRDG helped brighten up the sergeants' mess of Raiding Forces HQ in Mena. (Courtesy of the SAS Regimental Archive)

In fact, Lawson, along with 'about 36 other LRDG and 80 or 90 of other units with several officers', were clustered in a grove of trees on the Patella side of Porto Largo on the late afternoon of 16 November. When Croucher returned from his encounter with Prendergast, he and Lawson split the group into parties and set off for different escape points. 'I took 20 LRDG and went down the road to Porto Largo and then out across the hills to Patella,' remembered Lawson. It was, he added, 'a very rough journey and I had my big pack still full and heavy'.[21]

At 2330 hours on 16 November they reached a gun battery just below Monte Patella. Though Brigadier Tilney had officially surrendered, many British officers remained where they were, waiting for further instructions. One such unit was still in possession of the gun battery just below the summit of Patella. They provided the LRDG with food and water and some of the men joined their party. By dawn on 17 November, Lawson's party were well concealed above the escape point on the coast below. They spent the day observing German activity and 'at dark we moved down to the point above the rocks and recced a position down'. There were no Germans, but nor was there any sign of a Royal Navy vessel. It was cold, the men were hungry, and some began to grow despondent. 'Our men's training stood out a mile,' reflected Lawson, 'and apart from that their whole attitude was quite different from the majority who were helpless without their officer.'[22]

At dawn the next day a large Greek fishing boat appeared. Lawson suspected it was German. But by now their party had swelled enormously and as soon as the vessel approached the shore, 'there was a general movement and about 120 people appeared from bushes and rocks like the dead rising'. Lawson, as the officer in charge, felt compelled to investigate. But as he emerged from his hiding place and picked his way down the hillside, he saw the men on the boat were Germans. Turning, he saw also a line of Germans on the hill above. By sundown, Lawson and all the men with him were under armed guard in Porto Largo. 'Two German officers stopped in a jeep and asked if there were any LRDG,' he recalled. 'We gave a non-committal answer to which they replied that they were good fighters, and went on.'[23]

In the next 24 hours the number of prisoners in Porto Largo increased from, in Lawson's estimation, 500 to 1,000. That was just the British and Commonwealth soldiers. There were also hundreds of Italians in captivity, and the place was soon a squalid mess. Discipline began to break down as more prisoners arrived. Drawing rations was a terrible business, recalled Lawson, 'with little cooperation from many of the men who seemed devoid of sense'.

On 20 November Lawson obtained permission from the Germans to retrieve the body of Jake Easonsmith, which for several days had lain on the side of the road where he'd been shot. Lawson took a burial party with him, including Curle and Whitehead, who, having escaped from the Germans the previous month, were back in their hands once more. They found Easonsmith on the road leading to Leros. Lawson examined his friend's corpse and was relieved to see 'he must have died instantly'. Nonetheless, it was a distressing moment for the medical officer. 'A miserable feeling of loss and [I] could hardly believe it,' he remembered. 'Whitehead made a cross and the owners of the house in whose vineyard we buried him promised to look after the grave.'

Lawson returned to Porto Largo and thanked his captors for allowing him the opportunity to bury Easonsmith. 'When you get to Germany you will meet most unpleasant people,' replied the German officer. 'Remember us when you do. We are the real Germans.'[24]

When Lawson departed the island on a boat bound for a POW camp, he left behind a scene of humiliating devastation. In the five-day battle for the island, the British had lost an estimated 1,000 men, with another 9,000 wounded. Lawson was one of 3,000 British officers and men captured (along with nearly 6,000 Italians), and heading into captivity with him were 63 soldiers from the LRDG, including Gordon Broderick and John Olivey and most of the men of S1 Patrol. It was a huge number for such a small unit, but on the plus side, 70 had managed to evade the Germans' clutches, including their commanding officer: for the moment.

On the evening of 16 November, Lieutenant Colonel Guy Prendergast, having ascertained that there were no more LRDG personnel at Porto Largo, trekked to the top of Monte Scumbarda to check on a section he knew to be there. But the only man he found when he arrived at midnight was Private Lennox, who explained the rest of the patrol had vanished while had had reconnoitred a stretch of coastline. Prendergast and Lennox filled two rucksacks with rations and water, but just as they were leaving a band of Italian soldiers arrived. They were agitated and annoyed, their officer telling Prendergast 'the British had let them down and he was proposing to hand us

Corporal Alf Curle was one of the men captured by the Germans in October 1943 when the LRDG landed on the Aegean island of Kalymnos. (Courtesy of the SAS Regimental Archive)

over to the Germans'. Prendergast suspected the Italians had been drinking, and it was certainly not difficult to escape a couple of hours later. They hiked through the mountains and the next day, 17 November, stumbled upon a cave containing Captain Dick Croucher and Ron Tinker, another desert veteran, and three other LRDG men. 'For the next three days our routine was very monotonous,' remembered Prendergast. 'By day we lay, with stomachs rumbling, in the cave and waited for the next meal. By night we tried to sleep on the rocky shore and shivered in our inadequate clothing. We saw many German craft chuffing slowly round the coast, looking for escapees.'[25]

The Germans failed to spot Prendergast and his party but by the morning of 20 November the British soldiers were beginning to wonder if they would ever get off the island. They were also nearly out of rations, and so Prendergast decided that, as the only member of the party with rubber-soled boots, he would creep down to Serocampo Bay and see if he could pilfer some rations, and perhaps a small boat. He left the cave at dusk, and approached the bay without incident. 'I walked through the small village of Serocampo and could see that one of the houses was occupied by Germans as they had two jeeps there and were singing and playing an accordion,' he recalled.[26] Many of the other houses were deserted, but eventually Prendergast found one occupied by a local family, who opened the door to him but were nonetheless clearly scared by his presence with the Germans in such close proximity. Despite their fear, like all islanders in the Aegean, the family were fiercely anti-

Some of S Patrol's officers, including (left to right) John Olivey, Gus Holliman and Stan Eastwood. (Courtesy of the SAS Regimental Archive)

German, and having fed Prendergast, the man of the house 'agreed next day to patch one of the boats and to leave it at the water's edge with oars and a rudder'.

Prendergast returned to the cave and explained that, all being well, they would soon be off Leros. But the next night, 21 November, when Prendergast and the six others arrived at Serocampo Bay the wind was up and the sea rough. None of them rated their chances of crossing several miles of water in such conditions. Then, 'about midnight [we] heard a craft approaching the coast,' recounted Prendergast. They could just make out its shape through the darkness. 'We decided to risk everything and flash our torch,' said Prendergast. It was a moment of extreme tension for the seven men, 'as we did not know whether we should be greeted with a hail of bullets or whether we should be taken off'.[27]

On board the craft the atmosphere was also strained. Sergeant George Miller of the SBS had left Bodrum on the Turkish coast at 2145 hours with orders from Major George Jellicoe, his commanding officer, to scour the coastline for stragglers. Miller and the Royal Navy personnel on board the caique saw the signal, a series of Ns. It wasn't on the list of expected signals, and they suspected it was a German trap. The naval captain was all for withdrawing. Miller had a nagging doubt. What if? Miller, a south Londoner and one of the coolest operators in the SBS, persuaded the commander to let him take a dinghy in so he could be sure. He knew the risks. If he wasn't back in a few minutes, then they should get the hell out.

Miller climbed into the dinghy and started to row towards the signal. The man holding the torch, Prendergast, suddenly spotted a small boat 'and the occupant hailed us'. They were too far to make out what he was saying, so Prendergast cupped his hands and shouted their names. 'After a lot of hesitation he came in closely and eventually came right up to us.'[28] Miller introduced himself, and invited the first two men into the dinghy.

CHAPTER 15

A DIFFERENT TYPE OF WARFARE

Any hopes Guy Prendergast entertained of resuming command of the Long Range Desert Group in the wake of the debacle on Leros were soon dashed. He returned to England in early 1944 where he joined the staff of the Special Air Service Brigade as they began preparations for the invasion of France. No matter that the LRDG could have done with Prendergast's calm, efficient leadership as they counted the cost of their autumn in the Aegean. As well as the men killed or captured on Leros, the LRDG had lost 43 men on the island of Levitha, many of them New Zealanders. The LRDG had landed on the island – 20 miles south-west of Leros – to round up what they believed to be a small force of German sailors who had swum ashore after their ship was sunk. In fact the sailors had managed to send a message to German HQ in Kos requesting assistance, and a large force of Gebirgsjäger, the crack mountain troops who had as their cap insignia the white edelweiss, were sent to collect the sailors.

Jim Patch was one of the men who landed on Levitha under the impression that it was simply a matter of detaining a few bedraggled and unarmed sailors. 'As we were crossing the open ground, we came round some sort of bend, and we were confronted by a German machine gun,' remembered Patch.[1] 'We didn't try and get up to anything desperate, to do so would have been suicidal. So we gave up.' Patch's friend, Ron Hill, was on the other side of the island when he was

OPPOSITE
Captain Stan Eastwood and his patrol spent the autumn of 1944 in Albania 'chasing the enemy where he could'. (Courtesy of the SAS Regimental Archive)

confronted by the reality of the situation. 'I turned and found myself looking down the barrel of a German machine gun,' he said. 'I froze. My terror at that moment can only be described by the old clichés – my blood ran cold, my knees turned to water, the hairs on the back of my head bristled.' Hill was convinced he was going to be shot, but instead the German 'motioned me away from the cliff edge to join the others who, with their hands above their heads, were being searched by their captors. I let out a long, long breath of relief and thanked the powers that be for the Geneva Convention.'[2]

Patch, Hill and nearly all of the 50-strong LRDG group were taken prisoner, to the fury of the New Zealand government. '[We] are greatly disturbed over events in the Dodecanese Islands,' they cabled their British counterparts subsequently. 'His Majesty's government in New Zealand wish to observe that they were never consulted as to the use of their troops in this connexion nor, they are advised, was their Commanding Officer [General Freyberg] in the Middle East advised until the men had actually landed.'[3] The upshot was that on 29 December 1943, A Squadron, the Kiwi squadron, was withdrawn from the Long Range Desert Group.

The man responsible for steering the LRDG through this diplomatic mess was David Lloyd Owen. He had spent November in Cairo at the insistence of Jake Easonsmith, who had ordered his second-in-command to return to the Egyptian capital 'to collect more recruits and to start a training organisation for them'. Easonsmith was already 43 men down at this point because of the Levitha fiasco, and Lloyd Owen sensed that his CO foresaw a disaster of even greater proportions on Leros. When they parted, Lloyd Owen had a premonition that he wouldn't see Easonsmith again. Did he, too? Easonsmith 'talked about home, and about his family, to whom he was devoted', recalled Lloyd Owen.

Now that Easonsmith was dead, Lloyd Owen was more determined than ever that the LRDG would survive. In a reorganization of the squadron, Lloyd Owen – recently promoted to lieutenant colonel – appointed Major Ken Lazarus commanding officer of the Rhodesian A Squadron, with Major Stormonth Darling assuming command of the British B Squadron. Each squadron comprised eight patrols of one officer and ten men, with a signaller, medical orderly and trained navigator included. It was also decided 'to give up the all black beret for the beige type which Raiding Forces were going to adopt', the colour chosen by David Stirling for the SAS in 1941.

There was the problem of filling the ranks of the LRDG after the loss of so many men in the Aegean, and then of training them to operational standards. Lloyd Owen's greatest concern, however, was whether the LRDG still had a role to play in the war against Germany. Embedded with the unit at this time was Captain

Stuart Manning, described in contemporary reports as a 'Southern Rhodesia official observer', who came from the South African public relations department. He commented that

> for five months some of the senior officers of the unit added steadily to their collection of grey hairs in trying to establish a properly appreciated niche for the LRDG. It seemed that few at GHQ (Middle East) could achieve a clear-cut picture, as was essential, of the proper functions of such a unit. But Lloyd Owen and others worked with extraordinary diligence and even more praiseworthy tact to create the right impression in the right places of how the LRDG should be allowed to function.[4]

By February 1944 Lloyd Owen had moved the LRDG to Syria, where they underwent mountain training, and also attended a close combat school in Jerusalem. One of the Rhodesian officers, Lieutenant Cecil 'Jacko' Jackson, recalled that the 'chief instructor of the school was an American who had been training the FBI in how to use pistols and Tommy guns'.[5] The man in charge of physical training was

A member of the Rhodesian Patrol pedal-charging radio batteries during a shipping watch on one of the Dalmatian islands. (Courtesy of the SAS Regimental Archive)

Oscar Heidenstam, one of the pioneers of body-building, or what was known in the 1930s as 'Physical Excellence'. Heidenstam had been crowned Mr Great Britain in 1937 and seven years later he was still in formidable condition as he whipped the LRDG into shape. 'We started the day with an hour of PT to loosen up,' recalled Jackson. 'Then breakfast, after which we had small arms instruction, followed by more PT, including holds and bare-hand strikes. After a light lunch there was more PT followed by firing practice at the end of the day.'[6] The culmination of all their instruction was a test of what they had learned in a specially adapted house. Inside, remembered Jackson, were 'a series of rooms rigged out with dummies which leapt up from chairs and beds, and out of corners when the door was opened, or we trod on a certain part of the floor'.[7]

As his men honed their skills in Jerusalem, Lloyd Owen flew to Italy at the end of February where he spent a week discussing the possibility of LRDG operations in Italy in Field Marshal Alexander's headquarters. Soon the unit was moving into new quarters in Rodi, on the Gargano Peninsula, or as the soldiers liked to call it, the top of the spur on the Italian boot.

But the move failed to usher in a new phase of dynamism for the LRDG. Lloyd Owen continued to shuttle back and forth between Rodi and AAI (Allied Armies in Italy) HQ at Caserta, mooting plans of his own and listening to those of others. Captain Manning, the Rhodesian observer attached to the unit, articulated the frustration felt by Lloyd Owen during this period of inertia. 'It would seem natural

Jackson and Scott clean their teeth while a comrade checks the wheel of their vehicle. (Courtesy of the SAS Regimental Archive)

to believe that special forces needed special understanding and treatment for the sake of efficiency,' he wrote.

But it is not cynical to realise that such a happy state of affairs is a difficult thing to achieve under army regulations and drill. But as in the desert the LRDG worked on the unexpressed assumption that to achieve something, something had to be attempted, so now they believed that one got nothing they didn't ask for. They asked, and asked again.[8]

Lloyd Owen compiled a report on the skills of the LRDG, a CV of sorts, intended to sell the unit to the top brass. 'All operational and other essential personnel are trained parachutists,' he wrote.

The LRDG HQ was established here in Rodi in early 1944 in readiness for operations in Italy. (Courtesy of the SAS Regimental Archive)

They have also been trained to operate by sea in small boats landed from bigger craft. A large number of men have been trained on skis, and are capable of existing in snow conditions. Patrols are capable of walking distances of up to 100 miles and being self-contained in supplies for 10 days when on foot and can maintain communication to their HQ. All ranks are trained in demolition and a number of men have been trained in handling mules.[9]

Eventually their persistence paid off, and on 7 May 1944 it was agreed that Ken Lazarus's A Squadron, the Rhodesians, would be loaned to Force 266, the Allied organization encompassing the SBS, SOE (Special Operations Executive) and OSS (Office of Strategic Services, the SOE's US equivalent) then at work in the Balkans. By now Manning had spent several months with the LRDG and he was struck by the calibre of the men who served. 'If a man did not "fit" he went,' he wrote. 'That original rigid discipline, born and matured in the desert, reinforced by the bufferings on Leros, was very much alive. In the atmosphere of that code no man ever left a compass behind, or ran out of water, or got lost. Whatever happened, nothing could be due to carelessness.'[10]

Six months after the Leros shambles, the LRDG returned to action on 16 May 1944 when Captain Stan Eastwood and four men (including the irrepressible Gunner Edwards) were ordered to Corfu, the 35-mile-long island just off the Albanian coast garrisoned by more than 2,000 enemy troops. Their task was to gather intelligence on an enemy radar station believed to be on the island with the help of a Greek agent. They came ashore in a rowing boat and spent the first 24 hours observing the countryside while the agent went off in search of the radar station.

The LRDG's first parachute operations were in June 1944 when small parties of men dropped into central Italy to reconnoitre German troop strengths as they withdrew north. (Courtesy of Jack Valenti)

Having located its whereabouts, the agent returned to the LRDG hideout and next day set off again for the station accompanied by one of the LRDG soldiers, Private Marc, who like the agent was dressed as a local.

Once at the radar station, Marc not only made several rough sketches of it, but 'he even endeavoured to enter the enemy camp by pretending to sell fish but was forcibly ejected by a sentry'. Their mission accomplished, the LRDG men returned safely and provided Force 266 with 'very detailed information which included suitable landing places and routes to the target for Commando raiders at a later date'.[11]

At the same time that Eastwood was reconnoitring Corfu, events were occurring in Italy that would have significant repercussions for the LRDG. On 18 May the Allies finally seized Monte Cassino after five months of bitter fighting. The Germans withdrew from the Gustav Line, the defensive position that crossed the Italian peninsula from Garigliano in the west through Cassino and then to Sangro in the east. On 23 May the US VI Corps broke out of the Anzio beachhead and suddenly the Americans, as well as the Eighth Army, began advancing rapidly north after months of bitter and bloody stalemate. As the Allies pushed north, the LRDG were asked to insert four patrols by parachute on the nights of 11 and 12 June to obtain intelligence about enemy traffic on roads north of Rome.

The first two patrols from B Squadron to insert were those of lieutenants John Bramley★ and Simon Fleming. Fleming was an Irishman, from County Down, who

---

★ Bramley's was the most successful of the four. Inserting without incident, they spent a week radioing back information to Allied Armies in Italy [AAI] HQ. When the radio died, Bramley led his men back safely having provided information of 'considerable value to our advancing troops'.

had come to the LRDG from the Royal Artillery at the end of 1943. Lloyd Owen appreciated his 'glorious sense of humour' and his 'carefree attitude to life'. En route to Italy from the Middle East, the LRDG stopped one night at a transit camp at Port Tewfik, on the southern boundary of the Suez Canal. The unit was confined to barracks that evening ahead of its morning sailing to Italy, but Fleming and a couple of others slipped out of camp for one last spree. He was eventually tracked down to a hotel where he was coaxed down from a bar counter in the middle of a demonstration to a group of delighted naval officers of how not to do a parachute roll.

The drop zone (DZ) for Fleming and his eight men in M2 Patrol was Montepulciano, approximately 35 miles west of Perugia in Italy. Once on the ground, they were to gather intelligence on German troop movements during the Allied advance and then make their own way south through enemy lines. It was a challenging operation from the moment they took off from Foggia, and the mission became

These LRDG men don't look too enthusiastic about jumping from this training tower. (Courtesy of Jack Valenti)

even more onerous when Fleming vanished during the drop. The seven other men searched for their officer as long as they could, but time was of the essence and they had to get away from the DZ as quickly as possible.★ But it was already too late. There was a shout and suddenly 'there was a hail of bullets flying around our ears'. The LRDG dived for cover among the long stalks of corn, but four were soon in German hands. Three managed to escape, wriggling their way through the cornfield into the trees and, eventually, Allied lines.

Two days after Fleming's patrol had left Foggia, it was the turn of another LRDG stick to drop into occupied Italy. M1 Patrol, led by Captain Ashley Greenwood, took off at 0130 hours on 14 June with instructions to obtain information on roads and tracks, enemy troop movements and types of transport. One of the men with Greenwood was Vincent Murphy, known to his pals as 'Spud'.

★ It was subsequently learned that Fleming's parachute had failed to open because of a default static line and he had been killed on landing. His mother commissioned a brooch designed on the LRDG emblem and wore it for the rest of her life.

A group of recruits on their way to their first parachute jump from an aircraft. (Courtesy of Jack Valenti)

A former Coldstream Guardsman, Murphy was a skilled navigator who had been with the LRDG in the desert. He was also one of the most popular men in the unit, 'a cornerstone of reliable strength in all conditions'.[12] Murphy wrote a diary of the mission, which began with a description of their area of operations. 'We would operate at a place named Lama, a small village in Italy … 50 or 60 miles behind the German front line,' he related. 'The plan was to be dropped at a spot three miles outside the village and near to a wood in which we hoped to establish our rendezvous.'[13]

The aircraft approached the DZ at a height of 500ft, the LRDG men making their final preparations for the jump. Murphy heard the engine throttle back. Any second now. The despatcher yelled 'Action stations!' and the men began shuffling towards the despatch door, their eyes fixed on the red light as they waited for it to turn green. The moment it did, the first man, Captain Greenwood, was out of the door. His comrades followed in quick succession. Murphy had made several practice jumps from a plane, but this was his first combat drop. 'The slipstream hits me with terrific force,' he wrote in his diary. 'I am picked up and tossed about like a cork on the ocean. After what seems like an eternity – but is actually less than two seconds – there is a tug on my shoulders and I am airborne, swaying gently from side to side.'[14]

The surge of relief at seeing his chute open was fleeting. As Murphy looked down and picked out the village of Lama to his right, he heard a sound. Was it a shot? The next moment 'red and green Verey lights are seen going up in all directions'. Horribly exposed on the end of his parachute, Murphy willed the ground to come up to meet him. Then, to his further dismay, he saw that he wasn't landing in a field but on an orchard of small trees. 'I endeavour to protect myself as best I can against the branches,' he said. 'There is a sharp crack as my feet strike a branch and it breaks away from the tree and the next instant I am lying in a heap on the ground.'[15] In a second Murphy was up and wriggling out of harness, listening to the 'noise of motor cars and track vehicles' approaching. With his parachute rolled up and under his arm, Murphy set off to find his comrades, but despite a thorough search of the orchard he found no one. In the meantime, the Germans were pouring out of their lorries and conducting an extensive sweep of the area. Within a short space of time they had captured four of the seven LRDG men.

Murphy was spotted as dawn broke on 15 November, just as he was looking for a suitable spot in which to hide for the rest of the day. He turned and fled in the other direction towards a cornfield, 'when lo and behold seven Germans armed with automatic rifles popped up from the other side of the hill'. He ducked instinctively as the Germans opened fire, but 'fear of capture lent me wings and I was soon out of sight'. He sucked in some air, then made a sharp turn to his right for 100 yards before doubling back in the hope he would throw the Germans off his trail. 'It was successful,' he wrote. 'I heard them shouting below me and firing

Two of Eastwood's patrol take a break from calling in RAF strikes on German targets in Albania. In one such aerial assault 1,500 enemy soldiers were killed. (Courtesy of the SAS Regimental Archive)

as they went. Now to get over the hill and I should be safe.'[16] Murphy quickened his step, anxious to be clear of the Germans as the sun began to rise. He was almost at the crest of the hill. Once over, he would be out of sight and on his way back to the Allied lines. Suddenly, figures rose from the cornfield. Murphy started and then 'my heart sank'. They were Germans, all pointing their weapons his way. 'I was a prisoner.'[17]

Murphy didn't know it, but he was the last of the patrol to be captured. Greenwood and another soldier, Ford, had independently evaded the German net and in due course reached Allied lines. The other four LRDG soldiers had been rounded up before dawn, and when Murphy was marched back to the village word had quickly spread of the drama that had unfolded during the night. For the Italian villagers the sight of a British soldier, even a captured one, was like the first drop of rain after a long cruel drought. Soon, surely, the deluge would arrive. 'The whole village turned out to gaze silently upon me as I was marched past,' wrote Murphy. Most of them appeared sympathetic and tried to show their sympathy by a wave of the hand when my captors were not looking in their direction.'[18]

Like all recently captured soldiers, Murphy would have felt a sense of disorientation and apprehension, a man who for the foreseeable future would eat, sleep and talk at the discretion of his captors. But he had no reason to fear for his life. Fortunately for him and the rest of his LRDG comrades, the Germans believed they were aircrew who had baled from their aircraft. This assumption was partly based on the fact the patrol sergeant, Gordon Harrison, was wearing a USAAF (United States Army Air Force) cap that he had swapped with an American airman in Italy for his LRDG beret. It was probably just as well, for German forces had been under instructions for more than 18 months to liquidate all captured Commandos and paratroopers once they had been forcefully interrogated by the *Sicherheitsdienst* (SD, the intelligence service of the SS). The Commando Order came from the Führer himself, Adolf Hitler's response to an instruction allegedly issued by Allied commanders prior to the ill-fated Canadian raid on Dieppe in August 1942 to 'bind prisoners' captured in the operation. The Order was a closely guarded secret within the German military, but already a dozen SAS soldiers had been executed following their capture in Italy in 1943, and a fortnight after Murphy fell into German hands 34 SAS soldiers were murdered and buried in a mass grave in central France after their forest hideout was overrun by SS troops.

The Allies learned of the Commando Order in the spring of 1944 after the escape of an SAS officer from captivity. A sympathetic German doctor had informed the British soldier of his likely fate, and then connived in his flight from a military hospital. Yet the prevailing view among the Allied high command was one of scepticism, that it was probably nothing more than a scare tactic, 'an interrogation technique'.★

Murphy was taken into an upstairs room in a house in Lama. Nothing was said to him, and nor was he manhandled. But a German guarded the window and another the door. Appreciating that there was no chance of escape, Murphy 'sat on the floor with my back propped up against the wall. I soon found thoughts wandering back over my many and varied experiences since I had joined the Long Range Desert Group. It was a good life … there had been plenty of thrills and a great deal of excitement.'[19]

A local woman fetches water watched by members of Eastwood's patrol. (Courtesy of the SAS Regimental Archive)

★ Irrefutable proof of the Order came in August 1944 when two SAS soldiers miraculously managed to escape from in front of a firing squad in a French forest, running into the trees as the Germans gunned down the rest of their comrades. The pair were found by the Maquis who eventually spirited them back to England.

CHAPTER 16

VALOUR AND VERSATILITY

The responsibility for the failure of three of the four patrols dropped into Italy rested largely with Lloyd Owen. Understandably keen to see the unit back in action after the events of November 1943 on Leros, he had thrown caution to the winds in selecting drop zones too close to the enemy front line. He should have remembered the old maxim from the desert days: 500 miles behind enemy lines is safer than 50 miles. When a special forces soldier is 500 miles inside the enemy's territory his opponent's guard is down because they assume themselves to be safe, but at 50 miles they're on alert. In addition, what had been asked of the LRDG patrols in Italy wasn't what they'd been trained for. They had done a brief parachute training course, but landing in enemy territory with several canisters of weapons and supplies required experience. The brutal truth was the LRDG still had a desert war mentality; operating in vast uninhabited regions where survival more often than not depended on a man's will, wit and initiative. In Europe, one never knew what lay round the corner and one never knew who one could trust.

As for A Squadron, the Rhodesian Squadron, by the middle of June their role changed from carrying out purely reconnaissance operations on the Dalmatian Islands to combining them with offensive action against enemy targets. Wishing to have the self-sufficiency and independence that the LRDG had enjoyed in North Africa, Lloyd Owen procured the unit's very own vessel, the motor fishing vessel *La Palma*,

OPPOSITE
The LRDG pose for a photo with locals at Bolabani on the Istria Peninsula. (Courtesy of the SAS Regimental Archive)

which allowed them to operate without having to rely on the Royal Navy, who might not always be able to meet the LRDG's requirements. *La Palma's* maiden voyage was to the island of Vis in June, her crew of nine taking seven and a half hours to cover the 70 miles. It was the first of many such trips, the aim of which was to either report on enemy shipping so that the RAF or Royal Navy could launch an attack, or so that small raiding parties could harass enemy shipping or installations on lightly held islands.

In the same month, Captain Stan Eastwood and five men, including an interpreter and Albanian guide, landed at Orso Bay on the Albanian coast. A German observation post was believed to be located somewhere on the stretch of coastline, and Eastwood was 'to liquidate it' because it was reporting the movements of Allied shipping. They located the target, but it was too much for their party to tackle, comprising 'a rectangular concrete building of seven rooms with a flat roof camouflaged to look like an ordinary house with a pitched roof, the eastern portion giving the appearance of having fallen in'.[1] On the roof, noted Eastwood, was a square lookout with slits for guns, and one, sometimes two, sentries were also on duty in the tower. Additionally two corners of the buildings were augmented with pillboxes, 'the gun slits in which would permit their combined fire to cover a 360-degree radius'. If that wasn't formidable enough, a double apron barbed-wire fence encircled the position at a distance of 40 yards.

Eastwood radioed a report to Force 266 and it was decided to mount a combined operation with three RN Hunt-class destroyers as well as a couple of rapid Italian torpedo boats. David Lloyd Owen delegated command of the land operation to Captain Tony Browne, one of the original New Zealand contingent in the LRDG, who had just wangled his return to the unit after several months away. Then, at the last moment, Lloyd Owen came along for the ride. 'I had not been on active operations for so long,' he said, 'and I was beginning to feel stale and tired. I wanted a breath of fresh air again.'[2]

In all, there were 35 men from the LRDG in the torpedo boats that raced east across the Adriatic from Brindisi. Stan Eastwood signalled them in and when dawn broke at 0415 hours they were safely ashore. 'We had to get away from the beach and it took us nearly five hours to move a few miles over rough and rocky country to where there was thick cover under some trees,' recalled Lloyd Owen.[3] He, Eastwood and Browne left the rest of the party among the trees and climbed to a boulder-strewn ridge 1,200 feet above sea level. In the far distance they could see the town of Valona bathed in morning light. Nearer, just 1,000 yards across a scrub-covered ravine, was the target. It was indeed formidably defended, said Lloyd Owen, observing the target, but he was confident all the same that its obliteration wouldn't

LA PALMA

ABOVE, LEFT

La Palma was the motorized fishing vessel acquired by the LRDG in the summer of 1944 so they would not be reliant on the Royal Navy to transport them to targets. (Courtesy of Jack Valenti)

ABOVE, RIGHT

The maiden voyage of *La Palma* was to the island of Vis in June 1944 with the boat taking seven and a half hours to cover the seventy miles. (Courtesy of Jack Valenti)

LEFT

La Palma had a crew of nine and proved invaluable through the second half of 1944 and early 1945 as the LRDG stepped up their shipping watches from remote Adriatic islands. (Courtesy of Jack Valenti)

The traditional Albanian headwear kept the LRDG warm during their time in the Balkans, as did the captured German helmet of this soldier. (Courtesy of the SAS Regimental Archive)

pose much of a problem. The plan, he said, was simple: 'We would move to within seven hundred yards of the target at dusk and then await the blitz of the three destroyers. When these had done their best the final assault would be led by Stan. We were to be in touch with the destroyers by wireless, and had brought a trained gunnery officer with us to control their fire.'[4]

They spent the day under cover, checking their weapons, checking their watches, eating, dozing, thinking. At sundown Eastwood led the assault force into position, while Lloyd Owen and the gunnery officer climbed to a point where they could see the three destroyers. It was a moment of high suspense, one where the LRDG were at the mercy of the Royal Navy's guns. A few hundred yards of inaccuracy could have deadly consequences. 'The silence was a little weird, but fascinating at the same time,' reflected Lloyd Owen, as he stared at the 'dark and sinister forms on the gentle ripple of water'.[5]

At 2325 hours Lloyd Owen flashed the agreed signal, and the officer confirmed their position and that of the target by radio. Five minutes later, bang on time, a star shell illuminated the coastline, followed a few seconds later by 'the first ranging shot [which] tore through the air and struck the mountainside a little below the target'. Then the bombardment began and 12-gun salvoes from the three destroyers screamed down on the observation post. The ground shook beneath the LRDG men and great chunks of rock cascaded into the ravine. As for the target, that was obscured in a storm cloud of dust. Eastwood radioed for some more star shells. As they burst overhead, he saw that the observation post 'needed another dose'. After the second short bombardment, Eastwood and his men moved towards the target in a line abreast. Through the dust they saw 150 yards away four Germans staggering from the post. Eastwood called on them to surrender. They didn't respond, so they were shot. Three other Germans emerged with their hands above their head and were taken into captivity. Eastwood grabbed one and together they entered the ruins of the observation post. But there was no further resistance, and from the doorway of the house, Eastwood fired three long bursts of tracer into the air and then flashed three times with the torch towards Lloyd Owen's position. It was the signal for the successful completion of their objective. By 0300 hours, the LRDG were on the beach with 'three miserable weeping Germans', and half an hour later a whaler arrived and transported them onto one of the destroyers, HMS *Terpsichore*.

A change of clothes, a hearty breakfast and then a moment to reflect on the mission. Three prisoners, one casualty (a slight 'friendly fire' wound to one of Eastwood's party from a naval shell splinter) and the destruction of the observation post. It was hardly a major setback for the Germans, acknowledged Lloyd Owen, but the principal result of the first Allied raid launched from Italy 'lay in the uneasiness which the enemy was to feel along the whole of their Adriatic coast'. What was more, the Royal Navy had had a good time, the captain of HMS *Terpsichore* sending Lloyd Owen a letter thanking him 'for a good evening's entertainment and for providing the live exhibits in the form of the first Germans many of my sailors have seen'.[6]

There was a minor reorganization in August, with the LRDG being placed under the operational command of the Land Forces Adriatic [LFA] on the 14th of the month. The HQ of the LFA was in Bari, and it was here that missions and raids were planned. 'The prime task of the LRDG was to provide reconnaissance for the striking forces of all three Services [army, navy, air force],' wrote Captain Stuart Manning. 'When the LFA attacked targets, the LRDG had to be prepared to mark landing beaches or dropping zones and provide guides to lying-up places or targets.'[7]

One such target was a railway bridge over a gorge inland from Gruda, a village approximately 20 miles south of the port of Dubrovnik in Croatia. On 19 August, an LRDG patrol of five men, commanded by Captain David Skipworth, left Italy in a motor launch to reconnoitre the area. One of the men was Sergeant Fred Leach, erstwhile of the Scots Guards, and a veteran of the LRDG's desert days. 'Having found suitable landing 10 to 15 miles south of Dubrovnik [we] moved off inland to a thick wooded area,' he remembered. They made contact with a group of partisans who invited them to their camp. 'The offer was accepted,' said Leach. 'Trouble was to understand each other, but they had plenty of food, mostly British, and the site was ideal for the patrol's purpose.'[8] The next few days were spent surveying the area, and observing the target. 'The peace and quiet was uncanny,' recalled Leach. 'There was no sign of troops, army trucks or heavy weapons anywhere. The local farmers and others just carried out their work as usual.'[9]

Satisfied that the bridge was a viable target, the LRDG communicated the fact to the LFA HQ in Bari, and on the evening of 27 August a 12-strong raiding party came ashore from a motor launch. Eleven of the men were from the SBS, the twelfth a demolitions expert from the Royal Engineers. They were commanded by Captain Anders Lassen, a fearsome and fearless Danish officer who had three military crosses to his name, and also among their number was Sergeant Dick Holmes, a recipient of the Military Medal for his courage during an SBS raid on Crete the previous year. 'We were all carrying two rucksacks,' recalled Holmes. 'One contained our own kit and the other fifty pounds of plastic explosive.'[10]

The route inland was treacherous, particularly at night, but the SBS were guided to the partisans' camp by the LRDG. The next day the SBS observed the target in the presence of the LRDG and it was agreed that they would destroy it on the night of 30 August. Reaching the target without obstruction, the raiders attached electric charges to each of the bridge's abutments while the Royal Engineers' corporal made a junction box with a primer cord to each charge. Within a few minutes, 500lb of explosive were in place and ready to blow. Once the wiring from the charges to the plunger was in place, the men sheltered behind a large rock 200 feet from the bridge. Holmes was given the job of blowing the bridge. 'On the count of three I pressed down on the plunger but nothing happened, there was no proper connection,' remembered Holmes. 'I tried again but [had] the same result.'[11]

Three LRDG soldiers lunch at Chersicia on the Istria Peninsula. (Courtesy of the SAS Regimental Archive)

The Royal Engineer cleaned the plunger, unscrewing the terminals and polishing and replacing the wires, but that had no effect. Lassen looked at his watch. Dawn soon. He swore at the plunger, and at the sapper, but, ignoring the insults, the Royal Engineer scrambled down to the bridge to put Plan B into place. Running a safety fuse from the detonator back to the rock, he reached into his pocket for a box of matches. They watched the fizzing fuse for a few moments, then prudently crouched down behind the rock. 'Lassen was starting to get impatient again,' explained Holmes. 'He wanted to go down and have a look for himself. Then suddenly the whole lot goes up and great chunks of masonry begin raining down on us. One bloody big piece flew past over our heads. It's amazing no one got killed.'[12]

Leaving behind a thick pall of yellow dust, the British raiders hurried high into the mountains until they reached the sanctuary of the partisan HQ. There was a delicious hot stew waiting for them when they arrived, and once that had been polished off the men lay down to rest. But at first light the next morning their slumber was shattered by a breathless sentry, who ran into the camp to warn that a large force of Germans and Ustaše were close at hand. The Ustaše were the fascist Croat force, whose reputation for brutality surpassed that of the Nazis.

In the grey dawn light, Holmes saw between 50 and 75 Germans and Ustaše advancing up the mountain towards their hideout, the officer in charge blowing a whistle and exhorting his men to move quicker. Lassen ordered his men to take up defensive positions along the rim of a hollow. 'He decided to engage the approaching enemy troops, to the disgust of the rest of us,' said Holmes. 'I believe he was anxious to impress the partisans … we had done what we had been asked to do. Nothing would be gained by staying to fight.'[13]

The partisans, however, had no intention of staging a last stand. They took off up the mountainside and Lassen, realizing they were hopelessly outnumbered, ordered the SBS and LRDG to withdraw. Fred Leach was shot in the arm as he pulled back, and consequently was 'not a lot of use'. He, Captain Skipworth, the Royal Engineer and a partisan were captured, fortunately by the Germans and not the Ustaše.★

The British prisoners were driven to Mostar, north of Dubrovnik, and there they were separated. 'I was then taken to a room for questioning,' recalled Leach. Waiting for him were three officers from the SS. 'Having heard more than enough of the reputation of the SS I confess to being very unhappy indeed. However, these three turned out to be officers and gentlemen.'[14] It appeared to Leach that the trio knew the war was lost and were anxious to curry favour with any Allied soldier they encountered. Above all, they were relieved to be in Yugoslavia and not Russia.

★ The rest of the raiding party were picked up by motor launch on the night of 6 September.

'Having heard more than enough of the reputation of the SS I confess to being very unhappy indeed. However, these three turned out to be officers and gentlemen.'

Ron Crossfield

The LRDG continued to operate in Albania throughout September, with the ubiquitous Stan Eastwood blowing up roads, attacking vehicles and generally making a nuisance of himself at every opportunity. Despite his success, however, and that of other Rhodesian patrols, relations between the LRDG and the partisans were deteriorating. 'Albania had been a very successful phase of LRDG operations, but that had been due more to their own initiative and exertion than to so-called cooperation of the partisans,' commented Stuart Manning, the Southern Rhodesia observer. 'Throughout the local commanders, themselves willing to cooperate and be generally helpful, were everlastingly ruled by orders from above, which, as had been the case in Yugoslavia territory, they carried out blindly.'[15]

By now it was evident to all – not just the three SS officers who questioned Sergeant Leach – that the Third Reich was crumbling. Squeezed on two fronts, Germany began recalling its troops from the Balkans to defend its border from the Soviet troops advancing westwards, who had already captured the Ploieşti airfields, entered Bucharest and made the first push into Yugoslavia. As German soldiers streamed

Captioned 'Dick, Joe, Dod, Skinny', this photo was taken in Istria and shows Rhodesian members of the LRDG. (Courtesy of the SAS Regimental Archive)

north from Greece, through Albania and Yugoslavia, Winston Churchill demanded his chiefs of staff act quickly to ensure British troops reached Greece before the Soviets. The problem faced by Britain was a lack of resources; with so many soldiers fighting their way up Italy or across France, there simply were not enough troops in the Mediterranean theatre to meet Churchill's insistence that a force of 5,000 march on Athens. Instead, an amalgamation of units was raised under the moniker Foxforce. Commanded by Lieutenant Colonel Ronnie Tod of No. 9 Commando, Foxforce comprised the LRDG, SBS, Commandos, Greek Sacred Squadron and the Raiding Support Regiment. Tod was answerable to the 2nd Special Service Brigade, which came under overall control of Brigadier Davy's Land Forces Adriatic.

On 15 September Foxforce occupied the island of Kythira, six miles south of the Peloponnese, the large peninsula in southern Greece. The island was a good place from which to launch operations on the Greek mainland and the British established a naval base on the south of the island. From here the SBS and LRDG began reconnoitring the islands in the Bay of Athens, eradicating the last pockets of resistance, before, on 24 September, it was deemed the Peloponnese was sufficiently clear of the enemy to land a 450-strong force – codenamed 'Bucket Force' – at Araxos airfield in a fleet of Dakotas.

Lloyd Owen was asked to provide an LRDG patrol to act as Bucket Force's ears and eyes as they advanced east from Araxos, so he called on John Olivey and

A shave breaks the monotony of life on Istria. (Courtesy of the SAS Regimental Archive)

his Rhodesian Z1 Patrol. Olivey's 11 jeeps arrived in Greece by landing craft on 26 September, roaring ashore in their jeeps at Katakolon, 40 miles south of Araxos. The patrol soon became bogged down, however, Olivey noting as they drove north that 'the roads [are] very bad after the recent rain'. Four of the jeeps in the patrol pulled trailers, on each of which was 1,000lb of equipment for Bucket Force, and within a day of landing Olivey began to doubt that all the vehicles would stand the ordeal if the condition of the roads did not improve.

On 30 September Olivey's patrol arrived at Bucket Force's Forward HQ, a few miles west of Patras. L Squadron of the SBS were positioned on the high ground overlooking the port, and their commander, Major Ian Patterson, was endeavouring to persuade the garrison of 900 Germans and 1,600 Greeks from a collaborationist security battalion to surrender. During the night of 3/4 October word reached Bucket Force HQ that the Germans had started withdrawing from Patras. At first light a patrol of the SBS, travelling in the LRDG jeeps, raced into the port and discovered that all but a German rearguard had indeed sailed out of Patras, heading east up the Gulf of Corinth towards the Corinth Canal.

The SBS and the LRDG now set off in pursuit of the Germans. In a convoy of jeeps they roared along the headland overlooking the gulf, a captured 75mm German field gun hitched to the back of one of the jeeps. 'Chased the enemy who were withdrawing by boat,' wrote Olivey in his log, 'firing with .5 Browning and 75 mm gun, from positions on the Corinth Road.'[16]

They reached Corinth on 7 October, exchanged desultory fire with the Germans on the other side of the canal and then accepted the surrender of another battalion of Greek collaborators. From Corinth Olivey received instructions to push on to the town of Megara, several miles to the north-east over a mountain road, but to leave two jeeps' worth of men in Corinth to help in the clearance of German mines. Olivey's Z1 Patrol reached Megara on 9 October and at dawn the next day assisted an SBS unit to 'blow the escape road that the enemy were using'. With that done, they set about preparing a landing strip for the arrival of the 4th Independent Parachute Brigade led by Colonel George Jellicoe. They dropped into Megara on 12 October, a day when the wind was particularly stiff. 'We were rushed to Megara airfield to help by driving alongside the paratroopers on the ground with open chutes, swinging left or right to collapse the chutes, to enable them to get to their feet,' recalled Tommy Haddon, a Rhodesian trooper in Z1 Patrol. 'Even so, many parachutes were not collapsing and men were swept onto the rocks along the coast running alongside the airfield.'[17]

The next day, 13 October, Z1 Patrol was among the first Allied troops to enter the Greek capital. 'We proceeded over the Corinth Canal to Athens in convoys,'

A group of partisans on Istria. The female fighters were often more ferocious than the men. (Courtesy of the SAS Regimental Archive)

recalled Haddon, 'all the way being greeted by singing and joyful Greeks, shouting words of welcome.'[18] Once in Athens, Haddon and Z1 checked into the Grand National Hotel, though it wasn't for long. They were soon billeted in less salubrious surrounds – the old Ford factory on the main road to Piraeus.

Foxforce was now subsumed into 'Pompforce', a 1,000-strong amalgamation of the LRDG, SBS, 4th Independent Parachute Battalion, a unit from the RAF Regiment and a battery of 75mm guns. Commanded by Jellicoe, 'Pompforce' drove north towards Larissa, driving past the detritus of a large-scale German retreat. Glimpses of the Germans were rare, and what resistance was encountered was quickly crushed, as at Kozani and Florina.

John Olivey's patrol 'proceeded south of Florina and harassed the withdrawing enemy and proceeded to the flat country … firing at a range of 2,000 yards, at the enemy force withdrawing up the Florina–Havrokhoma Road. Florina was occupied/captured at 1600 hours.'[19] Hours after the capture of Florina, Jellicoe received a signal 'instructing us not to go into Yugoslavia or Albania, presumably as a result of a pact with the Russians'.

An LRDG soldier (left) with two partisans on one of the Adriatic islands in the spring of 1945. (Courtesy of the SAS Regimental Archive)

At the end of October Lloyd Owen withdrew most of the LRDG patrols from Albania, leaving behind Eastwood 'chasing the enemy where he could'. Much of his work was calling up air strikes on retreating Germans, such as the convoy moving south to reinforce the town of Tirana. Having first blown a bridge with his patrol, Eastwood radioed the RAF, who attacked the convoy as it waited for the bridge to be repaired. The convoy of '1,500 men, a few tanks, guns, MT and horse-drawn vehicles' was all but wiped out. Tirana subsequently fell to the partisans on 17 November, and a fortnight later Eastwood's patrol finally withdrew after four months of superlative work that only a unit with the LRDG's unique skills could have accomplished. Eastwood had been awarded a Military Cross for leading the raid on the observation post in Orso Bay, and his sergeant, Andy Bennett, was decorated for his work in Albania, the citation for his Military Medal describing his role during a battle with 200 Germans on the Elbasan-Tirana road:

> In a battle lasting some hours he showed magnificent courage under extremely heavy fire. He refused to leave his position only a few hundred yards from the road and thus enabled the combined force to compel the enemy to withdraw, leaving behind eighty dead and much valuable equipment. During the whole of these operations Bennett displayed great gallantry under fire.[20]

Back in Greece, the Germans had been chased out of the country by November and on the 12th of the month the LRDG, together with the SBS, returned south to Athens for what they imagined would be some well-earned rest and recuperation. Greece, its islands and its people, were hugely popular with both units, and in the preceding 15 months a strong bond had developed between the British special forces and the Greeks. It was a bond forged in war, unbreakable, or so the British assumed.

But it was quickly apparent in Athens that the indolent days of the past had evaporated. The antagonism was palpable between the government of 'National Unity', who were pro-monarchy, and EAM, the predominantly communist National Liberation Front, whose military wing was ELAS, the Greek People's Liberation Army. At first it was assumed that the trouble could be easily contained by the Greek authorities, and so Major Stormonth Darling led B Squadron (who had also been in Greece) back to Italy on the same day that John Olivey's Z1 Patrol arrived back in Athens, the men relishing the ten days' leave they had been promised.

An aerial reconnaissance of Zara harbour, from where the Royal Navy departed to attack German shipping identified by the LRDG shipping watches. (Courtesy of the SAS Regimental Archive)

When the LRDG visited Zara, 200 miles north of Dubrovnik, it bore the scars of heavy fighting. (Courtesy of the SAS Regimental Archive)

On 13 November leave was cancelled because of 'trouble, which was expected from ELAS', and six days later the LRDG were placed under the command of 23rd Armoured Brigade. A short while later they moved their base to Osiphoglion Orphanage, on the main road to Athens, but they rarely ventured out, their presence more symbolic than practical. Tommy Haddon 'witnessed many sordid events, as one does in a civil war', and it was Captain Stuart Manning's job to condense an unpleasant few weeks into a report on Z1 Patrol's stay in Athens.

They were in Athens when the trouble with ELAS started and their jeep patrols rescued police from posts under fire and raided an ELAS headquarters to capture petrol and arms. Several of the party were wounded and had to be evacuated. A Greek National Guard was then being hurriedly formed, and the Rhodesians and their colleagues helped to train them while assisting in maintaining order in Athens and the neighbourhood.[21]

In December ELAS began to consider the British fair game. On the 11th an LRDG truck taking sick men to the 97 General Hospital was ambushed. No one was killed, but one of the LRDG men in the cab was hit in the shoulder. ELAS claimed later it was a case of mistaken identity, they'd thought it was a pro-Royalist vehicle, but later on the same day John Olivey and his driver, Artie Botha, drove into Athens to stock up on supplies. As they turned up a quiet side street, a machine gun opened up from a window above. Botha was shot in the head and Olivey hit as he dragged his wounded driver to cover. The pair were rushed to the 97 General Hospital but Botha died on the operating table. Olivey was evacuated to Italy by air, and doubtless as he left behind Greece the irony wasn't lost on him that he had come through four years of fighting the Germans and Italians with barely a scratch, only to be shot by people who were supposed to be on the same side.

CHAPTER 17

UNTIL THE BITTER END

The LRDG withdrew from Athens at the end of 1944 and returned to their base in Italy. It had been a dispiriting few weeks in the Greek capital, and the Balkans campaign had had its unsavoury moments too. It made the veterans of the North African campaign appreciate the desert and its indigenous people all the more; no politics there, no treachery or deceit from spiteful, small-minded, self-important panjandrums.

Nonetheless, the LRDG wouldn't have swapped roles with any other army unit. They enjoyed their existence and appreciated their life. 'Firstly,' commented David Lloyd Owen, 'we practically never suffered the horror of a heavy barrage, the menace of a bombing raid or the carnage of the infantry run over by tanks. We did not live with constant gunfire, in touch with an enemy a few hundred yards away.'[1] But the real beauty of serving in the LRDG, considered Lloyd Owen, was that one was among like-minded fellows, who chaffed at the pettiness of army routine and sought not medals or glory but adventure. Above all, 'no one depended on us save ourselves. Our failure would reflect on us alone. We could move largely where we wished, and not just in conformity with some wider plan. There was no front line for us, because we were always behind and among the enemy.'[2] Yet by the very nature of their existence, the LRDG sometimes found themselves confronted with dangers no British infantryman would have encountered.

OPPOSITE
The LRDG are forced once more to dig out a vehicle, but on this occasion on the Riete to Aguila Road in Italy, January 1945, it's snow rather than sand causing the problem. (Courtesy of the SAS Regimental Archive)

These two photographs, believed to be somewhere in the Balkans in the winter of 1944/45, show some LRDG men loading an aircraft with one of their jeeps prior to their return to Italy. (Courtesy of the SAS Regimental Archive)

As the war entered its final year, the LRDG were scattered among the Dalmatian Islands, observing enemy troop and shipping movements from well-situated vantage points. One such patrol was situated on Ist, a sparsely populated island just 3¾ miles square that lay 20 miles west of the city of Zadar on the Croatian coast. Codenamed Kickshaw, the 14-man patrol drawn from both Y1 and Y2 was commanded by Sergeant Anthony 'Tich' Cave, one of the very first recruits to Y Patrol exactly four years earlier.

'Life on Ist was pretty good and light-hearted,' remembered Corporal Gilbert Jetley. 'The locals were extremely friendly and their loyalty extended to learning the patriotic song of the Allies.'[3] The men of Y Patrol allowed their mischief to get the better of them one day, tricking the locals into learning the words to 'She'll be Coming Round the Mountain' in the belief it was the British national anthem. They all then stood solemnly to attention, the British saluting the Union Flag while the villagers sang the words of the folk song with due reverence.

On the evening of 10 January, most of the patrol were in their billet playing cards. It was 2115 hours and Cave was about to turn in for the night. Suddenly he heard four shots. Thinking it might be the MFV *La Palma* arriving at the jetty, Cave went outside, but saw no lights in the sea, nor did he notice anything untoward coming from the radio room where he knew Ken Smith, the signaller, and Jock Watson to be. He returned to the billet and went upstairs to bed. Jetley, who was sick in bed with a fever, pieced together subsequent events from the testimony of his comrades. 'Something disturbed Watson and he went to the front door,' recounted Jetley. 'As he opened it, he heard something clank behind it. He saw that it was a large time bomb, which was ticking. There was a booster of extra explosive alongside in a canister.'[4]

Watson dashed across to the billet and knocked on the door of Tich Cave's room. In a voice that was calm but edged with excitement, Watson informed Cave upon entering that there was a bomb outside the radio room. Cave 'at first treated the matter as a jest'. Who would leave a bomb outside the radio room? Watson insisted it wasn't a joke. Cave, noticing the concern in his face, instructed Watson to return to the house and tell Smith to evacuate the radio room. The pair of them gathered up the radio and hurried outside.

'At some point Kenneth Smith must have remembered the family who were asleep in the back-room [of the billet],' recalled Jetley. 'He put down the [radio] equipment, picked up the bomb and made for a piece of waste ground between the house and the village church. Before he could get there, there was a tremendous explosion.'[5]

> *'He put down the [radio] equipment, picked up the bomb and made for a piece of waste ground between the house and the village church. Before he could get there, there was a tremendous explosion.'*
>
> **Gilbert Jetley**

Smith was literally blown to pieces by the power of the bomb, and though one other LRDG man received 37 shrapnel wounds, none of the villagers asleep in the house were hurt. 'Kenneth Smith's valiant deed was not the thoughtless action of the ignorant,' said Jetley. 'The whole patrol knew these time bombs and knew that, in addition to being unreliable if touched, many contained mechanisms to explode them immediately if moved. He was therefore a most gallant soldier who gave his life for his comrades and allies.'[6]

Smith's action in removing the bomb (which had been planted by a party of Ustaše, who had been seen and fired at by some pro-British partisans) earned him a posthumous George Cross, which was presented to his mother by King George VI in 1946. Outside Buckingham Palace she told reporters:

It was just typical of him to do what he did … he was a grand boy and never caused me any trouble. He always wanted to go into the army from a boy, and joined up at the age of 18 for 12 years' service. He was never happier than when he could get his dad to talk about his experiences in the Great War but his dad said: 'My boy, when you have been through what I have you won't be so keen'. But he went all the same.[7]

The LRDG were at a loose end at the start of February 1945. With the Allies unable to break through the Germans' Gothic Line (a 10-mile deep defensive line that ran across the breadth of northern Italy through the natural barrier of the Apennines) before the winter of 1944–45 descended, the LRDG had no role to fulfil in southern Austria and northern Yugoslavia. It was therefore decided to establish a small Combined Operations HQ at Zara, a town on the Croatian coast, 200 miles north of Dubrovnik. Known as the Land Forces Northern Adriatic, it comprised A Squadron LRDG, the SBS and a unit called the Raiding Support Regiment. Zara possessed a good harbour and what remained of the town impressed one of the Rhodesians, Staff Sergeant Stan Andrews: 'The town itself was quite large, with a palace, opera house and banks but the whole area had been heavily bombed,' he recalled. 'One would have to walk through the rubble of buildings and down streets full of bomb craters.' But not everything had been destroyed. 'There were stacks of empty German beer cases around,' said Andrews. 'We actually found quite a few full ones, too.'[8]

Demaine, Hawkins, Young and Lt Cecil Jackson in Zara, Yugoslavia, where the Combined Operations HQ was based in the spring of 1945. (Courtesy of the SAS Regimental Archive)

Reluctantly, David Lloyd Owen had concluded that there was not enough work for both A and B squadrons in the northern Dalmatian Islands, so B Squadron (commanded by Major Stormonth Darling) was withdrawn from the theatre and sent to train in mountain warfare in readiness for operations following the breakout from northern Italy. 'I chose that Squadron because the other one was committed more deeply, and it would have been difficult to extricate it,' explained Lloyd Owen. 'On top of this the Rhodesians knew the Dalmatian coast well and had made many contacts there.'[9]

At this stage of the war, though defeat was inevitable for the Germans, they were still clinging tenaciously to their garrisons on islands such as Pag, Rab, Losinj, Cherso and Krk. Additionally, the Adriatic had been heavily mined, and so the German Navy, sailing at night to avoid Allied air attacks, was able to move freely without fear of molestation from the Royal Navy. During daylight hours the enemy ships were camouflaged 'so that from the air and the sea, covered by bushes and branches stuck into vast nets, they looked part of the landscape'.

The LRDG was asked to help 'in the elimination of this sea traffic', and the first patrol to embark on this task was T1, skippered by Lieutenant Mike Reynolds and comprising ten men. They were landed by the navy on south-east Istria near the mouth of the Arsa Channel (also known as the Arsa Canal, it lies on the east coast of the Istrian peninsula), and were escorted by a partisan to a suitable lying-up area, a clearing that could only be reached by burrowing through deep bush. They erected their two-man Arctic tents and lived in comparative comfort and security,

Istria, near the mouth of the Arsa Channel, was used by the LRDG in the spring of 1945 to keep enemy shipping under surveillance and call up RAF air strikes when necessary. (Courtesy of the SAS Regimental Archive)

free from detection by sea or air, with their most vexing foe − initially, at any rate − the 'hairy caterpillars which set up a very nasty rash if they fell on the body'.[10]

Soon there was a constant flow of messages being radioed from T1 to the base in Zara detailing all the enemy shipping that sailed up and down the Arsa Channel, as well as the boats that were cunningly camouflaged on the coastline. The intelligence kept the RAF busy, and also occupied Reynolds as he strove to note down everything in his diary:

4th March: Hurricanes and bombers get hits on S.S. Italia

5th March: Hurricanes with rockets set fire to tramp and sink 500-ton coaster

6th March: Three Motor Torpedo Boats attack three E-Boats and one tramp. Tramp sunk

7th March: 800-ton vessel damaged and 100-ton lighter sunk by Mustangs and Hurricanes

9th March: 700-ton coaster sunk

10th March: 800-ton vessel sunk. Walked along beach and could see no ships afloat.

Staff Sergeant Major Sandy Bennett poses for Jackson's camera at Zara, Yugoslavia in March 1945. (Courtesy of the SAS Regimental Archive)

ZARA HARBOUR, 1945

ABOVE LEFT
A fishing boat in Zara harbour, May 1945. At times such vessels were used to transport LRDG patrols to remote islands off the Croatian coast. (Courtesy of the SAS Regimental Archive)

ABOVE RIGHT
The Bank of Italy building in Zara, which served as the billet of A Squadron, LRDG, in the spring of 1945. (Courtesy of the SAS Regimental Archive)

LEFT
Captioned 'Homeward Bound', this photograph shows an LRDG patrol returning to Zara after a shipping watch in the spring of 1945. (Courtesy of the SAS Regimental Archive)

13th March: Three [British] Motor Torpedo Boats engaged and damaged 'F' and
'E' Boats as they entered Arsa Channel. On three occasions the Motor
Torpedo Boats drove back enemy vessels trying to leave Arsa.

14th March: Hurricanes sink two E Boats

20th March: Three [British] Motor Torpedo Boats engaged and sunk a schooner

23rd March: Capture spy in our camp and hand him over to the Partisans

26th March: German patrol 100 strong beating bush near our camp.
Uncomfortable. Our watchers over jetty nearly captured.

27th March: Germans still trying to find us.[11]

David Lloyd Owen recalled that 'they were the most thrilling days as each new result was flashed back to us', and they were exciting, too, for the navy and air force tasked with destroying the targets provided by the LRDG. On one such attack an LRDG signaller, Robbie Robinson, was assigned to a RN motor torpedo boat (MTB) to provide direct communication between Reynolds' patrol and the naval commander. Departing from Zara at 1400 hours one afternoon, the flotilla of MTBs 'sheltered amongst the Dalmatian islands off the coast of Istria until dark then moved into Arsa Bay in a V-formation'.[12] On this particular night, no vessels came their way. Disappointed, the vessels returned to their shelter among the islands and spent the day hoping for better luck on the second night. But again no target sailed into view. Their luck changed on the third night, remembered Robinson. 'No sooner had we stopped with engines idling when a call came,' he said. The rear MTB had spotted the dome-shaped conning tower of a midget submarine breaking the surface. 'Immediately Monty [Montgomery, the commander of MTB 1] swung hard to starboard and roared away in a circle behind MTBs 2 and 3, and did as they had done, dropping depth charges on and around where a submarine had just surfaced for a sighting.'[13]

Then, on the far side of the bay, something exploded. Mike Reynolds' signaller came on the radio, demanding to know from Robinson what was going on. He was speaking in Shona, the native language of Rhodesia, a tactic used by the Rhodesian LRDG so that the Germans couldn't intercept their wireless communications. Robinson replied in like fashion, reporting that it was a torpedo fired from a submarine that had missed the three MTBs and exploded against the coastline. The MTBs then circled the bay, dropping more depth charges and a short while later 'debris appeared on the surface'.★

★ Commander Montgomery wrote in his log that 'midget thought sunk'. It was probably a Biber (German for 'beaver') submarine, which were 9 metres in length, crewed by one man and armed with two torpedoes.

While the three MTBs headed back to the security of their base in Zara, for Reynolds and his patrol each day brought more pressure and the possibility they might be found by the Germans. The spy who wandered into their camp was one of several employed by the Germans, and when they failed to deliver the British, the enemy sent in dogs. The last resort was to set fire to stretches of scrubland in the hope of flushing out their prey, but that too failed. All the while the locals supplied the LRDG patrol with eggs, milk and bread, did their laundry, and on one occasion sent a barber in the dead of night to give the men's hair a trim. Such co-operation was welcomed by Reynolds, but at the same time there was always in the back of his mind the worry that the more locals who knew of their presence, the greater the chances of betrayal.

At the start of April, two members of the LRDG patrol, Alf Page, a 20-year-old Rhodesian, and Len Poole, known as 'Zulu', left the camp to carry out a reconnaissance of the Arsa coal jetty from a hilltop. Their position was visible from the LRDG camp, and shortly after first light the following morning Reynolds watched in alarm as a fleet of German trucks arrived at the foot of the hill. Page and Poole had just crawled out of their sleeping bags and were now tucking into a breakfast of bully beef, oatmeal slab and compo tea, blissfully unaware of what their commanding officer could see. Through the dawn mist on top of the hill they watched two women approach, one of whom Poole recognized as Tosca, a 'young, short, jovial girl of about sixteen'. It was the older woman, whoever, who had a look of panic in her eyes. 'Tedesci, Tedesci!' she cried, the word both Poole and Page took to mean 'German'.

'We were told that an informer had given our presence away to the Germans who were mounting a hunt to catch us,' recalled Poole.[14] He and Page had a brief discussion and decided to remain where they were for the moment, 'until the threat became more defined'. Additionally, it was nearly 0700 hours, and they were scheduled to contact Mike Reynolds on the radio at that hour. Nonetheless, the pair arranged 'to meet Tosca at a point halfway to a farm house occupied by partisan sympathisers if we were forced to clear out'.

Poole was unable to raise Reynolds on the radio at the appointed hour, another source of concern on a morning when everything appeared to be going wrong. Tosca returned at 0730 hours to warn them that the area 'was alive with German troops'. The pair decided it would be prudent to pack up and get ready to move at a moment's notice, and once done they began their observation of the harbour now that the mist around their position had cleared. Page fixed the harbour with his binoculars, and, seeing nothing of interest began scanning the countryside. He started, and then whispered to Poole: 'I can see three Germans and you won't need glasses to see them.'

Poole followed the gaze of his comrade, and observed 'an extended search party coming up one side of our hill with other parties swinging in to complete the circle over the summit of the ridge connecting us to other high ground'.

The pair 'moved pretty smartly', running at a crouch out of the view of the approaching enemy and towards the farm halfway down the hillside. Tosca was waiting for them, as insouciant as ever, and she took Page into her care while another young woman, Amelia, beckoned to Poole. '[She] led me into a stone barn and across to a corner where I helped her move several stones at the junction of wall and floor,' he recalled. Underneath was a recess in the floor large enough to fit Poole and a partisan who had climbed in a few minutes earlier. Amelia and her mother and father rearranged the stones and waited for the inevitable arrival of the Germans. From his hiding place, Poole heard the Germans burst into the farmhouse, heard, too, their boots clatter over the cobbles into the stone barn and heard the barks of the officers in charge as they searched the building. 'What I found amusing was the fact the Germans looking for us took turns taking drinks from the water barrel in the barn,' said Poole.[15]

The Yugoslav partisans in Istria were helpful but in general the LRDG regarded their irregular allies with dislike and distrust. (Courtesy of the SAS Regimental Archive)

By mid-afternoon, Poole deemed it safe enough to emerge from his hiding place and a couple of hours later he was reunited with Alf Page, who told his comrade about his adventure. He had been taken by Tosca to the house of the village mayor, who'd gone into hiding several days earlier. The mayor had built a small room at the bottom of a dry well in his garden, and covered the well with a roof of earth and shrubbery. Page and the mayor spent the day playing cards at the bottom of the well until collected by Tosca. The two LRDG men held a council of war with the partisans and agreed that it was safe to return to their original observation post on the hilltop. It would soon be 1900 hours, the time of the evening radio schedule, and Poole was anxious to have news from Reynolds, having failed to make contact 12 hours earlier. They reached the OP without incident and Poole called up the patrol on his radio. 'I did so again and again without result and was preparing to close down when a reply came surging through the earphones,' he recounted. It was a brief message from Reynolds: 'Come back at once to the patrol and bring the radio. The Germans have been walking all around us and we dare not put up the radio aerial. The hunt parties have moved away.'[16]

Just as Poole and Page prepared to return to the camp, the wife of one of the partisans appeared on the hilltop with her two children in tow. She also brought some alarming news. German trucks were on their way to conduct another search. It was decided that the partisan, his wife and children would take the two soldiers to their house in another village. 'I'll never forget that walk,' recalled Poole. 'The four adults walked together through the village streets while the two children, Aurelio (about 12) and his little sister, about nine, skipped and ran laughing and shouting as they darted down side lanes and the road ahead. In their singing they were reporting on whatever other traffic there was about. What a grim game for two young kids.'[17] They rested briefly in the family's house, long enough for a cup of coffee and a cigarette, and then the pair moved off alone, skirting the village of Porto Carnizza and finally reaching the main camp by crawling through the thick bush.

The Germans kept hunting the spies in their midst and the LRDG kept sending their reports. On 7 April a 200-ton vessel and 100-foot barge were sunk by RAF Hurricanes, and two days later the aircraft returned and attacked another barge. On 11 April the Germans, by now at the end of their tether, mortared the headland in which, somewhere, the British were concealed. To no effect. Ultimately, what brought the LRDG reconnaissance to an end wasn't the Germans, but the partisans.

On 13 April Reynolds wrote in his diary: 'We are tricked by Partisans and placed under arrest.' The day had started routinely, with the arrival of eight partisans in mid-morning for a spot of 'elevenses' and a confab about what the rest of the day held. Without warning, the partisans raised their weapons at the LRDG and Reynolds had no choice but to comply with their instructions to lay down their arms. Fortunately, the partisans didn't spot the LRDG wireless operator, who had set up his post a little way off from the main camp. Observing events, he had the time to transmit a quick radio message to their HQ describing the partisans' action.

Alf Page had seen the situation grow tenser in Yugoslavia in the preceding month as the Germans began to withdraw and the various factions in the country began positioning themselves for a power grab. Marshal Josef Tito, head of the communist partisans, knew the strategic value of the Istrian peninsula and he feared that the British might try and secure it for themselves in the final weeks of the war. 'With the Germans seemingly on the run they were willing to accept only nominal Allied assistance,' he recalled.

An RAF rocket attack on the Slovenian town of Idrija that was called up by the LRDG. (Courtesy of the SAS Regimental Archive)

The partisans would issue 'passes' giving approval [to the LRDG] to operate in a given area for a set time. Their justification for detaining the LRDG members was that their passes had expired. It was ironic as many times I would go with an MI5 officer to pick up bags of gold which were used to pay the partisans with, there were no issues with passes on these missions.[18]

A furious David Lloyd Owen pursued the matter up the partisans' chain of command, and on 16 April Reynolds had his radio returned and was told a partisan vessel would take him and his men back to Italy. Reynolds immediately contacted Lloyd Owen and requested he organize their collection, because 'I would prefer to be picked up by the Navy rather than be shanghaied by these garlic-eating bandits'.[19]

Reynolds was awarded a Military Cross for his role in what had been a very fruitful operation. The citation ran as follows:

At great risk valuable intelligence relating to coastal and other defences was collected, and quick action by Reynolds resulted in at least five medium-sized enemy vessels being bombed and sunk. At the same time he provided the Royal Navy with quick and valuable information about the movement of enemy

The Venetian Gate in Zadar with the Lion of Saint Mark, a symbol of the Republic of Venice, above it. (Courtesy of the SAS Regimental Archive)

shipping and the laying of minefields ... in this, as in previous operations, Reynolds showed complete disregard for his personal safety in the execution of the tasks entrusted to him. His courage, determination, initiative and leadership were at all times an inspiration to his own and to other patrols.[20]

The treatment of Reynolds resulted in Lloyd Owen's decision – taken after much discussion with Allied Force Headquarters – to withdraw all LRDG and SBS patrols from Istria. On 21 April he sent a signal from Zara to the LRDG base in Rodi, in which he 'recommended the withdrawal of everyone except [Stan] Eastwood and [John] Olivey. The latter [was] playing idiot boy with great success and undoubted charm'. In fact Eastwood withdrew with the rest of the British special forces a few days later, leaving only John Olivey and his patrol in Istria, who had been warned to be on their guard against the partisans' duplicity.

Olivey didn't have long to wait until the partisans arrived to detain them. He complied with all their demands but insisted the partisans carry not just the LRDG weapons, but also their rucksacks during their hike to the partisan HQ. Once there, Olivey and his patrol were handed back their weapons after the intervention of a political commissar.

Olivey's patrol continued with their road watch north of Fiume, observing an adversary in its death throes. 'I remember seeing the retreating Jerries and what a pitiful sight they were too,' recalled Alf Page, who had joined the patrol. On 3 May the Germans were heading north in droves. Olivey reported 'head-to-tail as far as the eye could see were horses and carts, the enemy having strong flank guards of infantry and artillery. This went on all day through much snow that fell at intervals.'[21] On 4 May Olivey considered it safe enough to radio in a resupply by air, and two days later a mouth-watering array of delicacies floated down from the sky on the end of white canopies: tea, sugar, milk, chocolate and several bottles of whisky. 'We gave the food to the partisans and their thanks was to disarm us and lock us up in a machine shop in a village down the mountain,' said Alf Page, who recalled that Olivey, denied access to a lavatory by the guard, 'peed on his candle!'[22]

Olivey was now at his wits' end, but so, fortunately, was the European war. In the early hours of 7 May at SHAEF (Supreme Headquarters Allied Expeditionary Force) headquarters in France, General Alfred Jodl, the chief of staff of the German Armed Forces High Command, surrendered unconditionally. The document he signed authorized 'All forces under German control to cease active operations at 2301 hours Central European Time on May 8, 1945'. On 9 May Olivey and his patrol were brought before the local partisan commander, 'who released them with many apologies and much wine'.

The war was over in Europe, but the conflict in the Pacific still raged, and David Lloyd Owen believed that the LRDG would be deployed to the Far East to help in the fight against the Japanese. Since July 1944 he had 'been trying to get the authorities interested' in deploying the unit to that theatre, compiling a series of papers that were well received from Combined Operations in London. But to Lloyd Owen's immense frustration none of his recommendations were acted upon. He had even flown to London in March 1945 to put his case in person to the Combined Operations, informing them that SEAC (South East Asia Command) had asked for the unit in November. Allied Forces Headquarters (AFHQ) in the Mediterranean had turned down the request, however, refusing on the grounds that the LRDG were required in their sphere of operations. Lloyd Owen returned to the LRDG from London no nearer to knowing if the unit would be sent to the Far East at the conclusion of the European war. He continued to press Combined Operations for an answer, but it was not until 19 May that AFHQ finally discussed the future of the LRDG. The result of the conference looked encouraging for Lloyd Owen, and on 25 May he told the 300 LRDG personnel who had volunteered for deployment to the Far East that the War Office was studying a proposal to transfer the unit.

A group of LRDG soldiers celebrate VE Day with a dip in the Adriatic. (Courtesy of the SAS Regimental Archive)

Staff Sergeant Stan Andrews, a popular member of the Rhodesian Patrol, celebrates VE Day. (Courtesy of the SAS Regimental Archive)

Two members of the LRDG in Italy, May 1945, when many expected to be posted to the Far East only to be informed that the unit was to be disbanded. (Courtesy of the SAS Regimental Archive)

Three weeks later, on 16 June, Lloyd Owen learned from AFHQ that 'the War Office had definitely asked for us … to regroup and have some leave before going on to Asia'.

Within a week, however, the War Office reneged on its promise and it was Lloyd Owen's gloomy duty to inform the men that the Long Range Desert Group was to be disbanded. The news devastated Lloyd Owen, who had invested so much of himself, physically, spiritually and emotionally, in the unit over the preceding four years. Suffering the understandable pangs of self-pity, he wrote a plaintive letter to Field Marshal the Hon Sir Harold Alexander bemoaning their disbandment of the LRDG. The reply came on 26 June:

Dear Lloyd Owen

The news of the war office decision to disband the Long Range Desert Group must have come to you as a great shock – as it did to me. Long before I first went to the Middle East I had heard of the exploits of the LRDG in your original hunting grounds in Tripolitania and Cyrenaica, and it was with great pride that I first took you under my command in August 1942.

Since then you have continued your fine work with undiminished skill and enthusiasm and it is indeed with great reluctance that I say farewell and good luck to you all.[23]

This photo, taken in Istria in April 1945, is captioned: 'After 1st night's march'. (Courtesy of the SAS Regimental Archive)

It was a noble tribute from the field marshal, a crumb of comfort for Lloyd Owen during the six melancholic weeks it took him and his faithful adjutant, Captain Leo Capel, to disband the unit and organize the transportation home of men, paperwork and equipment. 'By the 1st of August, 1945, no more of anything remained,' reflected Lloyd Owen, 'only the vivid, wild and happy memories.'

The British LRDG headed north, the Rhodesians south, the air full of promises to keep in touch. The Rhodesians sailed on a troopship to Alexandria, and then on to Cairo, where they disembarked. They would make the final stage of their journey home by air, but until flights could be arranged they were billeted back where it had all started, in the Citadel, and the bed bugs were as bad as ever.

One of the first acts of the Long Range Desert Group on learning of its disbandment was to form an Association. An inaugural newsletter soon followed, a brief affair, admittedly, just two typed pages of A4 in which it was boasted that membership of the LRDG Association was already running at 381. It was hoped, stated the newsletter, that an annual dinner would be held, but the first wouldn't take place 'until possibly 1947 at the earliest'. With that in mind, 'until then the only link will be the News Letter or private correspondence. The question in point is this: we have started well … it is is up to us to keep our interest in the Association alive until such time as we can really get together and from then on there is no telling what further history may be made'.[24]

In fact, the editor of that newsletter had under-estimated the determination of the LRDG Association. The inaugural Annual Dinner was held on Saturday 13 July 1946 at the Connaught Rooms in central London, and 80 members were present. Apologies came from Brigadier Guy Prendergast and Lieutenant Colonel David Lloyd Owen, and particularly Brigadier Ralph Bagnold, 'who at the last minute was prevented from attending'. Nonetheless, there were plenty of men who were able to show their support in person. Gordon Broderick, who had been on Leros with John Olivey's patrol, was one, as was Spud Murphy, released after nearly a year in a POW camp. David Skipworth and Fred Leach were also able to regale their dining guests about life as a prisoner, while Bill Kennedy Shaw, Michael Crichton-Stuart and Richard 'Doc' Lawson were three of the officers from the days in the desert.

The 1946 Newsletter, by now a much more impressively designed journal with professional typesetting and binding, reported on the dinner, commenting: 'After the meeting and the speeches, members got down to the real business of the reunion – quaffing beer.'

EPILOGUE

By the time of the inaugural LRDG dinner in 1946, the unit had been disbanded for nearly a year, as had the Special Air Service and Special Boat Squadron. There had been an attempt by Brigadier Michael Calvert, commander of the SAS Brigade, to convince the powers that be to retain at least some kind of special force in the uncertain world they now faced. On 12 October 1945, Calvert sent a memo entitled 'Future of SAS Troops' to the 12 most senior officers of the three defunct units, including David Lloyd Owen and Guy Prendergast. Calvert had been instructed by the War Office to 'investigate all the operations of the Special Air Service with a view to giving recommendations for the future of SAS in the next war and its composition in the peace-time army'.[1] Calvert, who had made his name as a guerrilla fighter *par excellence* while serving with the Chindits in Burma, believed unequivocally that the special forces were now more important than ever. 'We all have the future of SAS at heart,' Calvert wrote in the memo, 'not merely because we wish to see its particular survival as a unit but because we have believed in the principles of its method of operations.' Therefore he asked the 12 recipients of the memo to co-operate fully with Major General Rowell, the Director of Tactical Investigation [DTI], and emphasize why special forces should be maintained. In particular, Calvert wanted the men to have answers to the following concerns of the War Office: 'Volunteer units skim the regular units of their best officers and men', 'Expense per man is greater than any other formation and is not worthwhile', and 'Any normal battalion could do the same job'. But despite Calvert's best efforts, the Director of Tactical Investigation concluded that Britain no longer required its special forces. The Soviet Union had yet to emerge as the threat it would become, while the British Empire had yet to fragment under the strain of countries clamouring for independence, either through diplomacy or violence.

OPPOSITE
The LRDG signal section, who performed sterling work for the unit, pose for the camera at Casa Rosa on 3 July 1945, shortly before they were disbanded. (Courtesy of the SAS Regimental Archive)

BELOW
An LRDG soldier writes home in the days after the Armistice. Many of the men hadn't seen their homelands for years. (Courtesy of the SAS Regimental Archive)

Though the Special Air Service was resurrected in the summer of 1947 as a result of a rethink by the Director of Tactical Investigation (of the first 200 recruits 59 had fought with the SAS in the war), the Long Range Desert Group was not. Nonetheless, the LRDG veterans regarded the SAS as their kith and kin, taking pride in their exploits in subsequent years. 'What a wonderful operation that was by the SAS!' commented the LRDG Association magazine in 1980, referring to the recent ending of the Iranian Embassy siege in London. 'I am sure all LRDG men would like to congratulate the SAS on showing the world how to deal with terrorists and demonstrating that the old magic is still there.'

Twenty years later, the LRDG Association met for the final time in London in October 2000. It was a good turnout, and those veterans unable to attend for whatever reasons sent their best wishes by letter. There was one message which

HMS *Colombo* leaving Zara harbour in May 1945 with its work attacking German shipping in the Arsa Channel at an end. (Courtesy of the SAS Regimental Archive)

Stan Eastwood finds a shady spot to enjoy his lunch on the Hon to Misurata road. (Courtesy of the SAS Regimental Archive)

aroused particular pride, a telegram read to the veterans and their families by Jim Patch, for 24 years the secretary of the LRDG Association. It was from Elizabeth R:

> I have received with much pleasure the message of loyalty and goodwill from the LRDG Association, meeting today at your final reunion. Your Association has since its foundation kept alive the memories of those who served with such courage and distinction in the LRDG during the last war. I send my warmest good wishes to you all as you gather together for the last time and wish to express my confidence that the remarkable exploits of the LRDG will never be forgotten.[2]

In December 2013, a memorial to the Long Range Desert Group was dedicated in the west cloister of Westminster Abbey, alongside similar monuments commemorating officers and men of the Submarine Service of the Royal Navy, the Commandos, and all ranks of the airborne forces and Special Air Service. Then, in October of the following year, another memorial was unveiled, this time in Doune, Scotland, in the shadow of David Stirling's statue. The SAS Regimental Association, who since 2000 have looked after the welfare of the LRDG veterans, organized the tribute that comprises a main recumbent stone and two flanking stones. The recumbent stone of Scottish whin evokes the desert, with lines cut to suggest LRDG vehicle tracks. The first flanking stone is engraved with the names of the LRDG's fallen and the second bears the inscription to the LRDG, with the words underneath, 'They Showed the Way'. As the SAS regimental website explains: 'This refers to the LRDG's provenance and their vital role as advance forces to the Eighth Army and British forces deployed in the Western Desert. It also refers to the part they played in the early days of the SAS, a part that enabled the SAS quickly to become established and to go on to become what it is today.'

Present at the dedication of the memorial in October 2014 were three men who had loyally served the Long Range Desert Group nearly three-quarters of a century earlier: Stuart 'Lofty' Carr, Jim Patch and Mike Sadler, a member of the Rhodesian Patrol who later transferred to the SAS. 'It was a wonderful occasion,' reflected Carr, who made the trip to Scotland from his home in the north-west of England. 'I met many relatives of men I'd served with, some of whom, like Jake Easonsmith, never returned home. It was pleasing to be able to pass on what anecdotes I could remember about their fathers and grandfathers.'[3]

As well as Easonsmith, another LRDG officer of Carr's acquaintance who fell in the war was Anthony Hunter, killed in action in February 1945 in Holland while serving with the Royal Scots Fusiliers. Of the others:

A group of LRDG veterans gather in London in 1958 for the premiere of the film, *Sea of Sand*, loosely based on the unit's exploits, which starred Dickie Attenborough. (Courtesy of the SAS Regimental Archive)

Ralph Bagnold: Retiring from the army in 1944 with the honorary rank of brigadier and an OBE for having formed the LRDG, Bagnold married a year after the war and for the rest of his life devoted himself to his scientific studies. He wrote many papers and received many awards, including an invitation in 1977 to give the keynote address at a NASA conference on the desert landscapes of Earth and Mars, drawing on his experiences in North Africa. He died in 1990 aged 94.

Pat Clayton: Spent the rest of the war in a POW camp and later remained in the army until retirement in 1953. He died in 1962 aged 65.

Michael Crichton-Stuart: Returned to the Scots Guard and was awarded a Military Cross in 1943. After the war he held a number of civic appointments and died in 1981.

Martin Gibbs: After leaving the LRDG in 1941 he served throughout the rest of the Desert War with the Guards and was captured at Tobruk in 1942. Later served as High Sheriff for Wiltshire and died in 1994 aged 78.

Richard Lawson: Resumed his medical practice after the war and kept close contacts with the LRDG Association. In the 1980s he returned to Leros to lay flowers at the grave of Jake Easonsmith. 'Doc' Lawson died in 2005 aged 91.

Bill Kennedy Shaw: His service with the LRDG ended in 1943 with victory in North Africa. He spent a further year in Tripolitania with the British Military Administration as an advisor to Arab Affairs. He returned to England in 1944 and wrote the first account of the unit in 1945. He continued to work for the civil service in various capacities and died in 1979 aged 77.

Guy Prendergast: Led a quiet life after the war on his estate in Scotland, close to Loch Ness. The father of five children, Prendergast was a devout Catholic after the war who attended mass every day. He died in 1986 aged 81 and in his obituary in the LRDG journal, David Lloyd Owen wrote: 'We admired his total dedication to the unit, his tenacity of purpose and his resolve never to send a patrol on any operational task unless there was a reasonable chance of it returning safely to base.'

Teddy Mitford: Left the LRDG to command 3 Royal Tank Regiment and remained in the army after the war, retiring in 1966. His last years were spent overseeing the 4,000-acre family estate. Married twice, but with no children, Mitford sold the estate in 1993 and died in 2002 aged 93.

Crosby 'Bing' Morris: Summoned back to the NZ Division in 1943, Morris became the chief instructor at NZ AFV School in

The LRDG Association held annual reunions, like this one advertised in 1968, until 2000 when it was wound down due to dwindling numbers. (Courtesy of the SAS Regimental Archive)

Waiouru. After the war he became a branch manager and he died in 1974. His granddaughter played hockey for New Zealand in two Olympic Games.

Alastair Timpson: Awarded an MC for his work with the LRDG in 1942, Timpson returned to the Scots Guards in 1943 and served them with distinction for the rest of the war, being wounded twice and twice receiving a mention in despatches. He became a stockbroker in later life and died in 1998 aged 82.

John Olivey: Returned home to his farm in Melsetter, south-eastern Rhodesia, and over the next few years fathered five children, including twin sons and daughters. He died in 1968 at the age of 62.

Nick Wilder: Left the army with the rank of lieutenant colonel and a DSO for his leadership during the Barce raid. Wilder returned to his 1600-acre farm at Waipukurau and died in 1970 aged 56.

Jack Davis: On his release from a POW camp he returned to New Zealand and died in Christchuch in 1988.

Jim Patch: Having been captured at Levitha, he and Ron Hill escaped from the train taking them to Germany and spent a year living with Bulgarian partisans. After the war he worked for the Post Office and for more than two decades was the secretary of the LRDG Association. He lives in the south of England.

Len Poole: Died in 2000 in Zimbabwe, having worked at a power station before starting his own business.

Spud Murphy: Spent the last year of the war as a prisoner of the Germans. He suffered from poor health in his declining years and died in 1980.

Frank Jopling: Captured during the Barce raid, Jopling spent the rest of the war as a POW. He died in New Zealand in 1987.

Edward Stutterd: One of the nine men who marched more than 200 miles to Allied lines in January 1942, he returned to New Zealand at the end of the war and died aged 58 in 1967. His gravestone says simply: 'E. C. Stutterd. Long Range Desert Group.'

Stanley Eastwood: Returned to Rhodesia to farm and entered politics, standing unsuccessfully for election in the 1978 Zimbabwe-Rhodesia general election. He died in the 1980s.

Lofty Carr: Worked in insurance for many years before deciding on a change of direction in the late 1960s. He retrained as an art teacher and finished his working life as head of the art department in a school in the north-west of England, where he still lives. 'We were regarded as an undisciplined and wild rabble,' he reflected in 2014. 'Anyone who didn't fit in, didn't meet the LRDG etiquette, was gone. For those of us who did serve in the unit, it was a privilege. The camaraderie was magnificent, it was a family.'

OPPOSITE
The LRDG's existence may have been short-lived but as Field Marshal The Hon Sir Harold Alexander said of them in 1945 they did much "fine work with undiminished skill and enthusiasm". (Courtesy of the SAS Regimental Archive)

NOTES

Introduction

1. John W. Gordon, *The Other Desert War: British Special Forces in North Africa, 1940–1943* (Praeger, 1987).
2. Bagnold's private papers, Churchill College Archives, Cambridge.

Chapter 1

1. 'A Lost World Refound', *Scientific American*, November 1939.
2. Bagnold's private papers.

Chapter 2

1. 'Destruction of an Army: The First Campaign in Libya' (Ministry of Information, 1941).
2. Bagnold's private papers.
3. Ibid.
4. Ibid.
5. Ibid.
6. 'Destruction of an Army'.
7. Bagnold, letter to the 1986 issue of the LRDG newsletter.
8. Kennedy Shaw obituary, LRDG newsletter, 1980.
9. Bill Kennedy Shaw, *Long Range Desert Group* (Collins, 1945).
10. Edward Mitford interview, Imperial War Museum, catalogue number: 29599.
11. Memoirs of Tim Heywood, LRDG newsletter, 1975.
12. David Lloyd Owen, *The Desert my Dwelling Place* (Cassell, 1957).
13. Kennedy Shaw, *Long Range Desert Group*.
14. Ibid.
15. Bagnold's private papers.
16. Ibid.
17. Ibid.
18. Kennedy Shaw, *Long Range Desert Group*.

19. Long Range Desert Group war diary, SAS Regimental Association Archives.
20. Bagnold's private papers.

Chapter 3

1. Kennedy Shaw, *Long Range Desert Group*.
2. The unpublished diary of Trooper Frank Jopling, SAS Regimental Association Archives.
3. Ibid.
4. Ibid.
5. Kennedy Shaw, *Long Range Desert Group*.
6. Ibid.
7. Edward Mitford interview, Imperial War Museum, catalogue number: 29599..
8. Jopling, diary.
9. Interview with Leslie Sullivan, Imperial War Museum sound archive, catalogue number: 30098.
10. Jopling, diary.
11. Bagnold's private papers.

Chapter 4

1. Jopling, diary.
2. Ibid.
3. Ibid.
4. Kennedy Shaw, *Long Range Desert Group*.

Chapter 5

1. Captain Michael Crichton-Stuart, *The Fezzan Operation* (1940), contained in the LRDG war diary and also reproduced in *Special Forces in the Desert War 1940–1943* (Public Record Office Publications, 2001).
2. Ibid.
3. Kennedy Shaw, *Long Range Desert Group*.
4. Jopling, diary.
5. Crichton-Stuart, *The Fezzan Operation*.
6. Kennedy Shaw, *Long Range Desert Group*.
7. Ibid.
8. Crichton-Stuart, *The Fezzan Operation*.
9. Kennedy Shaw, *Long Range Desert Group*.
10. Jopling, diary.
11. Ibid.

12. Ibid.

13. Ibid.

14. Crichton-Stuart, *The Fezzan Operation*.

15. Clayton, letter to his sister-in-law, 10 February 1941: republished in the 1967 edition of the LRDG newsletter.

16. Ibid.

Chapter 6

1. Lofty Carr, author interview, conducted between February and October 2014.

2. Ron Hill, unpublished war memoirs, SAS Regimental Archives.

3. Ibid.

4. Ibid.

5. 'Destruction of an Army'.

6. Michael Crichton-Stuart, *G Patrol* (William Kimber, 1958).

7. 'Some Points on Conduct When Meeting the Arabs in the Desert', Proclamation No. 1 of 1941, (Public Record Offices, WO201/809).

8. Ibid.

9. Guy Prendergast, 'History of the WACOS', LRDG newsletter (1986).

10. Ibid.

11. Ibid.

12. Alistair Timpson, *In Rommel's Backyard* (Pen & Sword, 2010).

13. Crichton-Stuart, *G Patrol*.

14. Carr, author interview.

15. Crichton-Stuart, *G Patrol*.

16. Carr, author interview.

17. An account of this operation by Crichton-Stuart is contained in *Special Forces in the Desert War 1940–43* (PRO Publications, 2001).

18. Ibid.

19. Ibid.

20. Ibid.

21. A copy of this article in the *Geographical Magazine*, volume 22 (1944) is housed in the SAS Regimental Archive.

22. Private papers of Dr Richard Lawson, contained within the private Papers of David Lloyd Owen, Imperial War Museum, collection number: 15623.

Chapter 7

1. *The Rommel Papers*, edited by Basil Liddell-Hart (DaCapo Press, 1982).

2. Crichton-Stuart, *G Patrol*.

3. LRDG war diary.

4. Crichton-Stuart, *G Patrol*.

Chapter 8

1. *Rommel Papers*, edited by Liddell-Hart.

2. Ibid.

3. Carr, author interview.

4. A copy of *Tracks* is housed in the SAS Regimental Archive.

5. Alexander Stewart, IWM Sound Archive, catalogue: 13127.

6. Spencer Seadon, IWM Sound Archive, catalogue: 19044.

7. Bill Smudger Smith, LRDG newsletter (1991).

8. Series of articles in the *Dundee Courier & Advertiser* (October 1970) entitled 'Dick Turpins of the Desert'.

9. Lloyd Owen, *The Desert my Dwelling Place*.

10. Jim Patch, author interview, March 2014.

11. Bagnold papers.

12. Minutes of a conference contained in the LRDG war diary.

Chapter 9

1. Lloyd Owen, *The Desert my Dwelling Place*.

2. Timpson, *In Rommel's Backyard*.

3. Kennedy Shaw, *Long Range Desert Group*.

4. Lloyd Owen, *The Desert my Dwelling Place*.

5. A copy of Mayne's report is reproduced in Hamish Ross, *Paddy Mayne* (Sutton Publishing, 2003).

6. Ibid.

7. David Lloyd Owen, *Providence Their Guide* (Pen & Sword, 2001).

8. Lofty Carr's report is contained in the LRDG war diary.

9. Ibid.

10. Ibid.

11. An account of Morris's operational report is reproduced in Kennedy Shaw, *Long Range Desert Group*.

12. Ibid.

13. Ibid.

14. Ibid.

15. Ibid.

16. Ibid.

17. Ibid.

18. Ibid.

19. Ibid.

20. Private papers of Dr Richard Lawson.

21. Kennedy Shaw, *Long Range Desert Group*.

Chapter 10

1. *Rommel Papers*, edited by Liddell-Hart.

2. Quoted in Lloyd Owen, *Providence Their Guide*.

3. LRDG war diary.

4. Timpson, *In Rommel's Backyard*.

5. Ibid.

6. Ibid.

7. Ibid.

8. Ibid.

9. Private papers of Dr Richard Lawson.

10. Ibid.

11. Ibid.

12. Ibid.

13. Ibid.

14. Ibid.

15. Ibid.

16. Kennedy Shaw, *Long Range Desert Group*.

17. Ibid.

18. *Special Forces in the Desert War*.

19. Timpson, *In Rommel's Backyard*.

20. Lloyd Owen, *Providence Their Guide*.

21. Malcolm James, *Born of the Desert* (Greenhill Books, 1991).

22. Ibid.

23. Ibid.

24. Gavin Mortimer, *The SAS in WW2* (Osprey Publishing).

25. Timpson, *In Rommel's Backyard*.

26. John Hackett IWM Sound Archive, catalogue number: 12022.

27. Timpson, *In Rommel's Backyard*.

28. Richard Dimbleby, *The Frontiers Are Green* (Hodder & Stoughton, 1943).

29. Timpson's speech was broadcast on the BBC on 29 July 1942.

30. Ibid.

Chapter 11

1. Lloyd Owen, *Providence Their Guide*.
2. Mortimer, *SAS in WW2*.
3. Jim Patch interview, IWM museum, catalogue number: 9961.
4. Timpson, *In Rommel's Backyard*.
5. LRDG newsletter, 1986.
6. Arthur Biddle's account of the Barce raid was in an unidentified newspaper clipping contained among the papers of Henry Horton, ex-LRDG, which were kindly donated to me by his daughter, Barbara Atherton, in 2014.
7. 'Against Impossible Odds', *Parade* magazine (1 May 1943).
8. Arthur Biddle's account.
9. 'Against Impossible Odds'.
10. Ibid.
11. Arthur Biddle's account.
12. Kennedy Shaw, *Long Range Desert Group*.
13. LRDG war diary.
14. Ibid.
15. 'Against Impossible Odds'.
16. Ibid.
17. Lloyd Owen, *The Desert my Dwelling Place*.
18. *Rommel Papers*, edited by Liddell-Hart.

Chapter 12

1. Mortimer, *The SAS in WW2*.
2. John Hackett, IWM Sound Archive, catalogue number: 12022.
3. Lance Corporal Jack Davis's journal, SAS Archives.
4. Ibid.
5. Ibid.
6. Ibid.
7. Lawson Papers, IWM.
8. Ibid.
9. Private papers of David Lloyd Owen.
10. Lance Corporal Jack Davis's journal.

Chapter 13

1. Ron Hill, memoirs.
2. Richard Lawson, 'All Change', LRDG newsletter, 1982.
3. Ron Hill, memoirs.

4. Lawson, 'All Change'.
5. Gavin Mortimer, *The Men Who Made the SAS* (Constable, 2015).
6. Ibid.
7. Ron Hill, memoirs.
8. Jim Patch, author interview.
9. Ibid.
10. Peter C. Smith, *War in the Aegean* (Stackpole Books, 2008).
11. Ibid.
12. Ibid.
13. Operation report, LRDG war diary.
14. Ibid.
15. Ibid.
16. Ibid.
17. Ibid.

Chapter 14

1. David Sutherland, *He Who Dares* (Leo Cooper, 1998).
2. Jonathan Pittaway, *Long Range Desert Group* (Les Martens, 2006).
3. Ibid.
4. Ibid.
5. Gavin Mortimer, *The History of the Special Boat Squadron in WW2* (Osprey, 2013).
6. Pittaway, *Long Range Desert Group*.
7. Ibid.
8. John Olivey, unpublished memoirs, SAS Regimental Association archives.
9. Pittaway, *Long Range Desert Group*.
10. Olivey, memoirs.
11. Pittaway, *Long Range Desert Group*.
12. Ron Cryer, LRDG newsletter.
13. Pittaway, *Long Range Desert Group*.
14. Ibid.
15. Smith, *War in the Aegean*.
16. Guy Prendergast's operation report, SAS archives.
17. Ibid.
18. Ibid.
19. Ibid.
20. Mortimer, *History of the Special Boat Squadron*.
21. Richard Lawson's account appears in the LRDG newsletter (1979).

22. Ibid.

23. Ibid.

24. Ibid.

25. Guy Prendergast's operation report.

26. Ibid.

27. Ibid.

28. Ibid.

Chapter 15

1. Jim Patch, author interview.

2. Ron Hill, memoirs.

3. *Special Forces in the Desert War* (PRO Publications, 2001).

4. Captain C. S. Manning, *The Rhodesian Squadron with the LRDG* (South African Public Relations, 1945).

5. Pittaway, *Long Range Desert Group*.

6. Ibid.

7. Ibid.

8. Manning, *Rhodesian Squadron*.

9. LRDG war diary.

10. Manning, *Rhodesian Squadron*.

11. Ibid.

12. Murphy's wartime diary, published in LRDG newsletter, 1980.

13. Ibid.

14. Ibid.

15. Ibid.

16. Ibid.

17. Ibid.

18. Ibid.

19. Ibid.

Chapter 16

1. Manning, *Rhodesian Squadron*.

2. Lloyd Owen, *Providence My Guide*.

3. Ibid.

4. Ibid.

5. Ibid.

6. Ibid.

7. Manning, *Rhodesian Squadron*.

8. Fred Leach's account of the raid appears in the LRDG newsletter, 1996.

9. Ibid.

10. Mortimer, *SBS in WW2*.

11. Ibid.

12. Ibid.

13. Ibid.

14. Leach's account.

15. Manning, *Rhodesian Squadron*.

16. John Olivey, memoirs.

17. Pittaway, *Long Range Desert Group*.

18. Ibid.

19. John Olivey, memoirs.

20. Pittaway, *Long Range Desert Group*.

21. Manning, *Rhodesian Squadron*.

Chapter 17

1. Lloyd Owen, *Providence My Guide*.

2. Ibid.

3. Gilbert Jetley's account appeared in the LRDG newsletter, 1971.

4. Ibid.

5. Ibid.

6. Ibid.

7. Mortimer, *The Men Who Made the SAS*.

8. Pittaway, *Long Range Desert Group*.

9. Lloyd Owen, *Providence My Guide*.

10. Ibid.

11. Ibid.

12. Pittaway, *Long Range Desert Group*.

13. Ibid.

14. Ibid.

15. Ibid.

16. Ibid.

17. Ibid.

18. Alf Page interview, Rhodesian Services Association http://www.rhodesianservices.org/user/image/publication01-2010.pdf

19. Lloyd Owen, *Providence My Guide*.

20. Pittaway, *Long Range Desert Group*.

21. The interview with Alf Page appeared in the 2010 edition of the Rhodesian Services Association, which can be found at: www.rhodesianservices.org/user/image/newsletter01–2010.doc

22. Ibid.

23. David Lloyd, papers.

24. LRDG newsletter No. 1, author's collection.

Epilogue

1. Mortimer, *SAS in WW2*.

2. Private video, author's collection.

3. Author interview.

BIBLIOGRAPHY

Books

Bagnold, Ralph, *Sun, Sea, War & Wind* (University of Arizona Press, 1991).

Bierman, John and Smith, Colin, *Alamein* (Penguin, 2003).

Cowles, Virginia, *The Phantom Major* (Collins, 1958).

Crichton-Stuart, Michael, *G Patrol* (William Kimber, 1958).

Dimbleby, Richard, *The Frontiers Are Green* (Hodder & Stoughton, 1943).

Feebery, David (ed.), *Guardsman & Commando* (Pen & Sword, 2008).

James, Malcolm, *Born of the Desert* (Greenhill Books, 1991).

Kelly, Saul, *The Hunt for Zerzura* (John Murray, 2003).

Kennedy Shaw, Bill, *Long Range Desert Group* (Collins, 1945).

Lewin, Ronald, *The Life and Death of the Afrika Korps* (Pen & Sword, 2003).

Liddell-Hart, Basil (ed.), *The Rommel Papers* (DaCapo Press, 1982).

Lloyd Owen, David, *The Desert my Dwelling Place* (Cassell, 1957).

Lloyd Owen, David, *Providence Their Guide* (Pen & Sword, 2001).

Maclean, Fitzroy, *Eastern Approaches* (Penguin, 1991).

Moorehead, Alan, *Desert War: The North African Campaign* (H. Hamilton, 1965).

Morgan, Mike, *Sting of the Scorpion* (The History Press, 2003).

Mortimer, Gavin, *The Daring Dozen* (Osprey, 2011).

Mortimer, Gavin, *The History of the Special Air Service in WW2* (Osprey, 2012).

Mortimer, Gavin, *The History of the Special Boat Squadron in WW2* (Osprey, 2013).

Mortimer, Gavin, *Stirling's Men: The Inside History of the SAS in WW2* (Weidenfeld, 2004).

O'Carroll, Brendan, *The Kiwi Scorpions: The Story of the New Zealanders in the LRDG* (Token Publishing Ltd, 2000).

Peniakoff, Vladimir, *Popski's Private Army* (Harper & Collins, 1975).

Pittaway, Jonathan, *Long Range Desert Group* (Les Martens, 2006).

Pitt, Barrie, *Special Boat Squadron* (Corgi, 1985).

Ross, Hamish, *Paddy Mayne* (Sutton Publishing, 2003).

Schmidt, Heinz W., *With Rommel in the Desert* (Constable, 1998).

Smith, Peter C., *War in the Aegean* (Stackpole Books, 2008).

Smith, Peter C., *Massacre at Tobruk* (Stackpole Books, 2008).

Special Forces in the Desert War 1940–1943 (PRO Publications, 2001).

Timpson, Alistair, *In Rommel's Backyard* (Pen & Sword, 2010]).

Young, Desmond, *Rommel* (Fontana Press, 1989).

Author interviews

Lofty Carr, February to October 2014

Jim Patch, March 2014

Imperial War Museum interviews

Cryer, Ron, catalogue number: 16849

Hackett, John, catalogue number: 12022

Heys, James, catalogue number: 16977

Lord, Frank, catalogue number: 10383

Matthews, Rod, catalogue number: 10214

Mitford, Teddy, catalogue number: 29599

Patch, James (Jim), catalogue number: 9961

Seadon, Spencer, catalogue number: 19044

Stewart, Alexander, catalogue number: 13127

Sullivan, Les, catalogue number: 30098

Swanson, James, catalogue number: 11385

Thompson, Lawrence, catalogue number: 20495

Upcher, Peter, catalogue number: 8006-26

Imperial War Museum documents

Diary of Walter Milner-Barry, catalogue number: 16758

David Lloyd Owen papers, catalogue number: 15623

Harding-Newman, Rupert, catalogue number: 1373

Websites

http://www.lrdg.org

http://www.popski.org

http://patria.homestead.com/patriadsoWILDERN.html

Articles and Journals

Bigio, Eric, 'Against Impossible Odds', *Parade* magazine (1 May 1943).

'Destruction of an Army: The First Campaign in Libya' (Ministry of Information, 1941).

Dundee Courier & Advertiser, October 1970.

The Egyptian Mail, 14 February 1941.

Kenn, Maurice, 'Ralph Alger Bagnold', reprinted from *Biographical Memoirs of Fellows of the Royal Society*, vol. 37 (1991).

Kennedy Shaw, Bill, 'The Oasis of Siwa', *Geographical Magazine*, vol. 22 (1944).

'Long Range Desert Group in the Mediterranean', *NZ in the Second World War*, Official History, 1948-1954, War History Branch.

Manning, Captain C. S., *The Rhodesian Squadron with the LRDG* (South African Public Relations, 1945).

The Times, 14 February 1941; 8 September 1944 and 22 September 1945.

West Sussex County Times, 3 December 1943.

SAS Archives

Diary of Trooper F. W. Jopling.

John Olivey, unpublished memoirs.

LRDG Diary (NZ Patrol), as kept by Lance Corporal Jack Davis.

LRDG newsletters, 1941 to 2000.

Mars & Minerva, regimental journal of the SAS, 1960 to 2010.

Papers of Ron Hill.

Report from Colonel G. Prendergast on his escape from Leros.

Churchill Archives, Cambridge

Bagnold Papers, GBR/0014/BGND

National Archives, Kew

File numbers: WO 373/8/500

WO201/807

HS 9/1036/1

WO 201/810

WO 208/5582-5583

WO 208/3326/2920

WO 201/799

WO 201/797

INF 2/44/87

WO 201/817

WO 201/818

WO 201/813

WO 201/729

WO 204/8495

W0 204/8492

WO 201/816

WO 201/817

WO 201/818

WO 201/813

WO 204/8459

WO 204/8500

DO 35/1696

WO 201/812

WO 201/738

WO 204/8460

T 161/1436/6

HW 1/1261

WO 218/90

WO 218/92

WO 201/2201

WO 218/94

WO 218/89

HW 1/648

INDEX